Downtown Planning for Smaller and Midsized Communities

Philip L. Walker, AICP

American Planning Association
Planners Press

Making Great Communities Happen

Chicago | Washington, D.C.

122 S. Michigan Ave., Suite 1600, Chicago, IL 60603

1776 Massachusetts Ave., NW, Suite 400, Washington, DC 20036-1904

www.planning.org/plannerspress

ISBN: 978-1-932364-67-5 (pbk.)

Library of Congress Control Number: 2008943665

Printed in the United States of America

Contents

List of Illustrations

Foreword

A vibrant downtown is recognized by civic leaders and planning professionals as an essential component of a healthy community and a resilient tax base, and often even as the catalyst for attracting new talent and investment to an area. Revitalizing traditional downtowns and commercial districts, however, has proven more complex than anything that any one sector—such as local government, real estate developers, or economic development professionals—can accomplish alone. After decades of being subjected to marginally effective single-solution approaches—specifically the dubious "catalyst projects" such as convention centers, aquariums, waterfront development, and ballparks—downtown is now viewed as a multifaceted organism of economic, physical, and social elements that must be addressed in a holistic manner. In short, planning, development, and management must be integrated in a seamless process. While there is no shortage of resources or publications on these topics individually, few provide a targeted focus on planning for the downtowns of small and medium-size cities. Even fewer recognize the relationship between the planning process and long-term comprehensive management of the revitalization process. This book does both. We find the principles and process outlined here useful to those who may be new to the field of downtown master planning and revitalization management, including our National Main Street Network of more than 1,800 local commercial-district revitalization programs from coast to coast that have used the principles of the Main Street Four-Point Approach over the past 25 years.

The Main Street Approach is a community-driven, comprehensive methodology used to revitalize older, traditional business districts throughout the United States. It is a commonsense way to address the variety of issues and problems that face traditional business districts. The underlying premise of the Main Street Approach is to encourage economic development within the context of historic preservation in ways appropriate to today's marketplace. The Main Street Approach advocates a return to community self-reliance, local empowerment, and the rebuilding of traditional commercial districts based on their unique assets: distinctive architecture, a pedestrian-friendly environment, personal service, local ownership, and a sense of community. It encompasses work in four distinct areas—design, economic restructuring, promotion, and organization—that are combined to address all of the commercial district's needs. The long-term strategic planning for both physical and economic development is seamlessly woven into each of the four points, and it looks to professionals from other fields, such as planning, to participate—and to help lead the process. Those seeking additional resources for Main Street can visit www.mainstreet.org.

This book provides a general overview on the process of developing a downtown master plan and the issues that a community has to consider when undertaking a planning process. These issues include land use, parking, design and historic buildings, infrastructure, market analysis, business development, and mechanisms for implementation. It also discusses organizational structures and funding mechanisms, such as Business Improvement Districts (BIDs), which can serve as ways to implement a downtown master plan. There are chapters on master plan preparation, the planning process, and the "substance of an effective plan" or what a plan should address.

There are excellent discussions here about how to time a planning process and how to select consultants. The book also touches upon other important considerations to be aware of when developing master plans, such as downtown organizational management, parking management, promotions and special events, business development, organizational development, and social issues. Main Street professionals might find this a useful book in understanding how downtown master plans are put together and the issues that have to be considered when developing one. In addition, readers will find an introductory discussion on economic development components to a downtown master plan, which are lacking in too many downtown plans.

This book addresses what have been previously treated as two different topics: downtown planning and downtown management. The downtown management aspect of the book may be useful to those who come from a planning field and are new to the maintenance and management aspects of downtown revitalization, especially those working in smaller and midsize communities. As a basic book on downtown planning and management methods, this publication can become a useful guide for public officials, planning commissioners, and citizens seeking a planning process that can prepare the community for long-term management of a downtown's resources.

Doug Loescher
Director, National Trust Main Street Center

Nick Kalogeresis, AICP
Program Officer, National Trust Main Street Center

Acknowledgments

There are many individuals, entities, programs, and schools of thought that have influenced the contents of this book. Building upon the foundation of my more than twenty years of experience in downtown planning, I was aided by the input of several professionals representing a diversity of disciplines and geographies, as follows.

Understanding that urban design serves as the physical backbone of downtown planning, I sought the input of Fernando Micale. A former colleague at Christopher Chadbourne and Associates and a classmate from the Harvard Graduate School of Design, Nando brought his years of experience with the Philadelphia office of Wallace, Roberts and Todd to a sound critique of my urban design concepts.

While the intricacies of urban design may seem like a mystical art understood by only a highbrow minority, every downtown user has strong opinions about traffic and parking issues. Consequently, I called on the expertise of transportation planner Ross Tilghman of the Tilghman Group, based in Seattle. Having worked with Ross on several downtown plans across the country, I trusted his judgment in balancing the movement and storage of automobiles with the safety, convenience, and pleasure of pedestrians.

Because all downtowns are essentially evolving historic artifacts whose historic character is their competitive edge with other commercial areas, the advice of historic preservationists was crucial. Consequently, I called upon Ron Emrich and Geoff Coates. Now the director of Preservation New Jersey, Ron worked with me on several downtown planning projects throughout Texas in his previous life as a preservation consultant. My former client for the Lower St. Charles Neighborhood Plan in New Orleans, Geoff served as the director of the Felicity Street Redevelopment Project before establishing the Urban Conservancy, a nonprofit organization dedicated to the preservation and enhancement of New Orleans's historic built environment.

Although physical planning issues typically capture the greatest public attention for any downtown plan, the economic issues are often more significant. I solicited the valued input of Randall Gross on market and economic topics. A planner and economist based in

Washington, D.C. (who also has an office in Johannesburg), Randy has a knack for challenging my ideas on economic issues to the point of irritation. However, he always proves to be correct in the final analysis.

Another important perspective was provided by Tom Phillips, a former fellow principal with the firm Community Planning and Research and a current project manager with the Seattle Housing Authority. Tom's diverse planning background ranges from an education at the New School for Social Research in New York, preference research for real estate developers, and his most recent vocation, leading the development of a HOPE VI project. Because a critical mass of housing units is a missing component for so many downtowns, Tom's insights were invaluable to me.

Though most downtown plans focus especially on what the public sector can do to enhance the downtown, the private sector must ultimately do most of the heavy lifting. Although I worked with him on numerous downtown plans in his earlier life as a land-use attorney and real estate economist, Bradford White offered me some perspective from his current role as a downtown developer with the Chicago-based Habitat Company. Just as every downtown plan should benefit from the input of developers, so should a book on the subject.

Unless successfully implemented, downtown plans are nothing more than expensive academic exercises. Consequently, I called upon the experience of two former clients who have effectively implemented downtown plans. Robin Taffler is the former executive director of the Main Street program in Murray, Kentucky, and Joey Dunn, AICP, is the deputy city manager for the City of Bryan, Texas. They each learned many lessons in implementing their respective downtown plans, and their collective knowledge helped to ground this book in that reality.

Because the adage "you can't see the forest for the trees" applies to downtown planning, I needed the views of a regional planner. Avera Wynne, AICP, the planning director of Florida's Tampa Bay Regional Planning Council, offered his broad perspective. Avera's ability to see the big picture of how a particular downtown fits into the larger regional scheme served as an important reminder that no downtown exists in a vacuum.

In addition to the major contributions of the people noted above, I conducted interviews with the following individuals: Susan Moffat-Thomas, executive director of Swiss Bear Downtown Development Corporation, New Bern, North Carolina; Julie Glover, director of Main Street Denton, Denton, Texas; Paul Drake, director of planning for the

New Jersey Office of Smart Growth; Donna Stenger, senior planner with the Economic Development Division of Tacoma, Washington; Sue Martin, director of the Main Street Chamber, Sigourney, Iowa; Val Giannettino, executive director of Downtown Partners in Burlington, Iowa; Charlotte McDonald, executive director of the Main Street Program, Eureka, California; Angie Hood, manager of the Main Street Program, Americus, Georgia; Julie Jackson, director of the Albany Downtown Association, Albany, Oregon; Jim Schuh, director of Chippewa Falls (Wisconsin) Main Street; Kathy Wellsandt, program manager of the Lake Rice (Wisconsin) Main Street Association; Beth Waddle, director of Main Street Corning, Corning, Iowa; Deborah Badhia, executive director of the Downtown Berkeley (California) Association; Ron Dentinger, director of the Dodgeville (Wisconsin) Revitalization Program; Ann Williams, manager of Franklin (Virginia) Downtown Development; Mary Pearce, executive director of the Heritage Foundation of Franklin and Williamson County, Tennessee; Bruce Gould, village planner, Pinehurst, North Carolina; and Sarah Pope, of the Virginia Main Street Program.

Providing general review and editing support on this book were friends William Collins, Ph.D., and David Popkin, Ph.D. As an economics professor at Vanderbilt University, Bill claims no expertise in downtown planning. However, his years of scholarly research and writing, as well as his fresh perspective unspoiled by the biases of the planning profession, were helpful. Similarly, as an English and philosophy professor at Nashville's Fisk University, David has an ability to convey complex ideas in a clear and concise manner, which more than compensated for his lack of expertise on the topic.

While my formal education helped to enrich this book's contents, perhaps no single "school of thought" influenced it more than the philosophy of the National Trust for Historic Preservation's National Main Street Center. This program's Four-Point Approach advocates a holistic strategy for invigorating downtowns, and a quarter century of tremendous success all across the country has proved it to be an effective methodology. While the Main Street Approach focuses more on "doing" than "planning," any downtown plan that overlooks the program's valuable lessons is, in my opinion, inherently flawed. I was fortunate to have Doug Loescher, director of the National Trust Main Street Center, and Nick Kalogeresis, AICP, then a program officer at the center, take a look at a draft manuscript. In addition to their constructive feedback, they were kind enough to write the foreword.

xvi *Acknowledgments*

My last measure of gratitude goes to my family. I thank my parents and brother for a lifetime of support in all of my endeavors. I thank my wife, Kathryn, for her patience, understanding, and encouragement. And I thank my daughter, Katie Rush, who never understood why daddy spent so much time typing on that electronic box.

Preface

Collectively, American downtowns are a grossly underused resource. Most possess "good bones" in the form of streets, infrastructure, public spaces, and buildings. Many are still privileged by the presence of important institutions, such as city halls, county courthouses, schools, and post offices. All are living historic artifacts that continue to evolve over time, adjusting to modern needs. It is no coincidence that, in many communities, the existing or emerging entertainment district for shopping and dining is located in the downtown. Savvy business people capitalize on the unique character of downtowns and their historic buildings as a venue for shops, restaurants, housing, offices, and other uses.

Despite this existing scenario, the vast majority of America's new development is occurring in an extremely generic form, described by some as "Generica." A new suburban convenience store in Kansas City, Missouri, differs little in appearance from a new convenience store in the suburbs of San Diego or Boston, depending upon the particular franchise architecture pulled off the shelf. As the character-defining remnants of our past are slowly chipped away, a faceless new landscape spreads like a wildfire. Accompanying this nondescript sprawling pattern of growth are numerous negative consequences, including: the loss of natural landscapes; the destruction of historic resources; the neglect of inner cities; fiscal inefficiencies; automobile-dominated environments that generate traffic congestion, air pollution, and groundwater contamination from stormwater runoff; and the social isolation of those too young, too old, or too poor to drive.

A segment of the market will always desire new places. However, public officials have little justification to promote development in undeveloped places until we fix existing places in need of repair. Empirical evidence proves that suburbs can no longer turn their backs on downtowns without harming their overall regional economy. Among numerous examples, the National League of Cities has published reports on this issue, including "City Distress, Metropolitan Disparities and Economic Growth," and "All In It Together: Cities, Suburbs and Local Economic Regions." Clearly, the prudent choice is to channel future growth to areas with existing infrastructure and public services, rather than allowing those resources to go underused and to deteriorate over time. The case for downtowns can be made on all fronts—economic, fiscal, environmental, and social.

This book will teach the reader how to resuscitate struggling downtowns through proactive planning as well as how to sustain the successful downtown. In particular, it focuses on small to moderate-size downtowns, defined here as those serving a metropolitan area of no more than 500,000 people. In a simple and straightforward manner, this book addresses a set of "best practices" for downtown planning. Chapter 2 explores the process of creating a downtown plan, while the subsequent three chapters address the substance of downtown planning. Readers seeking exceptionally novel ideas or "magic bullet" answers to downtown planning will be sorely disappointed, as experience proves that the cutting-edge concepts that occasionally surface quickly become "mainstream" once successfully implemented in a single downtown. Instead, this book examines planning approaches applied over the past few decades, some successfully and some not, and it draws conclusions that will benefit future downtown planning efforts for everyone.

WHAT IS A DOWNTOWN?

Given that this book will use the term "downtown" hundreds of times, a definition at the outset is in order. Without needing to be overly analytical, we can say that most people recognize a downtown when they see one, so a list of discernible clues may appear to be a waste of ink. However, when a downtown begins to lose the following seemingly obvious traits, it starts getting into trouble and moves away from being a true downtown.

Mixed Land Uses

Healthy downtowns host a wide range of activities, including commercial, institutional, and residential uses. The best downtowns manage to strike an equilibrium, usually not through conscious actions, that creates a synergy among different qualities, resulting in a dynamic and sustainable place. Downtowns that have fallen on hard times often become unbalanced and lose this mixture. For example, public institutions sometimes relocate to the suburbs, or a downtown may lose its appeal as a desirable place to live for a variety of reasons. Despite periodic upward and downward trends, a strong downtown features a balanced mixture of many uses. Unlike "multiuse" developments often found in the suburbs, downtowns are truly "mixed use" because their uses are physically integrated.

Diversity

Unless the downtown is located in an ethnically and economically homogenous community, which is a rarity, it is often the most socially diverse part of town. One of the most interesting characteristics and greatest strengths of downtowns is their diversity. Not only do downtown employees typically range from custodians to corporate CEOs, but downtown residents tend to be equally pluralistic. For example, depending upon their country of origin and associated cultural history, many immigrants are drawn to downtowns. The downtown housing market can range from low-income residents in affordable housing to struggling artists in lofts to young urban professionals in condominium apartments to retired "empty nesters" in expensive town houses. This diversity stands in stark contrast to socially segmented suburban areas where residents of each subdivision are surrounded by people who share their demographic characteristics.

Compact Development Forms

Downtowns constitute the most concentrated collection of buildings found in their community. A downtown's buildings are usually the tallest in town, and they have the shallowest front setbacks. Downtowns also tend to have the lowest ratio of undeveloped land relative to other parts of their community. Although some downtowns have their share of surface parking, most downtowns lack parking lots as expansive as those of suburban shopping centers. In fact, as downtowns grow in size and density, parking lots are eventually replaced by parking garages if their economics can justify a more efficient use of land.

Historic Buildings

More often than not, downtown saw the genesis of the original community. Although the community's earliest buildings may no longer exist due to "the great fire," "the great flood," or the rapacious developers, its oldest surviving buildings are frequently found in the downtown. Many downtowns started as a collection of modest one-or two-story wooden structures, only to be later supplanted by taller and more architecturally refined brick structures as a result of disasters or progress. As survivors of the natural evolutionary process, historic buildings are often the primary element that allows a community to retain its identity and sense of place, and the historic character of downtowns is frequently cited in consumer preference surveys as their most favorable attribute.

Central and Strategic Location

Community growth patterns generally exist as a series of concentric rings emanating from a central point—the downtown. Those rings are irregularly shaped because of topography and roads, as well as natural and man-made barriers, such as rivers and rail lines. Annexations and growth trends over the years can also alter the downtown's geographic position within municipal boundaries, and new mixed use centers may emerge, prompting their own set of growth rings over time. Regardless of these qualifying factors, downtowns are usually central to a city's historic growth patterns, and they are commonly located on or near a strategic natural or man-made resource. As the very genesis of their community, most were established at a river, bay, hilltop, canal, crossroads, or railroad.

"Downtown" Designation

While not a startling revelation, perhaps the most convincing clue in detecting a downtown is hearing the term "downtown" applied to the area in question. Despite the citizens of some towns and cities referring to their urban center as "uptown," "city center," "town center," "old town," or a similar term, the name implies that it is a distinct and important place in the community.

So who are the distant relatives and outright imposters that might be confused with bona fide traditional downtowns? The guilty parties include older commercial districts serving neighborhoods located outside of the downtown, and new urbanist "town centers" that have been developed within the past few decades. The most naïve among us might even be fooled by the latest trend—the "lifestyle center," which is essentially an open-air suburban mall with a superficial "ye olde" veneer. While older commercial districts and new town centers are important places for any community and should be nurtured, and many of the ideas in this book can directly apply to them, such places warrant distinction from genuine downtowns.

Nevertheless, "gray areas" exist in some communities. For example, the Pinehurst, North Carolina, village center was developed during the 1890s by a single developer, as was Palmer Square in Princeton, New Jersey, which was created during the early twentieth century and now serves as the heart of that eighteenth-century downtown. As with most generalizations about downtowns, there is no dearth of exceptions to the rule when answering the question, What is a downtown?

WHAT IS A DOWNTOWN PLAN?

In addition to the term "downtown," the term "plan" warrants definition in light of its frequent use throughout this book. First, it is acknowledged that numerous types of plans can be applied to downtowns. Examples include vision plans, strategic plans, physical master plans, urban design plans, transportation plans, community facilities plans, and economic revitalization plans, to name a few. On the West Coast, a plan for a particular area such as a downtown is often labeled as a specific plan. Although these various types of plans might be combined and coordinated as individual elements to form a single plan document, not every downtown is in need of a plan. Perhaps a particular downtown's current circumstances can justify expenditures only on a retail strategy. Regardless of the value that a special plan focusing on just one or even a handful of issues may bring to a downtown, such plans are not the focus of this book.

For many, the term "master plan" brings to mind a document that addresses only physical planning issues. For the purposes of the many pages that follow, however, the terms "downtown plan," "master plan," and simply "plan" are used interchangeably to describe the same type of plan: a plan that holistically considers all of the basic dimensions of a downtown—physical, economic, social, and political.

It is also noteworthy that effective downtown plans can and should address downtown management issues, such as marketing, promotion, business development, and special events. Some downtown practitioners view planning and management as two distinct issues. While they are indeed two separate processes, if planning did not occur to address the myriad of management issues, many downtown organizations would be blindly groping in the dark for answers. Consequently, even the ongoing management issues faced by downtowns and their championing organizations long after the planning process has ended should be incorporated into the downtown plan.

xxiiPreface

PREVIOUS WORK ON THE SUBJECT

Given the significance of downtown planning, it was surprising that a search of the literature identified no single book discussing the topics and perspectives addressed here. While several works on the process of developing "urban plans" exist, such as Larz T. Anderson's *Guidelines for Preparing Urban Plans* (1995) and T. J. Kent Jr.'s *The Urban General Plan* (1990 reprint of a 1964 edition), those books focus primarily on the planning process. Furthermore, they address citywide plans, rather than those focusing solely on downtowns. A related subject that has been covered thoroughly is the urban design facet of downtown planning, but those publications have a singular focus on design. Books about the function of downtowns and how to implement revitalization strategies also exist, but they tend to be program oriented and intentionally lack a master planning context. A good example of this genre is *Cities Back from the Edge* by Roberta Brandes Gratz and Norman Mintz (1998). In sum, this book fills a void.

This book addresses both the process of downtown planning and effective strategies for improving and sustaining downtowns through planning. It also views downtowns from a holistic perspective, believing that one-dimensional approaches to revitalization are generally ineffective.

INTENDED AUDIENCE

This book is meant for anyone interested in revitalizing a downtown through proactive planning. Foremost, it should be useful to public-sector planners and downtown organizations responsible for planning, enhancing, and sustaining their downtowns, particularly those professionals still relatively new to the field. Even seasoned professionals might learn something, as this work draws on the perspectives of many practitioners and academics, as well as the experience of specific communities referenced throughout the book. Those who are less directly involved with downtown planning but still downtown stakeholders can also gain important insights from this book. For example, public officials responsible for hiring consultants to prepare a downtown plan can learn what to expect once the planning begins, rather than having to learn as they go. And finally, this book can provide a solid foundation for students of planning and downtown revitalization.

RESEARCH BASIS

The information and ideas contained in this book are based upon a variety of sources. Much of the research comes from my two decades of experience assisting downtowns throughout the country, both in the public sector and as a consultant. Information found in relevant books and journals has also contributed to this work, as well as interviews with professionals and academics in the field. Research into the experience of communities has likewise proved invaluable, including the review of numerous downtown plans. And finally, the important efforts of groups, such as the National Main Street Center, the Urban Land Institute, and the International Downtown Association have greatly influenced this book.

Special mention must be made of the National Trust for Historic Preservation's National Main Street Center Four Point Approach, which focuses on the issues of organization, design, economics, and marketing and promotion for downtowns. That approach has certainly influenced my work when preparing downtown plans. While the ensuing chapters reflect the four-point approach, they also go beyond it. The Four Points Approach is primarily about programs for downtown management and sustainability. Planners, on the other hand, have done a good job of addressing physical planning issues, as well as some economic and policy issues, but it has been my experience that they often do not address other important aspects of downtown master planning in either as much depth or with as much comprehensiveness as they should. This book may be the first time that anyone has tried to couple the comprehensive and holistic approach of the Four Point Approach with best practices drawn from planning.

HOW TO APPLY THIS BOOK

This book is intended to provide the reader with a set of principles that can be adapted to their particular circumstances. Planning for downtowns is undoubtedly an art rather than a clear-cut science. Not every idea found in this book will be applicable to every downtown, but the general principles will apply to nearly all. Additionally, it should be relevant to older commercial and mixed use districts that may not constitute their community's "downtown" per se but that face many of the same issues. Among others, two key factors in applying the ideas of this book to a particular downtown are: (1) the scale of the downtown, and (2) the resources available to the planners and those implementing the plan.

This book is best suited to those involved with small to moderate-size downtowns. While it can be relevant to larger downtowns—defined here as those serving a metropolitan population of more than 500,000 people—greater adaptation may be required on specific issues to address the complexities of larger downtowns. For example, topics common to larger downtowns but less relevant to moderate-size downtowns and irrelevant to most small downtowns include highways as barriers, panhandlers, violent crime, skyscrapers, and large-footprint public facilities, such as arenas and convention centers. Those types of issues are addressed here, but not in great detail.

The resources available to a particular community for planning will dictate the scale and extent of the planning process. For example, a town with very limited funding for in-house planning staff or consultants will need to employ a streamlined methodology and should have lower expectations for the plan's level of detail. Limited planning budgets can affect various aspects of a plan, such as the degree of market analysis performed, the extent of public input, the volume of text written, and the provision of high-quality illustrations.

Regardless of the size of the downtown or available resources for planning, the following pages can provide a solid framework for any downtown planning effort. It is my goal that this book will be a useful tool for making beautiful and vibrant downtowns the norm, rather than the exception.

Figure P-1. This anonymous downtown could be virtually anywhere in America. It is typical of the thousands of downtowns to which this book applies. Source: The Walker Collaborative

THE BIGGER PICTURE

So how might downtown planning fit within the broader framework of community planning and growth management? What are its future prospects relative to current planning philosophies and trends? Should downtown planning be a top priority for planners and their communities, or are more pressing matters on the horizon of the contemporary city planning landscape? To answer these questions, one must first recognize today's most popular planning movements, which are unquestionably smart growth and new urbanism.

Smart growth has different meanings for different people. Judging from current debate on the subject, it may be easier to agree on what smart growth is *not* than what it *is*. The antithesis of smart growth is suburban sprawl, characterized by strictly segregated land uses and demographic groups, relatively low development densities, little consideration for the natural environment, architecture unrelated to a community's culture, and the recurring theme of automobile-driven planning. In short, Generica. Smart growth is often associated with the new urbanist movement, a development philosophy based upon pre–World War II principles of planning and design. Unlike the suburban sprawl paradigm, new urbanism promotes the physical integration of varied land uses and people, human-scale buildings, and an emphasis on the pedestrian realm. While automobiles can be easily accommodated by new urbanism, cars are not allowed to dominate the design of a community. Although the definitions of smart growth and new urbanism continually evolve, most planners view new urbanism as a subunit of smart growth, which focuses on the natural environment, fiscal efficiencies, transportation, and regionalism as much as it does on traditional urban villages and towns.

Regardless of their definitions and distinctions, smart growth and new urbanism have thankfully gained steady momentum over the past few decades in shaping the way communities are now planned. Much of the focus to date, however, has been on new development of "green field" sites, even though some of these properties are infill sites within otherwise developed areas. A growing number of new downtowns have also been planned and developed on essentially blank canvases, such as that of Kendall, Florida. In the five years after the adoption of its master plan in 1999, downtown Kendall witnessed approximately $250 million in new construction permits and 3,400 new residential units built on a 240-acre site that previously had no residential population (Katz 2004, 20). New downtowns such as this, at least in the near-term, will face a different set of issues from historic downtowns. Sadly,

Figure P-2. Although it resembles a traditional downtown in many ways—more so physically than economically or culturally—this town center in Southlake, Texas, was begun in the late 1990s. While this new town center is consistent with smart growth and new urbanist ideologies, it is imperative that greater attention be focused on the well-being of America's existing downtowns. Source: The Walker Collaborative

the critical role of existing downtowns has often been overlooked in the debate on smart growth and new urbanism. Taking a different tack, this book embraces and celebrates "old urbanism" and explains how existing downtowns can be reclaimed and sustained as part of a more comprehensive smart-growth scheme.

Auspiciously, the critical role of downtowns within the future of the smart growth movement is steadily gaining recognition. In "On Common Ground," the National Association of Realtors (NAR) stated, "When the Smart Growth discussion began in the mid-1990s among citizens, public officials and planners, the primary focus was on managing growth at the urban fringe. The conversion of large amounts of farm and forest land to low-density development was a major concern then, as it remains today. But over the past few years, it has become more widely recognized that the revitalization of existing communities is also a vital element of Smart Growth, and maybe a more fruitful arena for focused attention" (NAR 2005, 2). If an organization as politically conservative, credible, and influential as the NAR is recognizing and broadcasting the importance of revitalizing existing built environments, hope indeed exists for all of urban America.

1

The Groundwork
Before Planning

---

*Downtown holds together the most varied mix of economic, civic and social
functions. It is the place where everyone can meet and interact, where monu-
ments are located, where speeches are made, where parades are held and people
are entertained. More than anything else, downtown gives a community its
collective identity and thus its pride.*

— Richard Moe and Carter Wilkie, *Changing Places*:
Rebuilding Community in the Age of Sprawl

Faced with the question, Does downtown really need a plan?, some
officials who have shaped successful downtowns testified to the importance of a plan specific to downtown needs. Susan Moffat-Thomas, the
executive director of Swiss Bear Downtown Development Corporation in New Bern, North Carolina, said that, in 2002, it was vital, as
her organization employed a consulting team to prepare the successor
to the town's 1977 and 1990 downtown plans. In addition to addressing urban design issues, the plan included retail, housing, and transportation components, as well as a great deal of public input. "For so
long we were floundering and taking ad hoc measures, but the minute
I understood what a downtown plan really was I said 'We need one
of those!' As it turned out, it was the most fantastic vehicle I've ever
seen." Similarly, Julie Glover, the downtown director for Denton, Texas,
claims that the $150,000 downtown master plan prepared in 2002 "was
definitely worth it in that it got everyone engaged and fired up." Echoing
the same sentiment is Joey Dunn, AICP, the former director of planning

1

and development services for Bryan, Texas. According to Dunn, who helped oversee a $230,000 downtown master plan for Bryan in 2001, "Having a well-defined comprehensive master plan, coupled with sustained political and financial support, can mean all the difference in getting a downtown area going again." And there is more than mere anecdotal evidence that planning is an important activity for most downtowns. The Brookings Institution's 2005 research brief, "Turning Around Downtown: Twelve Steps to Revitalization," suggests that one of the most critical of the recommended 12 steps is "Step 2: Develop a Strategic Plan." In fact, it states that "having a strategy and management plan for downtown is absolutely imperative."

WHAT PROMPTS A PLAN?

While this faith in the power of planning is difficult to refute in general terms, and proactive downtown initiatives are certainly commendable, major planning efforts are usually undertaken only under certain circumstances. For most downtowns, the financial and human resources required for preparing a legitimate plan dictate that planning is a relatively infrequent occurrence. In fact, while an annual plan "revisit" is not unheard of and is often well advised, most municipalities and downtown organizations prepare a new downtown plan no more than once every five or 10 years, as is often the case with communitywide

Figure 1-1. City officials in Bryan, Texas, credit their 2001 downtown master plan as the catalyst for reinvigorating their downtown, including an extensive streetscape redevelopment, the rehabilitation of more than 25 historic structures, the establishment of numerous new businesses, and the creation of a new downtown redevelopment authority. Source: The Walker Collaborative

comprehensive plans. So how does one know when it is time to prepare a new plan for their downtown? There are a number of conditions that might prompt the creation of a new downtown plan, including those described in the following sections.

Passage of Time

No magic number exists for the frequency at which new downtown plans should be prepared or substantially updated. However, five-year planning increments are a reasonable rule of thumb, and that time horizon happens to coincide with the requirements of many states that mandate countywide and citywide comprehensive plans. For the typical downtown, the passing of a half decade usually results in enough change that the existing plan becomes obsolete, particularly with respect to economic and marketing strategies. During the period between new plans, an existing plan should be revisited and reconsidered on an annual basis. This exercise does not require that the plan be revised annually but simply reevaluated and kept alive in the minds of its users. Despite these rules of thumb, some downtowns are well-advised to allow for the passage of substantially more time than the norm before initiating a major downtown planning project. For example, the Brookings Institution suggests deferring downtown planning "if there has been a recent (within 20 years) failure of a previous attempt. It takes a full generation to get over the collapse of a revitalization effort and the injection of fresh leadership unencumbered with the 'we tried that once and it didn't work' mindset" (Leinberger 2005, 4).

Major New Developments

Major new developments can range from a welcomed opportunity (e.g., a mixed use building that provides a celebrated new downtown anchor) to a perceived threat to the downtown's vitality (e.g., a suburban shopping mall that directly competes with the businesses currently downtown). During the early 1990s, for example, numerous Midwestern, Mississippi River, and Gulf Coast communities commissioned downtown plans in response to the advent of casino gambling. Those plans typically sought to minimize the potential negative impacts, such as traffic congestion and competition with local dining and entertainment businesses, while maximizing the potential positive effects, such as tax revenues and the leveraging of economic benefits for downtown revitalization. Similarly, new public facilities can be as promising as a downtown convention center or as dreaded as a suburban post office to replace the downtown facility. Even seemingly benevolent new down-town facilities must be appropriately located and designed in order to help, and not harm, the downtown. Development clearly incompatible with a downtown's unique physical character or pedestrian orientation can underscore the need for planning and new regulations designed to avoid similar mistakes in the future.

Transportation Changes

Transportation changes are one of the most significant external forces that affect downtowns, and they come in a variety of forms. Given that many downtowns are traversed by state-designated roads, the widen-ing of streets, the conversion of two-way streets to one-way streets, and the elimination of on-street parking are common "improvements" inflicted upon many unsuspecting downtowns by their state depart-ment of transportation, transforming comfortable urban streets into undesirable barriers. Other transportation changes prompting the need for a plan include bypasses around a downtown or the introduction of mass transit, such as a commuter rail stop in the downtown. In the case of transportation changes that would negatively affect the down-town, the plan needs to offer alternatives or mitigating actions. In the case of positive changes, such as a commuter rail stop, the plan needs to assess its opportunities and devise a strategy to leverage benefits to the downtown. According to Randall Gross, a Washington, D.C., con-sultant with the firm Randall Gross/Development Economics, such a plan was crafted for Frederick, Maryland, when a new transit stop was planned as part of the Maryland Area Rail Commuter (MARC) system. Even commuter rail stops, however, can be a double-edged sword, requiring mitigation from impacts such as noise, traffic disrup-tions, safety issues, and large parking areas.

Changing Economic Conditions

While positive economic conditions can be a good reason for a down-town to plan its future, a serious and sustained downward trend more typically prompts planning. Increased building vacancies are usually a telltale sign of troubles ahead, but more subtle trends can be equally alarming. For example, the usurping of ground-floor retail uses by offices, or the inability to produce downtown housing, can be strong justifications for planning initiatives. Many downtowns facing these dilemmas have commissioned studies or plans intended to address those specific challenges either as part of a comprehensive downtown plan or as a special study limited to that particular issue. For example, several downtowns that experienced a trend of ground-floor retail uses being replaced by offices—including Pinehurst, North Carolina, and Franklin, Tennessee—hired real estate economists to conduct a study to address the issue, often with very positive results. Despite such reactionary measures, many communities already enjoying a strong economy have the foresight to plan for their downtowns as part of an overall communitywide economic development strategy, rather than waiting for hard times to arrive.

Image Problems

Occasionally, a downtown's image suffers setbacks that call for "damage control" in the form of planning. High-profile crime is one form of negative publicity that some downtowns experience. In fact, the location of media offices in downtowns, such as newspapers and television stations, can also be a double-edged sword. Although their employees are welcome customers for restaurants and shops, the convenience of covering even minor downtown crime stories can be a detriment. A series of publicized assaults and robberies might beg for a downtown plan, especially one emphasizing image development and marketing. The closing or relocation of a key downtown business, and the negative publicity that comes with it, can also be enough to prompt a plan. There can also be a combination of circumstances creating a generally negative image. In an interview with Fernando Micale of Wallace, Roberts & Todd, I learned that downtown Philadelphia's image had deteriorated so much by the 1980s that the "Central City Plan" was eventually commissioned, spurring the creation of a Business Improvement District (BID) and a public relations campaign that ultimately helped turn the area's image around.

Available Support and Resources

Sometimes the stars must be properly aligned for planning opportunities to arise. Even if no other special circumstances occur, newfound political support or financial resources can make embarking on a downtown plan possible. A single election or a successful grant application can suddenly make a pipe dream for a downtown plan become a reality. For Murray, Kentucky, as well as several other communities across Kentucky, a state program channeling funds to designated "Renaissance" communities made a comprehensive downtown plan possible in 2000. The results for Murray have included a new streetscape around

The Road Less Traveled to a Downtown Plan

State Route 206 through central New Jersey passes through a broad spectrum of conditions ranging from scenic rural landscapes to historic urban centers. The highway segment traversing Hillsborough Township, just north of Princeton, features strip commercial development as generic as any found in America. However, in the late 1990s, the New Jersey Department of Transportation (NJDOT) provided an unprecedented opportunity for positive change by supporting the township's plans to recreate a Main Street that had long vanished. NJDOT plans for a bypass for Hills-borough had existed for years and, if constructed, would provide a driving alternative to the strip commercial segment through Hills-borough. The bypass would also cause that segment of Route 206 to lose its state designation, along with the NJDOT standards that apply to such roads. The township was quick to recognize its unique chance to transform a poster child for sprawl into a new downtown or "town center."

One of the first steps taken was to conduct a computerized survey in which public preferences were solicited on various development issues for the corridor. The survey was placed on the township's website, and computer terminals for taking the survey were provided at a handful of locations throughout the community, including the Township Hall, the public library, and a coffeehouse. Topics such as density, building scale and form, the location of parking, streetscapes, and overall design character were polled, with more than 1,000 citizens taking the survey. The results were then used as the basis for a new master plan, zoning, and design standards intended to create a genuine urban center as the area redevelops over time. Although the real-estate market has been slow in helping the township's dream of a traditional Main Street come to fruition, the plan has continued to receive support from the state. Fortunately for Hillsborough, NJDOT has come to embrace smart growth concepts and stands by its commitment to assist the township in the development of its coveted Main Street.

the courthouse area, newly restored building facades, and numerous new businesses. Without the serendipitous financial support from the state, the downtown plan that triggered those improvements would likely have never occurred.

KEEPING PLANNING IN PERSPECTIVE

While almost any downtown can benefit measurably from a master plan, the value of plans must be kept in perspective. For example, a downtown with very limited funding that must choose between preparing a plan and establishing a management entity would, in most instances, be better served by the management entity. Not only is a plan of limited use without an entity whose primary mission is to implement it, but some of the recommendations contained in a downtown plan might likely have been hatched independent of a plan. Ideas such as streetscape redevelopments, new infill buildings, and marketing campaigns can certainly be generated outside of a master planning process, although without a plan they may not be coordinated for maximum benefit. In fact, most downtown plans include some concepts contemplated by stakeholders for years prior to the plan's preparation. Any good downtown plan will take advantage of such ideas, expand upon them, give them a context within a grander scheme, rank their order of priority, provide an implementation strategy, and lend them greater credibility than they would have otherwise.

Countless thriving and prosperous downtowns lack a master plan. Undoubtedly, some downtowns are blessed with such strong demographics, tourism traffic, or other attributes that they succeed without planning, and sometimes they succeed in spite of themselves. Likewise, plenty of downtowns have master plans, yet they are still not the strong and dynamic places they would like to be. While a plan, in and of itself, will not be the sole panacea for any downtown, its skillful and persistent implementation will undoubtedly allow the downtown to optimize its performance and to become a better place than it would be without a plan.

SELLING THE NEED FOR A PLAN

One of the most critical steps in preparing a downtown plan occurs before the formal planning process ever begins. If a core group of downtown supporters are unable to persuade the key decision makers and funding sources to embark upon a plan, all of the other related issues become irrelevant. Surprisingly, some of the toughest individuals to sell on a downtown plan are those who have lived in the community the longest. They can recall the downtown's former glory, and they can see the current problems, but they may not be able to envision future revitalization. Many elected officials fall into this category, seeing the downtown as a hopeless case. A history of past downtown efforts that failed can be particularly harmful and galvanize the skeptics. In fact, many downtown stakeholders who become actively involved in revitalization efforts are relatively new to the community, and they often have firsthand experience with other successful downtowns. An even tougher sell than a plan to resuscitate a struggling downtown is making the case for a downtown that seems to be doing fine. Convincing stakeholders a plan is necessary in order for the currently healthy downtown to sustain itself over time can be a major challenge, much like trying to convince federal legislators that an improved levee system was needed for New Orleans prior to the proof offered by Hurricane Katrina and the resulting flood. For all of these reasons, an ample amount of thought and strategy should go into selling the need for the downtown plan.

Before anyone can be sold on the need for a plan, they must first be sold on the need for an improved downtown. While most downtown advocates are already selling the value of their downtown to the community on a regular basis, a particularly important time to do so is when support is being generated for planning. On the other hand, given their broad responsibilities toward the entire community, municipal planners and economic development professionals must shift from a neutral stance on downtown and begin loudly praising its many virtues. The specific uses and benefits of a downtown plan are outlined later, so this section addresses the merits of a healthy downtown in general. Although the benefits of having a strong downtown may vary for each community, the following sections describe the common reasons for most.

Benefits to the Regional Economy

The adage "you can run, but you can't hide" is certainly applicable to the relationship between communities and their downtowns. As Larry Daughtrey, a reporter for *The Tennessean*, put it, "In most American cities, you can sense almost instantly and instinctively whether it is living or dying by its downtown" (4 December 2005). Nationally recognized real estate and economic development consultant Donovan Rypkema states, "I firmly believe that, until there is a healthy city core, the odds against having a healthy city overall are overwhelming" (2004, 2). Numerous studies, many prompted by the consideration of city and county governments merging to create metropolitan governments, have concluded that a strong and direct link exists between downtowns and their regional economies. In *Metropolitan Disparities and Economic Growth*, the National League of Cities (NLC) warned "The United States cannot move to a new path of economic growth unless driven there by the growth of the urban regions. . . . The need for a long-term strategy for investing in the growth and productivity of urban economies is urgent" (Ledebur and Barnes 1992). The NLC reiterated its point in *All in It Together: Cities, Suburbs and Local Economic Regions* (Ledebur and Barnes 1993).

Clearly, suburban bedroom communities can no longer turn their backs on their urban neighbors in the belief the central city's problem is not their problem. Like a drowning victim flailing in the water, a sinking downtown will take down everything within its reach. Therefore, anyone with an interest in their region's economy, which is most everyone, should have an interest in the economic health of their downtown. As a case in point, when a revitalization strategy was being developed for downtown Albuquerque, a senior executive with the Sandia National Laboratory, which employs 5,000 highly trained people, spent countless hours volunteering in the effort. Asked why he was committing so much time to the project despite the laboratory being located five miles from downtown, he replied, "If Albuquerque does not have a vibrant, hip downtown, I do not have a chance of recruiting or retaining the twenty-something software engineers that are the life's blood of the laboratory" (Leinberger 2005, 5). Undoubtedly, the links between a downtown and its regional economy are sometimes less obvious than the casual observer might realize.

Fiscal Efficiency

Fiscal efficiency is a topic that should get the attention of both elected officials and the average taxpayer. The fiscal costs of sprawl are well documented. Broadcasted by a wide range of smart-growth advocacy groups, those public expenses include new roads, sewer lines, water lines, electrical lines, and other types of infrastructure. Whether the initial cost of infrastructure is shouldered by the taxpayers or by developers, the ongoing maintenance is almost always a long-term public expense. When public infrastructure serves low-density suburban development, the costs per business or residence served is proportionally higher than the costs of serving higher-density urban development. Not only is building a mile of roadway, sewer line, or water line more fiscally efficient for urban areas than it is in suburban areas because that infrastructure will serve more users, but in most urban areas that infrastructure already exists and is being underused, although upgrades are sometimes needed. Fiscal analysis studies show that the financial savings offered by high-density, mixed use areas are not tied solely to one-time capital costs but to ongoing operating expenses as well. These facts should be vigorously touted when soliciting support for a downtown or a downtown plan.

Enhanced Quality of Life

While it may be the one facet of downtowns most difficult to quantify, robustness in a downtown undoubtedly adds to any community's quality of life. Not only is a vibrant and attractive downtown an amenity to be enjoyed by all, but it also contributes to civic pride. Quality of life may sound like an abstract concept to some, but there are solid economic reasons for being concerned with it. In past decades, large businesses considering relocations typically sought incentives, such as tax breaks and free land. The industrial recruitment landscape has changed substantially in recent years, although many industrial boards have yet to catch on. As is powerfully argued in Richard Florida's *The Rise of the Creative Class* (2002), one of the highest priorities for many businesses is the ability to attract bright and creative employees. That objective is difficult to achieve in a community lacking a high quality of life, including a desirable downtown. Furthermore, the executives making relocation decisions for their companies are also looking for a high quality of life for themselves and their families.

This issue was clear to Tom Bates, a bank executive and past Main Street program president for Sigourney, Iowa, a community of just 2,200 people. According to Bates, "We needed to bring in industry, but to do that we needed an attractive downtown filled with goods and services." It was the chamber of commerce and the economic development corporation that most vigorously urged Sigourney's municipal government to apply to Iowa's pilot Rural Main Street program in 1989. Since establishing the program, more than $2 million of investment has gone into the downtown, more than 50 building rehabilitations have occurred, a net increase of more than 50 businesses has taken place, and the building vacancy rate has dropped from 24 percent to less than 5 percent. In 1997, a downtown streetscape project was implemented, and nine new upper-floor apartments have been developed in the past few years. Equally important to many Sigourney citizens, including Bates, two new industries have located in the city's industrial park, and the demand for new housing in Sigourney has increased measurably. Thus, quality-of-life issues are significant to both current and future residents of a community.

Preserving a Sense of Place

Today's typical new development is often generic, homogenous, and sterile. Part of the blame can be placed on national retail and restaurant

Figure 1-2. Communities across the country are recognizing the contribution of a strong downtown toward their overall quality of life. Many chambers of commerce and economic development authorities are beginning to use their downtowns as recruiting tools to land major new employers. Source: The Walker Collaborative

chains, part of it can be placed on large home builders, and part of it can be placed on municipal development codes. But perhaps most guilty of all are elected officials unwilling to stand up to their local development community and impose better standards. However, in

Figure 1-3. Unlike a downtown, a generic strip commercial corridor tells little about what makes a particular community unique. There is no "there" there. Source: Sharyl Carter

all fairness to elected officials in economically depressed communities, some are well meaning but simply afraid of scaring off developers with more stringent regulations intended to yield higher-quality development. Regardless of the reasons, every day the average community looks more and more like its peers, as is well documented in James Kunstler's *The Geography of Nowhere* (1994). Downtowns, on the other hand, are one of the best opportunities for a community to retain its unique identity and sense of place. For some communities, downtown is their sole tangible link to the past, their only postcard location to take visitors, and their only source of genuine civic pride.

Downtown as an Industrial Recruitment Tool

It was the early 1990s, and the mayor of Murfreesboro, Tennessee, was courting a major industry to relocate to his city. Competing with several other communities across the country, he anxiously met the company's representatives at the local airport to escort them on a carefully planned tour of the city. Expecting to begin the tour with the top industrial site that might serve as the future home to hundreds of new employees, Mayor Joe Jackson was surprised to hear the executives request that the tour begin with the city's historic downtown. Puzzled but accommodating, Mayor Jackson proudly showed off the downtown's recently restored buildings and new streetscape improvements. All had been achieved through a downtown master plan, which was implemented as a joint effort of the city government and the local Main Street program. Following the downtown showcase, he then continued with the balance of the tour, including various industrial sites.

After the executives' trip, the intensive courting process accelerated, and the mayor was ultimately victorious in his efforts. Months later at a social event, the mayor finally had a golden opportunity to unleash the question that had bewildered him since their initial meeting and tour: Why were those executives so interested in Murfreesboro's downtown? The response was that the condition of a community's historic downtown was a litmus test for his company, as it reflects the community's general economic health, progressiveness, and level of civic pride. In short, some of the benefits of downtown planning and revitalization are not always obvious and easily measured, but they are often extensive and substantial.

2

The Process of Preparing a Downtown Plan

The pseudoscience of city planning and its companion, the art of city design, have not yet broken with the specious comfort of wishes, familiar superstitions, oversimplifications, and symbols, and have not yet embarked upon the adventure of probing the real world. . . . The way to get at what goes on in the seemingly mysterious and perverse behavior of cities is, I think, to look closely, and with as little previous expectation as is possible, at the most ordinary scenes and events, and attempt to see what they mean and whether any threads of principle emerge among them.
> —Jane Jacobs, *The Death and Life of Great American Cities*

Because a primary intended audience for this book is planners who are already familiar with the fundamental steps taken in creating a plan, it is not the intent of this chapter to detail the generic planning process. Instead, it will focus on topics related specifically to the process of planning for downtowns.

As with any daunting task, it is easiest to tackle a project the magnitude of a community plan—including a downtown plan—by breaking it up into distinct individual steps. Some steps may overlap in sequencing, and that is fine. While there are numerous ways to structure the planning process, the following time-tested steps are the most effective and straightforward approach for any type of plan:

- Research and Analysis
- Concept Plan Creation

- Draft Plan Development
- Finalizing the Plan

While there are many variations for adapting this basic approach to fit the specific needs of a particular downtown, each phase should be sequenced to build upon the previous phase. Using this four-step methodology as the context, the following pages will show how they are applied when creating a downtown plan for a small or midsize city.

DIAGNOSTIC PHASE: RESEARCH AND ANALYSIS

This initial stage of work serves as the foundation for the entire plan. While it is tempting to begin developing ideas for a downtown plan—or any type of plan—from the very outset of the project, it is best to refrain from preconceived notions that might steer the planning team down the wrong path. Instead, planners should do the necessary research and analysis to ensure that all ideas presented later in the process are grounded in the reality of the downtown's existing conditions and trends rather than in perceptions and hearsay.

What Data Are Relevant?

Data collection can be a time-consuming endeavor, and the thorough analysis of data can be even more so. Consequently, it is important at the front end of a planning project to determine what information is really critical to the plan. Often referred to as a "needs assessment," the planners should work with the plan sponsors and other stakeholders to identify the key issues for the downtown to help narrow and focus the collection of data. The type of information sought should be linked directly to the specific issues that will be addressed in the plan. While some of these materials may not be relevant to all downtowns or readily available when the planning process begins, the sidebar on the following page contains a list of data needed to ground the process.

This list is not radically different from the types of information needed for a communitywide comprehensive plan, an open space plan, a bicycle and pedestrian plan, a housing plan, or an economic development plan. However, there are some key distinctions. First, because of the historic nature of most downtowns, more information is typically needed regarding historic buildings, existing historic zoning and design standards, any financial incentives for historic preservation, and organizations involved in preservation. As in the case of economic development and housing plans, downtown plans also focus more on economic and market issues than other types of

Data Needed to Begin a Downtown Planning Process

Historic Information

- Historic photographs of downtown
- Historic maps of downtown, such as Sanborn fire insurance maps
- Inventory of historic sites
- National Register of Historic Places nomination materials

Physical Conditions Information

- Base maps depicting blocks, lot lines, building footprints, rights-of-way, streets, and sidewalks
- Aerial photograph map
- Existing land-use map
- Utilities map
- Topographical map

Socioeconomic Information

- Inventory of existing downtown businesses and institutions
- Inventory of downtown properties: ownership, size, improvements, use, value, zoning
- Retail sales statistics
- Housing inventory by unit types and occupancies
- Employment statistics and trends
- Property tax data: tax rate formulas and assessed values
- Real-estate market data: vacancy rates, absorption rates, average rents, land values, building permit trends

- Demographic profiles and population forecasts, including U.S. Census data
- Tourism statistics and trends
- Crime statistics

Public Policy Information

- Previous downtown plans and studies
- City comprehensive plan
- Zoning map
- Zoning ordinance and development codes
- Historic preservation ordinance and design guidelines
- Transit information: route maps, schedules, pricing, ridership data
- Capital improvements plan
- Municipal budget
- Funding programs and financial incentives

Political and Organizational Information

- List of elected officials
- List of relevant staff and volunteers for the city and the downtown organization
- List of key downtown stakeholders in the private sector
- Organizational flow chart of the local government
- Bylaws of the downtown organization

Figure 2-1. Historic photographs, such as this one of Murray, Kentucky, can offer useful clues to a downtown's past. In addition to their substantive value for revealing past streetscape and building designs, historic photographs can emphasize the importance of retaining the downtown's historic integrity and perhaps even strike an emotional chord with readers that will strengthen their support for a downtown plan. Source: Murray Main Street

plans. A citywide comprehensive plan, for example, is not typically intended to be a catalyst for new development. Instead, it is a public policy document with the perspective that, if and when future growth happens, "here is where it should be located, and this is how it should function and appear." One of its main implementation tools is zoning. On the other hand, downtown plans often have the goal of instigating redevelopment within the very near future. Thus, the time-sensitive nature of economic data that might be less relevant to a comprehensive plan may be very relevant to a downtown plan. If a plan intends to identify specific business types that should be recruited to the downtown, it must use current data.

The type of background information planners collect should be linked directly to the specific issues to be addressed in the downtown plan. The collection of data should not absorb an unreasonable amount of time and money, and it should not be a distraction from the larger task at hand—planning. Nevertheless, it must be anticipated that any errors in planning data might later be illuminated should plan detractors surface and attempt to undermine the plan's credibility.

Market Analysis

In order to understand how developers, business owners, and new residents might be attracted to a downtown, planners must fully understand the downtown's real estate market and the area's economic dynamics. A downtown's market and economic conditions are rarely as obvious as the physical conditions identified through fieldwork, but they are certainly as important. Market analysis is a specific type of economic analysis that determines the existing and future potentials for land uses and development. Market analysis can focus on housing, retail, offices, entertainment, tourist attractions, public facilities, and industrial uses, to name a few. The process involves an assessment of existing market conditions but also uses standard techniques to forecast the warranted demand for one or more specific uses within a target area based upon economic or demographic projections, absorption trends, and other factors. Market analysis does not simply determine "if" sufficient market demand for a particular use exists, which is sometimes a given, but rather the scale and characteristics of that use. The market potential for a downtown is often not captured by existing uses or is otherwise underdeveloped. A market analysis should identify this potential and answer the specific strategic questions relating to revitalization and ongoing management of the downtown.

Effective market analyses identify key opportunities if certain conditions are met. For example, a simple analysis might suggest that there is only limited demand for housing for sale in a downtown, based upon demographic forecasts and real estate trends. However, it should also explore the conditions necessary to result in greater demand for housing and explain the requirements for those conditions to be met. Market analysis describes a downtown's potential in terms of square feet of commercial space, number of housing units, acres of industrial land, or other measures, thereby linking directly to the physical planning process. Going beyond merely a handful of major land-use categories, the downtown's market potentials can determine very specific use categories, such as drugstores, shoe stores, and other business types. In addition to identifying the optimal tenant mix, market analysis can help to determine viable rent structures, sales pricing, marketing concepts, and target market segments. Market analysis not only provides the basis for remerchandising, retenanting, and other strategies to help existing businesses grow, but it often identifies unmet demand in the current market that could be captured by existing businesses through a targeted marketing strategy. Market findings can also be fed directly into recommendations for strategic marketing and promotion of downtown as a whole, as well as management of the downtown. As valuable as market analysis can be for local governments and downtown entities, it is certainly not a tool limited to the public sector. Because market analyses are also required by lenders to finance private development, it is important for downtowns to have a "bankable" assessment of real opportunities supported in the market.

The objectives of market analyses should be tied directly to the strategic questions and uses relevant to a particular downtown. Planners can forecast the potential for the market for the following uses in a downtown:

- Retail (including restaurants, public markets, and personal service businesses)
- Entertainment (theaters, galleries, family entertainment centers)
- Office space
- Industrial uses
- Housing (rental and for-sale)
- Museums and other tourism attractions
- Audience support facilities (civic centers, arenas, amphitheaters, convention centers)

They can also do forecasts of market potential for events, festivals, and other activities.

Often, market analyses are used to answer specific strategic questions, such as how to preserve or generate affordable housing, how to attract artists or create an arts district, how to attract corporate headquarters downtown, how to reuse obsolete industrial space, how to prevent chain stores from squeezing out small retailers, or how to generate tourism. Because of the importance of post offices and other public buildings as crucial traffic generators, one of the first questions asked at the outset of any downtown planning process should be, Are any governmental uses in the downtown considering relocating outside of downtown? and, Are any governmental uses existing or proposed for outside of the downtown that might be located downtown instead? Should the city identify any such public facilities, it is then incumbent upon the downtown planners to become familiar with the space and programmatic needs of the facility so that workable solutions can be found to benefit the downtown.

Once a qualified professional (e.g., a consulting firm, economic development department staff, or planning staff) has prepared a market analysis for a municipality or a downtown entity, that analysis should be made available to the local business community. Unless a market analysis is promoted among a wide spectrum of the downtown's economic stakeholders, its full value cannot be realized. One source of information for performing market analysis is Schmidtz and Brett (2001). However, because of the high level of expertise required to do reliable market analysis, it is recommended that such work be left to experts.

Public Input Before the Background Study Is Created

Downtown planning is no different than other types of planning in that public input is critical for a variety of reasons—to obtain useful information, to gain ideas for the plan, and to generate the political support needed for both formal adoption and subsequent implementation of the plan. However, relative to communitywide plans affecting a broader geographic area, downtown planning activities often attract more public participants. Stakeholders who live, work, or own property in the downtown often feel directly affected because all of the plan's recommendations will be targeted to a very finite area—their area.

Meetings with the public should occur at the very outset of any planning project. Information and opinions obtained early on from the community are indispensable to those preparing the plan. If the planning team fails to meet with the public until it is substantially into the project, the community will rightfully question the team's sincerity in soliciting input that will truly benefit the plan.

An endless range of vehicles exists for proactively securing public input. No single approach is necessarily "the" best approach, as every community is different, so the challenge is to identify the optimal approach for the subject downtown. One starting point is to discuss the subject with local leaders and planning staff to determine what types of public participation approaches have succeeded in the past. Examples of public input tools that have succeeded for many downtown plans include the following:

- A project steering committee comprising diverse downtown stakeholders to guide the planning process
- Stakeholder meetings with individuals representing a distinct interest or perspective
- Leadership interviews with key individuals whose buy-in is critical
- A project kick-off meeting with the public to initiate the broader participation process

Background Study Preparation

When manpower and budgets permit, background studies including the data described above are an effective means of assembling, organizing, and documenting a downtown's existing conditions prior to the actual planning process. The background study ought to be prepared prior to the preparation of the concept plan so that it can inform the people preparing the concept plan. In some cases, individuals involved with the concept plan's creation may not have any significant involvement in the project up to that point, so the background study can be used to brief them. Also, a review of the background study by the plan sponsor and other stakeholders can point out any incorrect information so that a completely accurate picture of the downtown is established prior to the planning phase. That step is valuable both for practical reasons and to inspire public confidence in the planning team and process. Despite its merits, a background study should not absorb too much time and resources. Otherwise, limited resources will be diverted from the more important subsequent planning stage.

THE BIG IDEAS: CREATING THE CONCEPT PLAN

Once planners have this solid foundation of knowledge about the downtown, the real work of planning can begin. The most practical way to arrive at a detailed downtown plan, as with other types of plans, is to begin with a very general "concept plan." The most basic ideas must first be conceived, evaluated, and either kept or discarded before the specifics can be expanded into a more detailed plan.

Although it is sometimes known prior to the concept planning stage that planners will need to consider alternative concepts or visions during the process, such concepts are likely to arise anyway once the process begins. Any concept planning exercise should remain flexible enough to accommodate more than one scheme before the various scenarios are honed down into a single concept. In some cases, this narrowing of options will require a formal presentation and review process in order for the plan's sponsors to determine the preferred scheme.

A concept plan can come about in a number of ways. The most popular approach and one that has gained widespread use over the past decade is the charrette, an intensive process in which multiple people brainstorm ideas over a limited amount of time. In communities where too many charrettes have occurred in recent years, particularly unsuccessful ones, the term "workshop" may be more palatable. Regardless of the nomenclature, the end product is the concept plan, which serves as the framework on which to build the complete and detailed downtown plan. Although charrettes are typically very public affairs involving numerous volunteer "citizen planners," they do not always need to be so hands-on for the public. The same intensive brainstorming process can be limited to the professionals preparing the plan or involve only a limited number of stakeholders, such as elected officials and municipal staff. While some communities choose this less public brand of charrette, it is usually not the best option, as it can severely limit the number of ideas generated, the level of public buy-in, and the enthusiasm that a more public process can generate. For more information on charrettes, see *The Charrette Handbook* (Lennertz and Lutzenhiser 2006).

Setting the Stage: Planning to Plan

Assuming that many important decisions must be made within a limited amount of time (usually just a few days), the process of starting the concept plan should be efficiently executed. Going into the concept plan phase, the following tasks should have already been completed:

- Completion of research and analysis
- Scheduling logistics
- Assembly of needed materials
- Definition of the desired outcome

This last point requires elaboration. To successfully create a concept plan as the basis of a detailed downtown plan, there must be a clear, desired outcome for the plan. The substantive ideas that will constitute the concept plan can still be unexplored territory prior to the work of actually drafting the plan, but the specific issues to be addressed and questions to be answered should not be. For instance, by this stage in the project, planners should have created a detailed plan outline or table of contents, and that outline or table of contents should have been approved by the plan's sponsor so that outline can be used as a guide. The concept plan should address, in broad terms, the most rudimentary sections of the plan outline. Below is a list of issues addressed by the typical downtown concept plan; they should all be addressed in the outline or table of contents:

- Land uses—general mix and locations
- Streets and alleys—cross-section designs, directional flow of traffic, extensions
- Streetscapes—general dimensions and character

- Public spaces—enhancements to existing spaces, proposed new spaces
- Key infill development opportunities—site locations, physical characteristics
- Key building rehabilitation opportunities—specific buildings and potential uses
- Organization—strengthening of existing entities, establishment of new entities
- Economic restructuring—strategies for tenant mixes and development incentives
- Marketing and promotion—strategies for marketing campaigns and special events

Note, however, that the last three issues (organization, economic restructuring, and marketing and promotion) may not need to be addressed in detail at this stage if the physical planning issues addressed in the concept plan are not contingent upon them.

The Process of Creating a Concept Plan

What follows is a summary of one logical, straightforward, and commonly used approach to preparing a concept plan. Because not all communities choose to vigorously engage the public during the concept planning stage, and because a separate discussion follows on involving the public, the approach summarized here takes a minimalist view on public participation.

1. Hold a project team meeting to organize and fine-tune the process
2. Revisit the study area to better understand it
3. Debate the key issues to begin giving the plan some direction
4. Put pen to paper to express the ideas to which those preparing the plan can react
5. Meet with the plan sponsors to test the ideas and get further direction
6. Refine the concept plan to present to the public

The process summarized above is only one alternative, and many variations are possible. The approach taken should be tailored to the specific needs of the subject downtown, its stakeholders and the overall project.

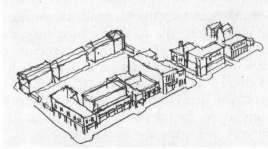

Figure 2-2a–b. While successful concept planning sessions usually benefit from participants representing a variety of planning-related disciplines, urban designers will be especially in demand. Sources: The Walker Collaborative (top); The Walker Collaborative / Barry Mahaffey (bottom)

Engaging the Public in the Concept Plan

While a meaningful public input process is strongly recommended for any downtown plan, the extent of citizen participation is ultimately the choice of each individual community. Judging from the experience of numerous downtowns, there is a direct correlation between the level of public participation and the prospects for successful plan implementation. Those communities that most vigorously engage the public seem to have the highest rates of success in implementing their plans. According to Joey Dunn, AICP, who helped lead the creation of the Bryan, Texas, downtown plan, "The downtown plan must set the vision with true stakeholder buy-in to convert the plan from paper to pavers. Downtown revitalization is all about momentum, and a good plan sets the stage." It is the combined duty of the planning team and the plan sponsor to ensure that, when the planning process is completed, the community has a true sense of ownership. In order for the plan to be actually implemented, it must be perceived as the community's plan, not the professional planners' plan.

Approaches to soliciting public participation during the early stages of planning were addressed above. While it is important to involve members of the public at the very outset of a downtown planning project, their involvement at the concept planning stage is especially crucial. This stage offers the most hands-on opportunity for participation. The public's active collaboration with the planners through charrettes and similar vehicles can result in the ideas of citizens making it into the ultimate plan.

There are many ways to actively engage the public in the concept plan development stage. The methods most frequently applied to downtown planning are equally effective for other types of planning. Some planners use an incremental process in which each stage of planning is followed by a "feedback loop" whereby the public can review the latest work and provide its input. Another method is to hold a series of open houses for the public to drop in on the planners and observe their work, ask questions, and provide input. That approach requires that the open house segments be limited in duration in order for the planning team to have periods of uninterrupted progress. One

Figure 2-3. One of the most magical moments for any downtown planning process, when included, is the public charrette workshop in which dozens of "citizen planners" exercise their democratic rights by planning their own destiny. Source: The Walker Collaborative / Russ Stephenson

of the most popular, time-tested, and effective methods is the "citizens as planners" workshop. While there are numerous potential variations, one approach involves:

- *Recruitment of public participants.* Several dozen individuals representing a broad cross-section of downtown stakeholders should be scheduled for the workshop.
- *Workshop orientation.* At the beginning of the workshop, the project team discusses the workshop purpose and agenda, key findings of background research, the results of the public input to date, and workshop "ground rules."
- *Planning session.* Participants are split into teams of approximately 10 people, and each team sits at its own table armed with a base map, colored markers, and other materials for preparing their own concept plan.
- *Plan presentations and wrap-up.* Stakeholder teams reassemble into a single large group and each team presents its plans.

Because this method of engaging the public in such a hands-on fashion is optional and up to the plan's sponsors, it was described here after the section on the "Concept Planning Process." However, if this or a similar approach is used, it should actually occur at the front end of the concept planning phase of the project. For example, within the context of a three-day charrette, it would typically occur on the first evening.

Presenting the Concept Plan

In the grand scheme, the one or two hours spent presenting the concept plan may be the most pivotal one or two hours of the entire downtown planning project. If the plan or its presenters are a failure, the results can range from needing to redo a great deal of work, to the plan sponsors losing confidence in the planning team, to the community losing faith in the sponsors and the process. If, on the other hand, the presentation is a resounding success, it can mean that the plan is destined for adoption so long as there is attention to detail and savvy political navigation during the balance of the project.

While the concept plan should be presented in a professional manner, it need not be overly polished. The focus of the multiday concept planning effort should be the preparation of the concept plan rather than its presentation. The meeting agenda should include introductions and background information to benefit those who have not yet been exposed to the project. However, the majority of time should be

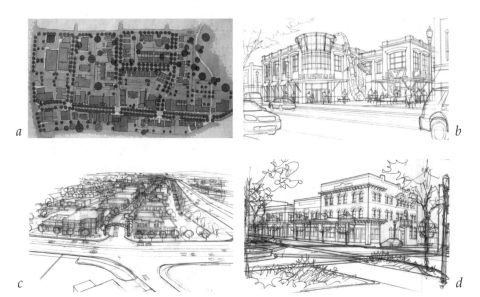

Figure 2-4a–d. This concept plan and supporting sketches for a portion of downtown High Point, North Carolina, when supplemented by a verbal description, provide the downtown's stakeholders with the most basic ideas being proposed. More refined graphics will later be prepared once a consensus is forged on the general direction that the plan is headed. Source: The Walker Collaborative / Third Coast Design Studio / Ben Johnson

reserved for presenting the concept plan and then discussing it with the public. It is important to emphasize that the ideas being presented are preliminary and subject to change once feedback is obtained.

ROLLING UP YOUR SLEEVES: DRAFT PLAN PREPARATION

Once the "big picture" planning has been achieved through the concept plan's creation, the detailed work must begin. Like with a newly constructed building consisting of only its foundation, framing, and roof, it is now time to add the exterior sheathing, doors, windows, and other key components. This phase of the project typically entails more individual effort among the various disciplines represented on the project planning team. For example, the landscape architects will begin working out details of the streetscape designs and public spaces. The architects and urban designers will be focusing on infill development concept plans and design guidelines for building rehabilitation and infill development. The traffic engineers will be developing alternative street cross-sections and devising traffic calming schemes, if relevant. The real estate economists will be evaluating the feasibility of a tax-increment financing district and developing the list of targeted new tenants to be recruited. And the historic preservation specialists will be evaluating the potential of historic district designation. They should all be communicating with one another as they conduct their work. Below is a summary of how the concept plan evolves into a legitimate downtown plan.

Introductory Material

If the background study prepared at the beginning of the planning process is not included as part of the draft downtown plan, a brief introduction should still be included. Many plans also begin with a set of principles that were adopted to guide the plan. Sometimes referred to as goals or objectives, the principles are the broad concepts on which the plan is built. For example, the Kalamazoo, Michigan, 2004 downtown plan used this approach. It includes a single page describing seven different "guiding principles" that served as the plan's foundation. Such principles are useful to revisit during the planning process if the project loses direction and a compass point is needed. This prelude to the actual plan will provide the reader with context.

The Physical Plan

The components of a downtown plan related to physical enhancements are generally the most memorable and easily understood because they can be conveyed graphically, as opposed to financial incentive programs and similar revitalization strategies. The specific topics included in the physical plan will depend upon the scope of work established at the beginning of the project. There is usually a direct relationship between that scope and available funding for the plan's preparation. However, taking a comprehensive perspective and assuming there are no unusual funding constraints, the physical plan elements summarized below should be featured in the most thorough downtown plans. These components apply to the plan recommendations portion of the document and do not include the existing conditions analysis that may have appeared in the background study, if one were included. Also, the ideas below are limited to an overview of the components for the

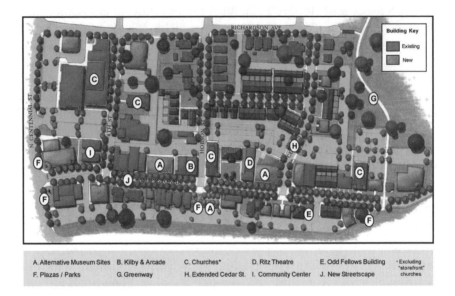

A. Alternative Museum Sites | B. Kilby & Arcade | C. Churches* | D. Ritz Theatre | E. Odd Fellows Building | *Excluding "storefront" churches
F. Plazas / Parks | G. Greenway | H. Extended Cedar St. | I. Community Center | J. New Streetscape

Figure 2-5. This illustrative master plan for a portion of downtown High Point, North Carolina, uses color coding and letters corresponding to legends to describe the plan's key ideas. This type of graphic is the single most important one for most downtown plans, and it serves as a plan synopsis that is explained by the balance of the plan document. Source: The Walker Collaborative / Third Coast Design Studio

physical plan in light of the planning process, while Chapter 3 addresses the substantive facets that make for an effective physical plan.

Illustrative plan. Serving essentially as a graphic table of contents for the plan's physical planning recommendations, this critical element illustrates some of the plan's most central ideas within a single map of the study area. The pages that follow the illustrative plan should explain it in greater detail.

Land uses. This section of the physical plan should include a color-coded proposed land-use map and accompanying text that describes each land-use category, including suggested uses and densities. Because of the mixed use nature of downtowns, such maps sometimes address only the ground-floor uses, recognizing that the options for most of the upper-floor space in a downtown should be limited to offices and residences.

Circulation, streets, and streetscapes. In addition to the explanatory text, the following graphics should be provided in the physical plan:

- Circulation and street improvements map—streets by type, directional flows, key improvements
- Street cross-sections—driving lanes, on-street parking, sidewalks, landscaping, building facades
- Street segment designs—concept plans for specific street segments
- Streetscape furnishings—images of recommended benches, street lights, trash receptacles

Parking. A map and supporting text should address the following types of downtown parking:

- On-street parking—distinguishing between parallel and angled parking
- Parking lots—conveying lot locations, access locations, and number of spaces
- Structured parking—if applicable

In addition to the types and location of parking, this section should address the design of parking lots and garages.

Infill development and rehabilitation opportunities. The text and graphics for this section should include the following:

- Infill and rehabilitation sites map—distinguishing between infill and rehabilitation sites
- Urban and architectural design principles—text and graphics for infill and rehabilitation
- Schematic renderings of infill and rehabilitation—sample elevations or perspectives

Public spaces. One of the key issues that section of the physical plan should clarify is the proposed function and character of public spaces.

Graphics supported by explanatory text should address the following issues regarding public spaces:

- Public spaces map—location of existing and proposed parks, plazas, and greenways
- Public space concept plans—depicting improved and new public spaces

Figure 2-6. This deteriorated and partially vacant old building may have tremendous potential, but that potential is not apparent to many people.
Source: The Walker Collaborative

Figure 2-7. Computerized visual simulations can be a powerful tool to vividly convey how a building and its context can be dramatically improved.
Source: The Walker Collaborative / Juan Ayala—Invisioneering

Utilities. To the extent that utilities are a significant issue for the downtown, the following utility types might be addressed through one or more maps depicting line and facility locations:

- Drainage—map of existing stormwater drains, storm sewer lines, and proposed improvements
- Sanitary sewers and water—map of existing lines and proposed improvements
- Electricity and telecommunications—map of existing lines and proposed improvements

The Economic and Marketing Plan

Although some downtown plans fail to address the important topics of economics and marketing, years of focusing on streetscape and facade improvements has led many communities to realize that such a one-dimensional approach will not bring long-term change to their downtown. That understanding has been reinforced by the efforts of the National Main Street Center and its Four Point Approach, which advocates economic restructuring and marketing and promotion, as well as organization and design. Below are some of the typical components of an economic and marketing strategy for downtowns. As with the discussion of the physical plan above, the ideas here address the contents of the economic and marketing plan as part of the planning process. Chapter 4 covers the substantive aspects of this topic.

Market positioning. This section of the economic development and marketing plan evaluates the downtown in relation to the region's competing commercial and mixed use areas, and existing models within the area are often used in describing the desired market position.

Tenant mix and business development. Because the primary reason that people visit a downtown is for its specific destinations, this plan section is critical. A market analysis is the most effective way to determine the optimal tenant mix. Business development strategies offer steps to retain and expand existing downtown businesses, as well as recruitment strategies for new businesses.

Housing development. Many downtown programs focus on retail and service uses, but housing is a component that cannot be overlooked. While the plan's land-use strategy in the physical planning section should address potential locations and housing types, this plan section should address targeted market segments, pricing, marketing, and financial incentives for housing development, if applicable.

Management, marketing, and promotion. This plan section explains how downtowns can employ the same general management strategies used by suburban shopping malls but in a manner appropriate for a downtown. Centralized retail management (CRM) approaches might address days and hours of operation and common area maintenance (CAM) programs, while marketing and promotion strategies frequently consider a downtown logo, joint advertising among businesses, sales promotions, special events, and downtown marketing campaigns.

Social Issues

Examples of social issues that might be addressed in a downtown plan include crime, homelessness, panhandling, and gentrification. In practice, however, social issues are not addressed by most downtown plans except in the largest cities where the problems tend to be more magnified. Although social issues are often overlooked in downtown plans, they should be addressed much more often than they are. Even the most attractive and vibrant downtowns in affluent midsize cities have panhandlers who can scare off shoppers and potential residents, thereby damaging the downtown's economic viability. Not only are there selfish reasons for the downtown to want to address social issues negatively affecting them, but there are obviously humanitarian justifications as well. There are also many existing models that can be studied and adapted from communities (e.g., Berkeley, California, which, according to its mayor, in 2007, had more services for homeless people per capita than anyplace in the U.S.).

Implementation Strategy

As with marketing, management, and social recommendations, plan implementation is another topic frequently overlooked by downtown plans focused on physical solutions. Without this vital plan section, many communities will be mystified on how to get from the planning stage to the "doing" stage. The substantive facets of this issue are addressed in Chapter 5. Among the implementation issues that need to be addressed are the following:

Organization. The role of existing entities responsible for the plan's implementation, such as the municipal government or downtown organization, should be spelled out here, as well as suggestions for the creation of a new entity to help implement the downtown plan.

Public policy amendments. Policies commonly recommended as amendments to the downtown plan are the community's comprehensive plan, zoning ordinance, development regulations, and building codes. In particular, barriers to the plan's urban and architectural design recommendations should be addressed, as well as restrictions on desirable uses, permitted inappropriate uses, and overly stringent parking standards.

Development strategy. This portion of the plan provides the link between the economics and the physical plan, as it makes site-specific recommendations on building reuse, redevelopment, and new development in the downtown based upon the market analysis. This strategy also provides an assessment of the marketability of those buildings and sites, and it should have a strong relationship with the plan's recommendations for urban design, infrastructure, and marketing and financial incentives.

Funding and financial incentives. At the most basic level, planners need to understand private-sector development financing in the context of downtown development. If developers are having trouble obtaining financing to create downtown housing, for example, even the most aggressive public funding mechanisms and incentives may be of limited value. By exploring private funding issues with local developers and the financial community, strategies can be pursued to remove financing roadblocks. In addition to addressing private-sector funding, this plan section should identify potential public funding sources at the local, state, regional, and federal levels. It should explore ways to improve existing programs, in addition to potential new funding sources.

Implementation matrix. This user-friendly chart should summarize all of the plan's key recommendations by issue. It should reference the plan's page numbers for detailed information about the basis for the recommendation. It also needs to indicate the proposed timeframe and the sequencing for carrying out the actions necessary to fulfill each recommendation, and it needs to designate the parties responsible for implementing each recommendation. Some implementation matrixes go a step further and indicate the level of priority for each recommendation, as well as the cost or general cost range and funding sources.

FINALIZING THE PLAN

Presenting the Plan

Once planners have submitted the draft downtown plan to the plan's sponsor, sufficient time needs to be allowed for a review to suggest revisions. After an initial round of revisions is made, the plan needs to undergo public review. Alternative approaches include the following:

Public presentations. A serious effort should be made to attract a large turnout for all public presentations. Because of the importance of building momentum to push the planning phase into a fruitful implementation phase, presentations should kindle public enthusiasm. In fact,

Figure 2-8. The public presentation of the downtown plan warrants thoughtful preparation in order to attract and sell the audience on the plan's merits. Source: The Walker Collaborative

some communities generate a festive atmosphere by incorporating the plan presentation into a larger event. Main Street Murray, Kentucky, used the presentation of its new downtown plan in 2000 as the "main event" for its annual reception and membership meeting.

"Dog and Pony" show. To expose many different groups to the downtown plan without spending money on consultants, some plan sponsors present the plan themselves at various venues, such as the regular meeting of service organizations.

Internet. Even the smallest organization lacking a website can usually find a hosting entity, such as the local government, economic development agency, or chamber of commerce, to post the plan on the Internet.

Television. Many plan sponsors record the main presentation to show on local television networks.

Newspaper inserts. Local newspapers often include a special insert summarizing the downtown plan by including key graphics, summarizing text, and conducting interviews with those involved in the planning process and those most affected.

Plan Revisions and Adoption

After the public has weighed in on the draft plan and the plan sponsors have reviewed the document in detail, revisions will usually be needed. The appropriateness of formally adopting a downtown plan will usually depend upon the plan's sponsoring organization. In most cases, governmental entities will adopt the plan so it becomes part of their official public policy, and it paves the way for more far-reaching policy changes, such as zoning. Nongovernmental organizations, on the other hand, may choose not to adopt the plan because its adoption would achieve no particular advantage nor extend them any further authority within the study area.

The potential for the plan's formal adoption should be considered at the very beginning of the project, as it may affect specific plan contents. Many states have legislation with specific requirements for the contents of "redevelopment plans." Such plans are often required in order for the organization that will implement the plan (e.g., a downtown planning authority) to have specific powers and privileges within the study area, such as condemnation authority. Adopting a downtown plan as an official redevelopment plan can also qualify an organization for certain state and federal funding that might be unavailable otherwise.

WHAT HAPPENS AFTER THE PLANNING?

What does it mean to actually implement a plan? Some downtown plans currently sit on shelves, and many people consider them as not having been implemented, but "implemented" is a difficult term to define within the context of planning. In most cases, at least some ideas contained in these "unimplemented" plans have indeed been put into action. For instance, it may be difficult to secure hundreds of thousands of dollars to redevelop a streetscape, but amending a zoning ordinance and installing new awnings are achievable tasks for virtually any community. In fact, few downtown plans have been either entirely implemented or entirely neglected. Implementation of most plans requires both public and private-sector actions, and they typically occur over a considerable amount of time—five, 10, even 20 years. So, is the threshold for achieving bona fide implementation 50 percent, 70 percent, or 90 percent of the plan's recommendations? There is no definitive answer, but it is clearly not an "all or nothing" issue. Summarized below are steps for implementing, and later revisiting, a downtown plan.

Ready, Set, Go: Plan Implementation

By the time the downtown plan is completed, in most cases it either still has a chance for substantial implementation or it does not. If, for example, there was insufficient public participation and buy-in, it may be dead on arrival. If key leaders, particularly elected officials, are not entirely on board, the plan may have no chance of successful implementation. If there were serious credibility issues about those who prepared the plan, the plan may be ready for a premature retirement. Below are the eight rudimentary first steps for embarking on successful plan implementation:

Establish an implementation committee. A relatively standard procedure is to convert the planning project's steering committee, if one existed, into the implementation committee. If there was no steering committee, one will need to be formed. If the committee is affiliated with a local government, it should be given official status and should be given some level of responsibility in order to attract capable individuals to serve on it. The implementation committee will need to meet regularly—at least monthly—and it should be staffed to ensure that progress is made.

Get all of the implementers on board. It should be a primary objective of the planning process to achieve buy-in from all key players who will be critical to the plan's implementation. Although that goal will hopefully be reached before the plan is completed, it may be necessary to revisit some of those groups and individuals to reconfirm their commitment to the plan.

Start with the plan's "low-hanging fruit." Given the wide range of recommendations contained in the typical downtown plan, some are much easier to accomplish than others. Public policy amendments, such as zoning revisions not calling for major code rewrites, often require little funding or manpower. There are also some high-impact but low-cost aesthetic improvements that can enhance the downtown's appearance, such as adding decorative planters to streetscapes and colorful new awnings for storefronts.

Prioritize the plan's organizational recommendations. To accomplish the plan's more challenging ideas, a high level of organization will be needed. Depending upon the specific recommendations of the plan, if a downtown entity does not already exist it will likely need to be established. After Bryan, Texas, adopted its new downtown master plan in 2001, one of the first plan recommendations that it implemented was the creation of a downtown redevelopment authority. That entity was critical to the subsequent streetscape redevelopment, facade rehabilitations for more than 35 buildings assisted by the plan's recommended financial incentives, and the opening of numerous new businesses.

Do something visible. Although it may go by some other name, many downtown plans include a "quick victory" project within the implementation section of the document. This project is one with high odds for success and high visibility, and the intent is to help jump-start the plan's implementation. An early success sends out a clear message that the community is serious about implementing the new plan, and it can help to build needed support and momentum. When Greenville, Texas, created a downtown plan in 1999, its "quick victory" project was the city's acquisition and rehabilitation of the "white elephant" Henson Building, sending out a strong statement to the community.

Pressure, entice, and partner with the private sector. Once the local government or downtown organization has done its part to create a plan, it is time for the private sector to follow. In fact, some communities will strategically stall the initiation of a downtown plan until there is sufficient commitment from existing businesses and property owners. Upon

Figure 2-9. Purchased by the City of Greenville, Texas, during the latter stages of its downtown master-planning project, the restoration and leasing up of the "white elephant" Henson Building became the quick victory project of the plan's implementation section. That move generated additional excitement and momentum for the plan before it was even adopted by the city council. Source: The Walker Collaborative

the plan's completion, it is equally reasonable to withhold costly public improvements, such as streetscape redevelopments, until a sufficient number of adjacent property owners agree to make at least minimal improvements to their properties.

Pursue grant funding. Despite the commonly heard mantra, "We'll just get a grant to do that," grant funding is not nearly as available as many would believe. While there are numerous grants available through most levels of government, as well as private foundations, pursuing them is a competitive endeavor. Even if acquired, the red tape and strings attached can sometimes outweigh their value. Regardless of the advantages and disadvantages of grant funding, a downtown that has recently completed a planning process has a much greater chance of winning grants than those that have not.

Celebrate and publicize the victories. Every downtown achievement, no matter how large or small, should be treated as a precious jewel that cannot be wasted. For the most challenged downtowns, successes can be few and far between, particularly in the early stages of revitalization when momentum may not exist. Communities should reward themselves for their hard work and celebrate even the smallest downtown victories. They should also publicize them through newsletters and press releases.

Avoiding Complacency: Revisiting the Plan

So how long is too long to go between downtown plans? The trend of most communities and the correct answer are two entirely different matters. While some communities never develop a downtown plan, those that do tend to go from approximately 10 to 20 years between plans. In fact, they should at least revisit their plans annually. An annual revisit would not necessarily need to include actual revisions to the document, but the plan's ideas should certainly be reconsidered and priorities reevaluated in order to keep the plan current and valid.

Because of the extent of change that can occur to a downtown over a mere five-year period, it is recommended that the downtown plan be updated a minimum of every five years. In fact, for those states that mandate periodic citywide comprehensive planning, five years is the most common required period for updates. For those communities trying to determine when a new downtown plan is needed independent of standardized schedules, they should consider the rules of thumb outlined in the beginning of Chapter 1.

3

The Physical Plan

It is no longer a mystery how to start a downtown revitalization process, though it is more complex than suburban real estate development, and takes longer than most politicians are in office.

—Christopher B. Leinberger, *Turning Around Downtown: Twelve Steps to Revitalization*

The physical plan component of a downtown plan should attempt to balance the following objectives:

- Protecting and enhancing the downtown's historic or otherwise unique character
- Developing new buildings and adapting existing buildings to host uses that attract people
- Enhancing the pedestrian environment, while still accommodating automobiles
- Maintaining a human scale through the design of streetscapes, buildings, and public spaces
- Ensuring a safe atmosphere that protects pedestrians, in particular, from crime and automobiles
- Maximizing downtown's aesthetic qualities to make it more appealing and interesting
- Creating a diverse mixture of people, uses, and activities to make the downtown vibrant

These objectives not only are based upon a consensus of downtown experts but also seem to be what people perceive a "good downtown" to be, as reflected in hundreds of public input sessions from across

Top 10 Downtown Planning Myths

The true essence of every downtown plan is a collection of ideas. The misinformed notions below are among those frequently voiced by citizens, sometimes voiced by elected officials, and occasionally voiced by professional planners and downtown "experts" who should know better. Many have some element of truth, but none is accurate in its entirety:

1. *Our downtown just needs one "big ticket" development to turn things around.* Rarely does a "quick fix" really repair a downtown on a long-term basis. Developments such as sports facilities and casinos can vanish as quickly as they arrived, and even if they stick around, their novelty to the public may not. Downtowns that have reversed their downward spirals to become success stories have typically done so incrementally, through numerous small steps over time. Most struggling downtowns did not reach their current conditions overnight, so turning them around overnight is unquestionably unrealistic.

2. *Replacing some existing buildings with parking lots will bring more shoppers downtown.* Buildings are the most fundamental element of any downtown. Generally speaking, more buildings in a downtown—particularly occupied ones—are better than fewer buildings because the activities that occur inside them attract people and their money. People do not visit downtowns to park their cars. Furthermore, in the case of historic or unique buildings, it is their character that helps make the downtown so unique. While parking lots located interior to their blocks are necessary, those fronting directly onto streets create dead spaces along the streetscape and are visually unattractive. Parking is a challenging issue for most downtowns and one that must be addressed, but razing buildings is rarely the long-term solution.

3. *Our strategy for revitalizing downtown should focus on retail.* Successful downtowns enjoy a rich mixture of diverse uses, including offices, housing, institutions, entertainment and, yes, retail. However, a singular focus on retail is usually an ill-advised strategy, despite that fixation

for so many downtown revitalization programs. In fact, given its importance to most downtowns, housing is often the best bet of any component of downtown to promote—though success with housing is frequently difficult to achieve. In addition to providing further market support to retail and other uses, residents make their downtown feel inhabited and safe, thereby attracting those living outside of the downtown to visit for shopping, dining, cultural events, and other activities.

4. *Attractive new brick sidewalks will bring more people downtown.* New sidewalks, as with streetscape improvements in general, are certainly useful in broadcasting a message that downtown is important to the community. As part of a comprehensive urban design strategy, they will sometimes even stimulate adjacent private development, which can indirectly attract more people to the downtown. However, very few people visit downtowns simply to enjoy their high-quality sidewalks, so their value must always be kept in perspective.

5. *Downtown needs a large national department store to compete with the suburban malls.* Unless a downtown is large enough to enjoy the market support of thousands of people on any given day, in most cases time should not be wasted trying to recruit a national department store. Their numeric criteria for trade area employees, residents, and vehicular traffic, as well as sales volume potential per square feet, are typically too high for all but the largest downtowns to meet. Instead, most downtowns are better served by focusing on niche retailing that suburban malls are not filling, in addition to other uses such as offices, housing, and institutions. This principle does not preclude targeting smaller stores that happen to be national chains or franchises, as a limited number of such tenants are usually desirable to supplement locally owned businesses. However, unique independently owned stores are among the strongest draws for most downtowns.

6. *On-street parking should be converted to another driving lane to improve traffic flows for the benefit of downtown.* The inability of vehicles to flow quickly through its streets is not the root of a downtown's problems. A lack of destinations to

attract vehicles and their drivers to the downtown is more likely the challenge. On-street parking is important as a convenience to shoppers and diners, as a traffic calming device for drivers, and as a physical and psychological barrier protecting pedestrians from moving vehicles. The conversion of on-street parking to driving lanes simply results in faster moving traffic that makes downtowns less pedestrian-friendly and less business-friendly.

7. *Existing one-way streets should be maintained for traffic flows that will benefit downtown.* Even more alarming than simply maintaining the status quo, some communities that are still stuck in a 1960s mind-set will proactively contemplate the conversion of existing two-way streets into one-way couplets. One-way traffic is more beneficial to through traffic than it is to traffic for which downtown is the destination. For most downtowns, one-way streets prove unnecessary and even counterproductive because they encourage speeding, limit the visibility of retailers, and are confusing to new visitors to downtown. Confused visitors can easily become irritated

visitors, and irritated visitors may never return. From a traffic flow perspective, one-way streets create many of the same problems caused by the conversion of on-street parking into driving lanes, which, in turn, can generate the need for remedial traffic calming measures.

8. *Downtown special events are a waste of time and money because few dollars are spent in businesses during the events and a great deal of preparation and cleanup are required.* In most cases, special events are more important for their long-term benefits than for their short-term gains. Special events often attract some people who rarely or never frequent downtown, but their attendance at a downtown event makes them aware of businesses or activities that they might seek out at a later date. Furthermore, a positive visitor experience during special events can reap tremendous future rewards, including word-of-mouth advertising. Given the relatively low costs of preparation and clean up, particularly if volunteers are mobilized, special events are a worthwhile form of promotion when strategically linked

to the downtown's particular marketing strengths.

9. *One of downtown's primary streets should be closed to traffic and converted into a pedestrian mall.* While that concept was in vogue during the 1970s, downtown experts are now recommending that these streets be transformed back to drivable ones. Most Americans are still, and might always be, too automobile dependent to completely abandon their cars. Pedestrian malls typically work only in downtowns that have a high resident or employee density, large volumes of tourism, or some other unique circumstance, such as an adjacent university. Charlottesville, Virginia, and Burlington, Vermont, are two examples of downtown pedestrian malls benefited by nearby universities. State Street in downtown Madison, Wisconsin, works because it is doubly blessed—it is located in a high-density downtown and is adjacent to the University of Wisconsin.

10. *Too many regulations will kill downtown's businesses.* Perhaps in theory it would be possible to regulate a downtown to death, but not in political reality. Politicians enacting a detrimental level of regulation would likely be voted out of office. Well-crafted and detailed codes, such as design standards for buildings and signs, might be considered overly stringent by some, but they can clearly elevate the quality of the built environment if used properly. A physically and aesthetically enhanced downtown typically results in increased property values because of one simple principle: real estate values are ultimately based upon the degree of a place's desirability. While the associated increased rents can result in some businesses having to relocate, they are usually replaced by more profitable ones. Some of the most highly regulated downtown districts in America, such as Princeton's Palmer Square, Charleston's King Street, Cambridge's Harvard Square, and New Orleans's French Quarter, are also some of the most commercially successful. In fact, in 2005, the Old Town district in Alexandria, Virginia, added yet another regulatory layer to limit chain stores and ground-floor offices, yet its virtues as a fertile environment for prosperous businesses show no signs of abating.

Figure 3-1. Although all of the key components of a downtown plan are important, including economic, social, and policy issues, the physical planning recommendations tend to be the facet most readily understood and appreciated by the public. Source: The Walker Collaborative / Ben Johnson

the country. Some downtown planning projects use a variety of techniques for soliciting input on the public's perceptions and preferences related to the downtown. The most frequently cited favorite attribute of downtowns is its historic character, but the other objectives listed above are also commonly referenced. Therefore, a successful physical plan should be built upon a foundation that carefully balances all of these goals to create a single cohesive vision for the future.

LAND USES: MIX THEM UP

One of the most distinguishing advantages of downtowns over the suburbs is their walkability. However, research conducted by the Brookings Institution's Metropolitan Policy Program has determined the following:

> People will walk 1,500 feet or more only if they have an interesting and safe streetscape and people to watch along the way—a mix of sights and sounds that can make a pedestrian forget that he is unintentionally getting enjoyable exercise. . . . Fostering such walkable urbanity is the key to the revival of any struggling downtown. But doing so can be a challenging process, requiring the development of a complex mix of retail boutiques, hotels, grocery stores, housing,

offices, artists' studios, restaurants, and entertainment venues. (Leinberger 2005, 2)

The city planning movement's legacy of strictly segregated land uses stemming from the early twentieth century and reaching its zenith during the 1950s and 1960s is the antithesis of how land-use patterns should occur in downtowns. The majority of urban land uses should be physically integrated both vertically—within the same multistory buildings—and horizontally, within the same geographic areas. The distinction between "multiple uses" and "mixed uses" must also be recognized. Multiple-use developments are commonly found in the suburbs. Although they include more than one land use on a single development site, they are usually not physically integrated. They are not bona fide mixed use developments in the truest sense of the term.

A prerequisite for diverse land uses to harmoniously coexist is the appropriate use of building scale and design. In fact, from a compatibility perspective, the scale and design of neighboring structures is generally more important than the uses that occur within them, which is why the popularity of form-based zoning has grown rapidly in

Figure 3-2. The majority of downtown buildings should be mixed use, with ground-floor retail and service uses and upper-floor office and residential uses. This combination optimizes parking facilities and keeps downtowns in use 24 hours a day. Source: Gould Evans Associates

recent years. With the exception of uses that generate excessive truck traffic, such as warehousing, or unusually high parking demands, such as the inventory storage of automobile dealerships, a wide range of differing land uses can usually coexist peacefully in a downtown, and often within the same structure. The most common mix of differing uses within the same building tend to be ground-floor retail or services, combined with upper-floor housing or offices. In particular, the combination of commercial and residential uses is mutually beneficial, as each has contrasting peak-hour parking demands, allowing for nearby parking facilities to be optimized through shared parking. In fact, well-written zoning ordinances recognize the mixed use nature of downtowns and include special provisions for shared parking arrangements.

Retail and Services

Examples of common downtown retail uses include apparel stores, gift shops, furniture stores, bookstores, restaurants, bakeries, and coffeehouses, while services include hair salons, shoe repair shops, and photocopying establishments. Retail and service uses are strongly linked to the genesis of many downtowns. For thousands of years, the securing of goods and services—in a word, "trade"—has been one of the most fundamental activities giving rise to the establishment of urban settlements. Because of their high visibility on the ground floor of key streets, retail and services are still first and foremost in the minds of most people when they think of downtowns.

Here are two important principles to consider when planning for retail and service uses:

1. Unless enough population density and market strength exist to make upper-floor retail and service uses viable, these uses need to occur on ground floors to help activate the street.
2. Retail and service uses should be located on discernible shopping streets in order to receive sufficient visibility and traffic to succeed.

In theory, destination retail uses on upper floors could generate the same level of foot traffic for downtown streetscapes as ground-floor retail could. However, upper-floor retail requires customers to fight gravity to reach their destination, so impulse purchases would be less likely to occur. Also, storefront window displays are one of retail's greatest contributions to downtown streetscapes. Exceptions to this rule include large downtowns with high population densities that feature upper-floor retail and service businesses, as well as multistory businesses in even small downtowns that manage to lure shoppers to upper floors once they have entered the business from the street level.

A minority of downtowns and downtown plans make an attempt to strategically locate specific retail and service businesses in a manner that will optimize sales volumes for the entire downtown. As in suburban shopping malls, which can easily accomplish such a strategy because of their single ownership and control, anchor uses are generally spread out within a downtown to benefit the smaller businesses located in between. Another tenant location strategy is to cluster complementary businesses, such as a women's shoe store next to a women's clothing store. Although tenant location strategies may sound attractive on paper, the effective implementation of them can be extremely challenging in light of a downtown's numerous landowners. It can be achieved only through the cooperation of willing owners and the orchestration of a downtown entity. Centralized retail management is discussed in more detail below.

Offices

While telecommunications and other modern technology have increased the mobility of today's office workers, downtowns have remained a vital arena for the business world. Despite the popular image of tomorrow's white-collar workers sitting at home in their pajamas in front of their computers, even most futurists believe that downtowns will long continue to be important centers of commerce. Although many businesses have relocated to suburban office centers during the past several decades because of proximity to workers' homes, lower rents, and free parking, certain professionals, particularly attorneys, bankers, and accountants, have felt compelled to stay downtown for reasons of image and practicality. Attorneys, for example, often locate downtown because of their need to be near the courts and other public offices. This fact underscores the importance of keeping civic facilities downtown.

For the purposes of downtown planning, most office uses should be located in the upper floors of buildings because, relative to retail and service uses that can stimulate considerable foot traffic, offices tend to dampen street-level vitality. In fact, some communities preclude ground-floor office uses within their downtown core through special zoning measures. Banks, which function as tremendous activity generators for downtown streets, are at least one glaring exception to the principle of restricting office space to upper floors.

Lodging and Meeting Facilities

Hotels, motels, inns, and bed-and-breakfasts are important elements for a successful downtown. Tourism-oriented communities, such as Mendocino, California, and Kennebunkport, Maine, go to great lengths through special zoning to accommodate inns and bed-and-breakfasts within their urban neighborhoods because of their contribution to the economic viability of their historic downtowns. In fact, lodging can be so critical to the survival of nearby shops and restaurants that some city governments and downtown authorities are partnering with the private sector in hotel development. Examples include the partnership of Bryan, Texas, with a private developer during the late 1990s to restore the historic LaSalle Hotel to its former glory, as well as the participation of New Bern, North Carolina, in the development of a $13 million Sheraton Hotel on the Trent River in 1987. New Bern's Sheraton has been so successful that it has spun off an adjacent 75-room inn, built a new Comfort Suites hotel in the early 1990s, and in late 2008 completed a building with 121 condominium units.

Figure 3-3. Natchez, Mississippi, prepared design guidelines for large-footprint buildings several years before the construction of this new downtown conference center to ensure that its scale, massing, design, and materials would be compatible with its historic setting. Source: The Walker Collaborative / Daye Dearing

Cheaper Isn't Always Better

It was the first trip for a team of consultants to begin a downtown planning project for Natchitoches, Louisiana, a small, picturesque town used as the backdrop for several movies over the years, including *Steel Magnolias*. At the helm of the town's ship was beloved Mayor Joe Sampite, a colorful and energetic leader known for placing "I Love Natchitoches" stickers on anyone who would stand still long enough, including the deceased at their funerals.

Upon the consultant team's initial meeting with Mayor Sampite and several downtown leaders, they learned that the community had recently received a sizable grant from the state to develop a much-needed conference center. When the consultants asked which downtown site had been selected for the center, they were shocked to learn that it would be located on a highway on the edge of town because the owner of a national franchise hotel had generously donated the property next to his hotel. Being fiscally conservative, as good elected officials should strive to be, the city had graciously accepted the hotel owner's offer.

After extensive inquiry, the consultants finally succeeded in coaxing the city leaders to acknowledge that the conference center's location was not yet etched in stone. To change the site at that point, however, would require going through many hoops and over many hurdles with the state, potentially jeopardizing the grant altogether. The city would also have to spend approximately $250,000 to acquire a downtown site. Despite those considerable challenges, the consultants persisted and eventually managed to convince the mayor and other city leaders that developing the facility on the highway would: (1) be a huge missed opportunity for downtown, (2) potentially shift the community's economic center of gravity, and (3) create a new commercial area to compete with downtown.

Much to the credit of the elected officials, they agreed to take the more difficult and costly route—which was the one most beneficial to their downtown. The conference center has since been constructed, the additional foot traffic has helped the retail and service sectors of downtown, and today the community has no regrets about the extra effort, risk, and expense it incurred. The Natchitoches experience proves once again that cheaper is not always better.

Meeting facilities, including convention centers and conference centers, are a use often coupled with lodging. In some instances, they can have an even greater impact on the retail and entertainment sectors of a downtown than lodging does. Typically, a convention or conference center is physically adjoined with, or adjacent to, one or more hotels. When a community considers the development of a new convention or conference center, it is critical to the long-term health of the downtown that it be located in the downtown. Likewise, there will need to be a balanced relationship between the size of the meeting facilities and the number of hotel rooms available. Unless it is intended for a "day tripper" market, a conference center accommodating 500 people is of limited use if there are only 200 lodging rooms in the area. Another serious challenge can be integrating the building footprint, scale, and massing of a convention or conference center into a downtown's historic and human-scale environment. It is particularly important to fit the building onto a single block without having to vacate streets, thereby disrupting the downtown street system and pedestrian-friendly qualities.

Housing

The demand for housing in U.S. downtowns has increased steadily. A study of 45 major U.S. cities found an overall 14 percent increase in the number of households in their downtowns from 1990 to 2000 (Leinberger 2005). Regardless of this positive trend, some communities have found that financial incentives for residential development are needed much more than inducements for any other downtown uses.

With the exception of single-use residential buildings located on nonretail streets, most downtown residences should exist on upper floors. Upper floors are quieter and safer for residents, and they allow more vibrant uses, such as retail and restaurants, to activate the street level. In addition to housing located within the downtown proper, it is also important that the perimeter of downtowns have relatively high-density residential neighborhoods for the market support they provide to the downtown's commercial uses. In fact, surrounding neighborhoods often provide greater market support than do actual downtown residents, depending upon the specific downtown and its neighborhoods. Beyond location considerations, downtown housing also needs to meet a wide range of price points, as well as both rental and purchase options, in order to capture the greatest number of potential residents.

The market strength that downtown residents provide retailers and services is sometimes overestimated, but regardless of their actual level of market support residents provide their downtown with a 24-hour atmosphere that can be much more valuable than merely their purchasing power. By creating an environment that feels safe and comfortable, downtown residents help to attract nonresident visitors who will shop, dine, and otherwise enjoy the downtown. Also, although their numbers may be quite limited in many downtowns, the positive economic impact of a single resident far outweighs the impact of a single employee, as downtown residents typically spend three to four times the amount of downtown employees (Rypkema 2005). Furthermore, according to Randall Gross of the consulting firm Randall Gross/Development Economics, downtown residents have a greater positive economic impact on an annual basis than do visitors or destination shoppers.

Institutions and Public Facilities

Historically, institutional uses, including governmental, academic, and religious uses, are primary anchors for downtowns. Their affiliated lawns and plazas are often the most important public spaces in a downtown, embodying the essence of democracy and the civic realm. County courthouses, city halls, post offices, schools, and houses of worship are vital traffic generators that can help to keep retailers and services in business. In addition to people who visit such civic sites, their employees can be important assets as well. When Collierville, Tennessee, considered relocating its town hall in 2000 from downtown to a suburban site, a survey of town hall employees revealed that, on average, they spent significantly more money in downtown businesses than was initially estimated. Similarly, nearby universities can provide important foot traffic for downtowns. Some institutions are also magnets for certain office uses, such as the clustering of law offices near courts.

Within the context of downtown planning, new public facilities should be located to maximize economic spin-off benefits. The relocation of post offices to more spacious suburban sites is one of the greatest threats that many downtowns face today. Fortunately, federal policies currently require post offices to seriously consider downtown sites and historic structures before locating elsewhere. Downtown advocates must be vigilant in using such policies to their advantage. They must also be highly organized and political. When the idea of relocating the Encinitas, California, main library from downtown to

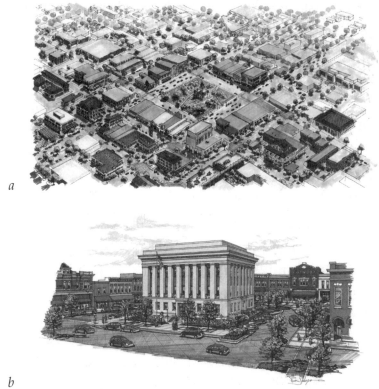

a

b

Figure 3-4a–b. Centrally located county courthouses and their surrounding public spaces served as key focal points of the downtown plans for Denton, Texas (top), and Gallatin, Tennessee (bottom). The existence of such traffic-generating institutions can be the very lifeblood of adjacent businesses. Source: Fregonese Associates (top); The Walker Collaborative / Ben Johnson (bottom)

a suburban location was entertained, the Downtown Encinitas Main Street Association (DEMA) formed a special committee and enlisted the services of political consultants to wage a grassroots campaign to keep the library downtown. Their efforts clearly paid off, as the subsequent communitywide referendum resulted in Encinitas's new $20 million downtown library, which was completed in 2008. Public transportation facilities, such as train stations and ports, can also be important catalysts to downtown revitalization. For example, the redevelopment of the port of Erie, Pennsylvania, over the first decade of this century has stimulated the development of downtown housing that offers spectacular views of Lake Erie and resulted in a $110 million waterfront construction project.

Entertainment and Cultural Facilities

Entertainment and cultural facilities can be a major draw for downtowns and encompass a variety of facilities, including museums, cinemas, symphony halls, opera houses, theaters, arenas, art galleries, stadiums, and aquariums, to name a few. Entertainment venues featuring live performances, in particular, can often be among the few uses that keep downtowns alive after 5:00 p.m. They, in turn, can be the lifeblood of nearby restaurants during evening hours.

Large-scale facilities, such as sporting arenas, can benefit downtown businesses tremendously, but they can have negative consequences as well. Undesirable aspects can include: building footprints that spill beyond the parameters of a single block, resulting in a loss of street segments; a building scale and massing at odds with the surrounding context; expansive parking areas that go unused or underused most days; and traffic congestion during major events. Conversely, parking areas for such facilities can sometimes be used to satisfy other downtown parking demands during the week, and the grid street network of downtowns can usually move traffic more efficiently than suburban street systems. Therefore, despite their various benefits and detriments, as well as the planning challenges they pose, the gains for downtowns from the presence of large entertainment and cultural facilities are usually worth the costs.

Cashing in on Sports Facilities

Many of the arenas and stadiums built in America during the 1960s and 1970s were located in suburban areas, often at highway interchanges for optimal automobile access. But since 1985, nearly all of the 60 major new sports facilities have been sited in downtown locations. The reason is quite simple: money. Studies have found that the economic spin-off benefits are substantially higher for arenas and stadiums located directly adjacent to businesses rather than those neighbored by highways, expansive parking lots, low-density suburban development, or open fields.

As observed by Timothy Chapin, an associate professor at Florida State University who studies the issue, "It's much more compelling when you envision an arena in a dense urban environment, rather than putting it in a parking lot." Bruce Katz, vice president and director of the Brookings Institution Metropolitan Policy Program, emphasizes that good locations and good design are critical to leveraging economic benefits, such as the $100 million of new housing, offices, and retail businesses that resulted from Louisville's Slugger Field, home of that city's minor-league baseball team.

Chris Nelson, a planning professor, agrees. His 2002 study examined the economic leveraging benefits of professional sports facilities in 25 metropolitan areas. He concluded that those facilities located in or near downtowns leveraged the greatest benefits, while those located in the suburbs yielded the least economic spin-off. He cites the Arlington, Texas, suburban baseball stadium as an example of a sports facility that reaps limited economic benefits compared to its urban counterparts. In contrast, Indianapolis located its $183 million Conseco Fieldhouse, home of the Indiana Pacers basketball team, in the heart of its downtown, and the city opened Lucas Oil Stadium for the NFL's Indianapolis Colts in 2008. According to a former spokesperson for the mayor, Jo Lynn Garing, "It would not serve any purpose to have that stadium anywhere but downtown."

Source: Poynter 2005

Industries and Wholesaling

For years, conventional wisdom told us that industrial and wholesaling uses should be tucked neatly away from residences and other more genteel uses. In many cases, this mind-set makes sense. For example, if industrial uses generating large volumes of truck traffic and belching clouds of smoke were to be juxtaposed by tranquil and spacious estate lots of an upper-end residential subdivision, a conflict would undoubtedly occur, even though zoning and real estate dynamics would probably not allow such a scenario in the first place. When people choose to live in a downtown, however, their expectation levels need to be quite different from those of their counterparts in the suburbs.

There are numerous examples across the country of downtown residents who are perfectly content living adjacent to industrial uses. Before Baltimore's Inner Harbor gave way to a festival marketplace, an aquarium, condominiums, and similar uses, the first wave of urban pioneers viewed their vibrant industrial waterfront as a novelty to be fondly observed. Similarly, those living in Virginia's Old Town Alexandria were content for years living near a torpedo factory prior to its conversion into chic art galleries and restaurants. Clearly, good downtown planning should make an effort to keep residences separate from the most noxious uses, including noise and heavy truck traffic. However, industrial uses with few negative effects can serve as an interesting backdrop that reminds residents why they chose to live downtown in the first place, and they can be important contributors to a community's jobs and tax base. Furthermore, if and when specific industrial and warehouse users eventually abandon their buildings, adapting such structures, especially if the buildings are architecturally interesting or historically significant, for "loft" residences and artist space has proven to be a very successful strategy.

BLOCKS, LOTS, STREETS, AND ALLEYS

The new urbanist movement has made great strides in steering the country toward a better form of growth than the one that dominated the sprawl-happy second half of the twentieth century. While much of the movement's focus has been on "green field" development on the edge of existing communities, it has also encouraged infill development for undeveloped or underdeveloped urban sites. New urbanism has also reminded us that blocks, lots, streets, and alleys are the most fundamental components within the physical framework of urban places. To maintain and reinforce "good urbanism" in a downtown, it is critical that the scale and design of these four basic elements remain faithful to their historic origins.

Blocks

By definition, a block is simply a group of adjoining lots bound by streets. It would be somewhat unusual, but even a single lot bound entirely by streets would be considered a block. While blocks are typically rectilinear in shape, they are not always. Downtowns with undulating topography and meandering rivers result in the occasional odd-shaped block because of their irregular street patterns. Many historic New England downtowns, in particular, have street networks that are more faithful to their topography than to an imposed grid design. Perhaps the most noteworthy shortcoming of irregularly shaped blocks is their resulting irregularly shaped lots, which can be difficult to market and inefficient to build upon. On a positive note, however, irregularly shaped blocks can yield distinctive landmark buildings, such as "flatiron" buildings in Troy, New York, Asheville, North Carolina, and of course New York City.

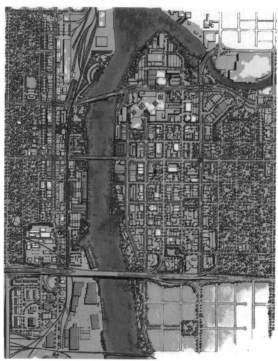

Figure 3-5. This physical master plan for downtown Green Bay, Wisconsin, emphasizes the important role of blocks, lots, streets, and alleys in serving as the organizing framework—the "skeletal system"—for the downtown. Source: Gould Evans Associates

The most important consideration in preserving existing blocks or designing new blocks is their size. To maintain a downtown that is pedestrian friendly, as well as capable of moving vehicular traffic efficiently, blocks should be relatively short in length. There are varied opinions regarding optimal block sizes, and it often depends upon their specific context. For example, blocks intended to accommodate the larger footprints of institutional and commercial buildings are often larger than residential blocks. Typical block sizes found in most American downtowns range between 300 feet and 600 feet in length. Block widths tend to be narrower, ranging between roughly 250 feet and 300 feet. Those dimensions allow for internal alleys, which are approximately 10 to 20 feet wide, flanked by lots 115 feet to 145 feet in depth.

Law of the Indies

Today's planning and zoning regulations enforced by thousands of municipalities across the country are certainly not new concepts. Throughout history, there have been governing guidelines, in one form or another, for the design of cities. The Romans had specific planning principles for the layout of the towns they established in newly conquered territories, as evidenced by many western European towns today. Likewise, the Renaissance era witnessed the evolution of detailed planning standards that superimposed symmetrical plazas and grand boulevards over the earlier irregular street patterns of medieval towns throughout Europe.

Spain was the leader during the post-Renaissance era in establishing a formal set of documents mandating specific town-planning standards for the territories it colonized in the New World. The first "instructions" were written in 1501 at the request of King Ferdinand, and they were refined in 1573 under the guidance of King Phillip II, who issued them as "The Royal Ordinances for the Laying Out of New Towns." In 1681, an extensive volume of Spanish laws pertaining to the New World was adopted. Known as the Law of the Indies, this set of principles for city planning expanded upon the 1573 standards.

The Law of the Indies criteria for laying out towns included a grid street system, a central plaza surrounded by governmental and religious buildings, peripheral defensive walls, uniform building styles, and a military parade ground. Examples of American communities that were influenced by the Law of the Indies, either in their original design or subsequent phases, include St. Augustine, Florida; Natchez, Mississippi; New Orleans; Santa Fe, New Mexico; and Tucson, Arizona. Today's Congress for the New Urbanism (CNU) Charter can be figuratively viewed as the most recent iteration of the Law of the Indies, and many municipal zoning and design guidelines are based upon similar town-planning principles. For today's communities that were never governed by the Law of the Indies, the spirit of those standards can still serve as a guiding light for downtown planning. For the handful of communities that were indeed laid out in accordance with Spain's very own design standards, extraordinary efforts should be made to continue their adherence to the Law of the Indies within the context of their contemporary downtown plans. The "laws" are not merely a useful tool for good urbanism, but their manifestation as a distinct pattern of blocks, lots, and streets constitutes a historic artifact worthy of preservation.

Source: Adapted from Veregge 1993

Figure 3-6. An irregularly shaped lot in Troy, New York, yielded this "flatiron" building. Although oddly shaped lots do not lend themselves to the most efficiently designed buildings, this historic structure has served the citizens of Troy as a treasured landmark for more than 100 years. Source: The Walker Collaborative

Lots

Although building parcels are one of the most rudimentary components of a downtown, they rarely garner much attention, perhaps deservedly, within the larger picture of downtown planning. Lots constitute the legal ownership boundaries on which individual developments occur, and they are physically oriented perpendicular to the street. Historically, urban lots tend to be narrow along their street frontage and deep in order to maximize the value of the street, although many of today's retail developers are seeking wider frontages. Regardless of recent trends, because lots can be legally subdivided and combined as needed, their greatest physical constraints are usually related to existing buildings.

As noted, irregularly shaped blocks yield irregularly shaped lots. While such lots can prove challenging to build on, they can also result in some of the most memorable landmarks in a downtown. Those downtowns fortunate enough to feature an acutely angled street intersection that yields a wedge-shaped "flatiron building" are blessed with a landmark location that orients the downtown user. These postcard buildings often serve as visual termination points anchoring important vistas. In fact, despite the understandable objections of traffic engineers, some new urbanist town centers on green field sites will intentionally include such intersections and irregular lots in order to achieve this effect.

Streets

Streets and their associated pedestrian areas, streetscapes, are the essence of the public realm. Within a well-designed urban streetscape, many different activities can occur. In addition to the movement and parking of vehicles, streetscapes play host to inanimate objects that make downtowns more user-friendly, such as benches, trash receptacles, newspaper racks, shade trees, and informational kiosks. Most important, streetscapes are a habitat for living beings, including pedestrians, leashed pets, street performers, bench sitters, and street vendors. Thoughtfully designed downtown streetscapes host all of these users, furnishings, and activities with ease.

With respect to the street itself (i.e., the asphalt surface lying between the curbs and intended for wheeled vehicles such as automobiles and bicycles), both functional and design issues need to be addressed in any downtown plan. The first street-related issue to typically be addressed is function. In other words, What role does each street play within the downtown's overall street network? Related issues to address include the existing street hierarchy, how the downtown street system interacts with the balance of the community's streets, and the relationship between streets and their abutting land uses. It is often the mismatch between a street's travel function and adjacent land uses that causes conflict for urban streets. For example, a thoroughfare accommodating relatively high volumes of fast-moving through traffic can be at odds with adjacent boutiques and outdoor eateries that might benefit from traffic that had to travel at slower speeds. With respect to the design of downtown streets, there are at least six characteristics to consider in any downtown plan: connectivity, two-way traffic flow, narrow driving lanes, on-street parking, pedestrian-friendly intersections, and well-designed streetscapes. Each is discussed below.

Street connectivity. The issue of well-connected streets is directly related to block lengths. The smaller the blocks within a given area, the more streets. In order to be pedestrian friendly and circulate vehicles efficiently, streets need to be connected and feature relatively short blocks. Otherwise, walking and driving options become more limited, which

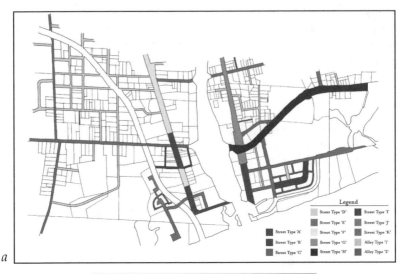

a

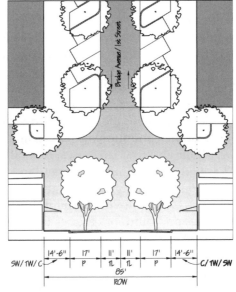

b

Figure 3-7a–b. An effective downtown plan will address the current and proposed street design for all key streets or street types. For the master plan for downtown Northport, Alabama, street types were color-coded on a map (top), which was linked to proposed street cross-sections and plan sections for each street type (bottom). Source: The Walker Collaborative / Third Coast Design Studio

is inconvenient for pedestrians and causes traffic congestion for drivers because fewer streets disperse the traffic. That is why public facilities with large building footprints should be thoughtfully designed to avoid removing streets, which chips away at the downtown street grid. Despite this commonsense principle, nearly every downtown has, at some point in time, experienced strong political pressure to vacate a street segment to accommodate a large new structure. According to urban historian Spiro Kostof (1992, 192), such "demapping" of streets has been occurring since at least the late fifteenth century, when Italy's powerful Strozzi family brokered a deal with the Florentine state to vacate a piazza and alley to make room for their palatial new home—or "palazzo." While downtown plans should loudly and preemptively condemn street vacations that result in "superblocks," they should also advocate for expanded pedestrian connectivity.

Directional flow. Despite the many one-way streets found in downtowns across the country, two-way traffic is more beneficial to downtowns. It provides greater visibility for retailers and is less confusing to visitors unfamiliar with the downtown. Given the importance of visitors having a positive experience and returning to a downtown for subsequent visits, happy visitors should be a goal for any downtown. Also, it is human nature to drive faster when the adjacent driving lanes are moving in the same direction. Whether it is a conscious or subconscious thought, drivers know that the risk of serious injury is much lower when two cars come into contact while moving in the same direction compared with a "head-on crash." Consequently, two-way flows help to calm traffic so that driving speeds do not endanger or annoy pedestrians. In addition to traffic calming benefits, two-way traffic reduces "out-of-direction" travel so that fewer miles will be driven, thereby reducing fuel consumption and air pollution. For all of these reasons, the conversion of one-way streets to two-way streets, wherever practicable, is often a key downtown planning recommendation, as it was for Kalamazoo, Michigan, in its 2004 downtown plan.

However, despite the many virtues of two-way traffic, it is recognized that some existing downtown streets are simply too narrow to convert to two-way traffic and still accommodate needed on-street parking. Unusually narrow streets are especially common in America's oldest East Coast downtowns, such as Boston, Charleston, South Carolina, and St. Augustine, Florida. Because of constraints caused by adjacent historic buildings, such narrow streets are usually best left as designed. If insufficient right-of-way widths exist, two-way street conversions can also be problematic for downtowns lacking alleys to access rear loading areas, as the resulting "double parking" of trucks in driving lanes can temporarily paralyze traffic while loading or unloading occurs.

Lane widths. One-way streets are not the only culprits, as people also drive faster when the perceived lane widths are wide. When one-way traffic flows and wide driving lanes are combined, the margin for error is especially high, and the driver can travel relatively fast with only limited risks of an accident. In addition, the driving speed of many drivers is dictated more by their own perceived safety than by the posted speed limit. Therefore, driving lanes that need to accommodate trucks and buses should not exceed a width of 12 feet, and 10- to 11-foot lanes are even better for streets used primarily by automobiles.

On-street parking. The most important role of on-street parking is to provide conveniently located parking for shoppers, diners, and other short-term users. It also serves as a protective barrier between pedestrians on sidewalks and moving vehicles, although the psychological comfort that parked cars gives pedestrians may be more valuable than the actual safety benefits they afford. As with two-way traffic flow and narrow driving lanes, on-street parking offers traffic-calming benefits. Even when parked cars do not encroach into the adjacent driving lane, the perceived narrowing of the driving lane caused by on-street

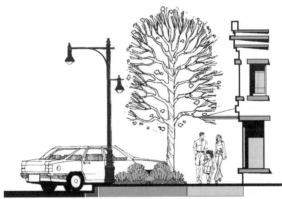

Figure 3-8. Where the street function, traffic levels, vehicle speeds, and curb-to-curb street widths allow, angled parking is usually preferable to parallel parking because it is easier to access, it yields more parking spaces per linear foot of street frontage, and it provides greater traffic-calming benefits.
Source: Gould Evans Associates

When in Doubt, Experiment

Because downtown planning is not an exact science, many downtown issues are subject to debate. For example, will the establishment of more stringent on-street parking regulations benefit the downtown by increasing parking efficiencies, or will it hurt the downtown because it discourages people from coming there? Will the addition of a skateboard facility give downtown a vibrant atmosphere that attracts more shoppers, or will the behavior of unruly teenagers scare downtown visitors?

When crystal ball predictions are not possible, a little experimentation can go a long way, as San Francisco's Noe Valley district can attest. For several years, merchants along a stretch of Castro Street had been debating whether their parallel on-street parking should be converted to angled parking so that more vehicles could be accommodated. In 1997, the transition nearly occurred when more than 1,000 signatures were gathered in favor of the concept, but municipal engineers snuffed out the idea when they determined that buses would have too much difficulty negotiating turns within the decreased driving-lane widths.

The concept resurfaced in 2001 when a new merchant to the area

Figure 3-9. As this photograph of San Francisco's Noe Valley district reveals, the block of Castro Street shown in the foreground is wider than other blocks on the street. Although the city had resisted merchant pressure for years to convert the parallel parking to angled parking, it was eventually convinced to give it a try for six months. Although not all downtown issues lend themselves to such experimentation, when possible, it is an effective approach to ending long-standing debate. Source: John J. DeMarsh

began promoting it. Upon learning of the past roadblocks, the merchant asked his customers to park diagonally on his block as a temporary experiment, and he videotaped buses successfully driving down Castro Street and negotiating the turns. The film was then used to coax the city's department of parking and traffic to conduct its own experiment using traffic cones, which it did from June to December 2005. In early 2006, the city passed a resolution permitting angled parking on a section of Castro street. Credit must be given to the merchants there for encouraging some harmless experimentation that ended up benefiting their district in the long run.

Source: Poger 2005

parking, as well as the chance that a parked car might enter the driving lane, causes drivers to slow down.

"Head-in" or 90-degree parking is not recommended for any downtown street, as it is too difficult for drivers to negotiate when backing out, and it is too disruptive for vehicles in the driving lanes. Ninety-degree parking is considered by traffic engineers to be a generally unsafe condition that should be avoided.

The two preferred options for downtown on-street parking are angled parking and parallel parking. The best choice depends upon the available curb-to-curb street width, traffic volumes, traffic speeds, and the street's function in the overall hierarchy. Parallel parking is appropriate on higher volume and higher speed streets. Although it provides fewer spaces than angled parking, it tends to be safer. Exiting a parallel space is easier than with angled parking because of greater visibility and the need for only a single motion, instead of two. However, entering the space can be more challenging, especially if the vehicle behind the parker does not provide enough room for the parker to back into the space. Where designated, parallel parking lanes should measure between seven and eight feet in width.

Where conditions permit, angled parking yields a greater number of parking spaces per linear foot of street frontage, and it is easier for drivers to negotiate than parallel parking. Although angled parking provides less visibility than parallel parking for drivers exiting their parking space and it requires two motions, that same issue—the risk of drivers backing into the street at any given moment—also provides greater traffic calming benefits than parallel parking. Parking angles should range between 30 and 60 degrees, and parking lane widths, measured perpendicularly from the curb, should range between 16 and 20 feet. The vast majority of angled parking is designed so that vehicles pull forward into the space and then back out to exit, but a rare exception to this rule is found in Pottstown, Pennsylvania, where the parking space angles are configured to be backed into so the driver can later exit by pulling forward. Although this approach is rarely used, many of those familiar with it believe that it is the easiest for drivers to negotiate.

Whether parallel or angled, all types of on-street parking should be clearly delineated through pavement striping. Supplementary small signage is also often used to help designate on-street parking, but aesthetic issues for the streetscape should be considered.

Alleys

Alleys are often viewed as the "ugly underworld" of downtowns, yet they play a vital role. Downtowns insufficiently served by alleys and rear loading zones often experience trucks parked illegally in driving lanes of streets while they load or unload. This situation can result in a serious disruption to traffic flows and safety concerns, especially on two-way streets with only one driving lane in either direction. In addition to loading areas, alleys also provide access to rear parking areas for employees and residents of adjacent buildings. Other benefits of alleys include the storage of refuse for garbage trucks to access, and the location of utility poles if burying overhead lines is not an option.

Fairly or unfairly, alleys are branded with a negative image in some minds as dark places inhabited by rats, criminals, and trash. While there is a genuine basis for this bad reputation, alleys can be greatly enhanced through proper design and management. Design strategies should include good lighting, as well as an attractive design for adjacent parking lots, including landscaping and Dumpster screening. Going a step further, Rock Island, Illinois, has created an "art alley" in which volunteers have created murals and other types of public art to animate a downtown alley. Another consideration is the design of the rear of buildings. By providing sufficient windows, and even balconies, Jane Jacobs's "eyes on the street" concept to deter crime can be adapted into "eyes on the alley." Management strategies for alleys should include routine security patrols and maintenance for cleanliness. Combining a social program with maintenance needs, in 1997 Seattle's Pioneer Square helped start a business, Cleanscapes (www.cleanscapes.com), that, in addition to other services, hires homeless people to clean streets and alleys.

Because of the many benefits of alleys, it is important that they be retained wherever possible. Over the years, alley segments in numerous downtowns have been vacated for private use, often with unfortunate results for the smooth functioning of the downtown. Downtown planning efforts sometimes provide an infrequent opportunity to reclaim vacated alleys or to even create new alleys where they never existed. Since it is rarely practical or desirable to eliminate existing rear building sections to create or reclaim alleys, it is clearly much easier and inexpensive to retain existing alleys than to develop new ones.

MAKING YOUR DOWNTOWN PEDESTRIAN FRIENDLY

One of the most appealing characteristics of a downtown is its walkability. Unless it is a place that is safe, comfortable, interesting, and enjoyable for walking, the downtown has no competitive advantage to distinguish it from suburban shopping areas. Likewise, many downtown businesses depend upon "impulse shopping," when shoppers make unplanned purchases. Pedestrians are clearly good candidates for impulse shopping given the ease in which they can make unplanned stops, while drivers are less inclined to act upon their split-second impulses. Pedestrian activity is also important to making streets safe and free from crime, while also sending out a message that the area is vibrant and worth visiting.

Pedestrian-friendly Intersections

One of the key tests for a downtown pedestrian system is the level of ease with which people can cross a street. Transportation consultant Ross Tilghman in Seattle maintains that pedestrians should not have to cross more than four lanes of traffic, and streets carrying more than 20,000 vehicles per day are generally perceived as barriers to pedestrians.

Although the number of driving lanes and the volume of traffic is often beyond the control of planners preparing a downtown plan, the design of intersections is usually not. Intersections warrant particular attention in the course of downtown planning. The two main devices for increasing pedestrian safety at intersections are "pedestrian bulbs" and crosswalks.

Pedestrian bulbs are paved and curbed extensions of the sidewalk system that project several feet into the intersection, still allowing

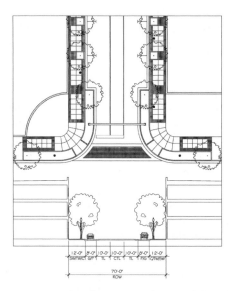

Figure 3-10. This streetscape plan for downtown High Point, North Carolina, features all of the trademarks of a good urban street: pedestrian bulbs at street corners, intersection crosswalks, street trees, and on-street parking. Source The Walker Collaborative / Third Coast Design Studio

The Dubious Blessing of State Roads and Bypasses

Downtowns traversed by state-designated roads are both blessed and cursed. Historically referred to in some regions as "farm-to-market roads," these two- or four-lane rural roads evolve into a mature urban "street" by the time they enter a community's core. Once arriving in the downtown, they are typically one of the most important downtown streets. Often named Main Street or Broadway, they sometimes intersect a courthouse square or town green, becoming part of the most significant public space in the community.

The greatest benefit that such streets bring a downtown is traffic. While excessive automobile congestion and truck traffic are not desirable consequences, the visibility and accessibility that high traffic volumes bring to downtown businesses are clearly wanted. Another benefit state designation can bring is state-funded road maintenance, depending upon the agreements between the state and local governments.

In some cases, however, the negative aspects of state designation outweigh the positive. If the state's department of transportation (DOT) declines to offer flexibility in road design, the result for downtown may be a through road rather than the more appropriate urban street. Typical state road design treatments unsympathetic to the unique needs of downtowns include:

- excessively wide driving lanes;
- excessively wide turning radii to accommodate trucks and fast-moving traffic;

- reluctance to allow landscaped medians, street trees, and pedestrian bulbs at intersections;
- prohibition of, or limitations on, on-street parking; and
- resistance to stop signs and traffic lights if traffic counts do not warrant them.

In addition to state DOTs, many local governments are also still clinging to these types of design treatments, particularly in their reluctance to add new stop signs and traffic lights. Although some states do not widely broadcast this fact, some DOTs are allowed to work with a variety of design requirements. Fortunately for America's downtowns,

Figure 3-11. By the time state-designated roads intended solely for moving vehicular traffic reach a historic downtown, they have often matured into the most significant streets in the community. Such roads, when perpendicularly juxtaposed, often intersect at the downtown's core to form its most significant space. Source The Walker Collaborative

DOTs have been encouraged by the Federal Highway Administration in recent years to employ flexible design and context-sensitive design. A handful of states, including Oregon and Vermont, are making great strides and beginning to serve as models for other states struggling to better harmonize state road planning with existing downtown character.

One solution to avoid DOT standards and unwanted truck traffic is to build state-designated bypasses that allow state status to be eliminated from key downtown streets. A proposed new bypass was used successfully by Hillsborough, New Jersey, during the late 1990s as an impetus to drop the state designation in hopes of creating a new pedestrian-friendly Main Street. In an effort to deal with peak-hour congestion, Petoskey, Michigan, created a bypass for through traffic just blocks from the center of its downtown to keep the popular shopping district from being overwhelmed by summer tourist traffic.

While the bypass solution can work in many instances, it can also be a detriment to some communities. In order to survive economically, downtowns desperately need traffic. Therefore, bypasses that will siphon off the vast majority of traffic, both undesirable and desirable, should be avoided unless the downtown can clearly attract enough strong tenants to become a major destination not relying economically on through traffic.

enough space for vehicles to make their turning movement, but only within a relatively narrow driving path. In addition to slowing down vehicles and protecting the end vehicle within the adjacent row of on-street parking, bulbs can also significantly reduce the distance that pedestrians must walk when crossing a street. Although pedestrian bulbs are wonderful for those on foot and tolerable for those driving cars, for large trucks they are a different matter. When designing pedestrian bulbs, consideration must be given to truck traffic, as long vehicles often have trouble negotiating pedestrian bulbs because of the tighter turning radii they create.

Pedestrian bulbs and crosswalks are often provided in tandem as mutually supportive streetscape elements. Crosswalks are simply paved or painted strips oriented perpendicular to the street segment that they traverse. Their main purpose is to designate the safest point for pedestrians to cross a street, as well as to remind drivers of the presence of pedestrians. Depending upon the local laws and customs, pedestrians often have the right-of-way priority over vehicles. Crosswalks are usually at least six feet in width, distinguished by paint striping or a material different from that of the street surface and located within a few feet of the intersection corner. Downtowns with especially long blocks, as in Salt Lake City and other Utah communities, often feature midblock crosswalks out of necessity. If the crosswalk is paved, its material often matches that of the sidewalk system, so that the crosswalk is essentially an extension of the sidewalk. This choice can give pedestrians a false sense of security, however, so such design should be considered carefully. Crosswalks are sometimes paved with a textured material that, combined with a slightly raised elevation above the street surface, purposefully causes the driver to feel the crosswalk under their tires. Although such a design can be effective in reinforcing the presence of crosswalks, the needs of elderly pedestrians, wheelchair users, and other disabled people must also be kept in mind.

Sidewalk Design

Within the context of downtown planning, "zoning" is not a term limited solely to the regulation of land uses. The portion of downtown streetscapes designed for pedestrians—that area between the street curb and building facades—needs to be wide enough to comfortably accommodate two distinct areas: the "utility zone" and the "pedestrian zone."

The utility zone should occupy the portion of the sidewalk closest to the street curb. The elements contained in this zone include street trees, streetlights, benches, trash receptacles, kiosks, newspaper racks, and street vendors, although streets more peripheral to the downtown core typically have narrower streetscapes and, consequently, will feature fewer streetscape elements.

Utility lines and power poles should also be located within the utility zone if burying them or relocating to alleys is not an option. Some utility zones include planting beds for shrubs to provide aesthetic relief between utilitarian features. Clearly, this zone is intended for the location of stationary objects, as well as stationary people, which would otherwise be disruptive to the flow of pedestrian traffic. It should be located on the outside portion of the sidewalk for multiple reasons, including the protective buffering that the zone's width and objects provide to pedestrians, as well as the fact that trees cannot be planted

Figure 3-12. The spacious sidewalks of Broadway in downtown Saratoga Springs, New York, are wide enough to accommodate a clearly defined utility zone on the right, a dining zone on the left, and a central pedestrian zone.
Source: The Walker Collaborative

too closely to buildings. Utility zones are typically two to three feet in width, although broad sidewalks often feature wider utility zones.

The pedestrian zone is the corridor located between the utility zone and adjacent building facades. It should be unobstructed to accommodate pedestrian flows. Ideally, the pedestrian zone should be a minimum width of four feet in even the tightest downtown streetscapes in order to accommodate wheelchairs and to allow pedestrians to pass one another. The utility zone and pedestrian zones, collectively, should be at least six feet wide. However, some of the most successful downtown streets, such as segments of King Street in Charleston, South Carolina, have sidewalk dimensions more constricted than even these minimal standards. Historical trends may tell you which sidewalks can exist at a "lower" standard.

A downtown streetscape does not have to be particularly wide in order to accommodate yet a third zone—the "dining zone." While its design can be much more flexible and adaptable than the other two zones, the dining zone can be as narrow as a small table for two. Most dining zones are located directly adjacent to their associated buildings, but some are integrated into the utility zone on especially wide streetscapes. In order to give diners a greater level of comfort and sense of separation from pedestrians, dining zones are often delineated by large planters, low fencing, an elevated grade level, or some similar feature that buffers them from the pedestrian zone.

In general, sidewalk widths should reflect the scale of adjacent buildings and the significance of the particular street. For example, Broadway is the primary street for downtown Saratoga Springs, New York, and it has an approximately 15-foot-wide sidewalk, of which approximately five feet is dedicated to the peripheral utility zone. Connecticut Avenue in downtown Washington, D.C., on the other hand, features a sidewalk approximately 25 feet wide, of which approximately three feet constitute the utility zone. Although Connecticut Avenue's sidewalk is punctuated by the occasional encroaching restaurant that narrows the pedestrian zone at points, it is flanked by much taller buildings and serves a higher volume of foot traffic than does Broadway in Saratoga Springs. Regardless of such factors as street significance and building heights, which may have factored into the original design of downtown streetscapes, the design options for addressing preexisting streetscapes today are much more limited. In fact, streetscape designs and sidewalk widths are often driven more by the right-of-way width available after driving and parking lanes are accommodated than by urban design ideals.

Materials. Far too much money is frequently spent by communities that want to "gold plate" their downtown with the finest sidewalk materials. One trip to Boston's Beacon Hill or Princeton's Nassau Street convinces many downtown leaders that brick or slate are the only options worth considering. While there may be historic precedents in those communities that make their sidewalk materials appropriate, some of the greatest downtowns in the world, including New York, Paris, and London, have predominantly concrete sidewalks. Rich sidewalk materials are certainly effective in broadcasting the message that downtown is treasured by the community, and they may occasionally help stimulate adjacent private development, but it is doubtful that many people visit downtowns to simply enjoy their high-quality sidewalks.

Cost-effective alternatives to exclusively brick sidewalks include concrete with brick accenting strips, as well as scored concrete that creates geometric patterns to visually break up the expanse of concrete.

Approaches such as imitating brick with tinted and stamped concrete should generally be avoided. Not only do they tend to look like cheap imitations conflicting with the authenticity of a historic downtown, but the inevitable patching that will be required to accommodate future underground utility improvements will not match the original paving. Another material to avoid is tile, as it becomes a safety liability when made slick by rain.

Streetscape furnishings. Streetscape furnishings include streetlights, benches, trash receptacles, newspaper racks, mass transit shelters, bicycle racks, and kiosks. Two key considerations need to be applied in the selection of any streetscape furnishings: function and appearance.

With respect to function, location and design are important factors. For example, a bench with its back against a building facade and

---

The Mauling of Main Street

The 1970s were an innovative era in design for many facets of American life, including clothing, hairstyles, architecture, and, yes, urban planning. By the early 1970s, a number of forces were already in full play, resulting in unparalleled residential and commercial growth in the suburbs and a steady spiral downward for many downtowns. In a desperate attempt, numerous downtowns across the country jumped onto the pedestrian mall bandwagon. In an effort to compete head-to-head with suburban shopping malls, these downtowns blocked off vehicular access on their primary retail streets in order to create open-air pedestrian malls. Because the market forces that were causing the downtowns' downfall were much larger than the issue of vehicular access, these panic-stricken efforts,

not surprisingly, did little to reverse the fortunes of these downtowns.

In fact, in most cases, the "malling" of Main Street only exacerbated downtown's problems, resulting in a slow and painful death for many. During the 1970s, Burlington, Iowa, a town of 26,839 people, fell prey to the pedestrian-mall snake oil. It converted the block of Jefferson Street between Main and Third streets into a pedestrian mall. By the late 1990s, it was clear that the pedestrian mall was not helping businesses along that block, so the downtown organization, chamber of commerce, and business association pressured the city to reopen the block to automobiles. Evansville, Indiana, an Ohio River community whose downtown is under the watchful eye of the Downtown Development Division of the

Growth Alliance of Greater Evansville (GAGE), had a very similar experience. Downtown Allentown, Pennsylvania, erected a canopy along Main Street on the same day that its first suburban mall opened, but it was recently dismantled and replaced with historic streetscape furnishings. Even major cities with seemingly critical masses in their downtowns, such as Louisville, Memphis, and Seattle, have undone their downtown pedestrian malls to reintroduce vehicular traffic.

These failed examples are not an indictment of all pedestrian malls. Some large downtowns, such as New York City and Baltimore, can support them. College towns, such as Charlottesville, Virginia, can support them. Those cities constituting both, such as Madison, Wisconsin, can clearly support a pedestrian mall, as evidenced by State Street there. However, because the "mauling" of Main Street resulted in failure for so many other communities across America, not to mention the tragedy of "urban renewal" programs that razed countless blocks of historic architecture, the 1970s are rarely recollected by most downtown advocates with any degree of nostalgia. In short, any downtown master plan proposing a pedestrian mall should be met with extreme scrutiny before receiving a stamp of approval.

Figure 3-13. Louisville, Kentucky, learned the hard way about converting a key downtown street into a pedestrian mall. Blocked off from vehicular traffic during the 1980s, this section of Fourth Street was finally reopened to automobiles two decades later. Consequently, it has experienced much greater commercial success. Source: The Walker Collaborative

a   *b*   *c*

Figure 3-14a–c. The trash receptacle on the left has a dated "1970s" appearance that would be unflattering for virtually any downtown, while the middle one conveys a strong historic character. The receptacle on the right represents a creative alternative that makes a bold statement about its hip, artsy context. Source: The Walker Collaborative

facing a sidewalk will be used much more than a bench placed near the curb with its back to the street simply because of what makes a user feel comfortable. Similarly, a trash receptacle placed too closely to a bench will attract insects and emit odors during summer months, making the bench an unpleasant place to sit. An important design facet of benches is their seating materials. Although a surprisingly large number of downtown benches feature metal seating, their absorption of heat and cold during extreme weather conditions make metal a less desirable material than wood, although wood has shorter life and requires greater maintenance. Perhaps the most significant design feature of a streetlight is its height. There should be some degree of correlation between the streetlight height and the scale of the street, with broad streets flanked by tall buildings calling for taller streetlights. Regardless of the street's scale, however, lights should generally not exceed a height of approximately 16 feet to emphasize a human scale.

The appearance of selected streetscape furnishings should be based upon two considerations: the specific character desired for the streetscape and the preference of downtown stakeholders. Ideally, decisions regarding the desired character of a streetscape should be linked to a downtown's marketing strategy for developing the downtown's identity, but in fact that is rarely the case. However, even if no plan exists to improve identity, it is still relatively straightforward to match the desired character for a downtown with specific streetscape furnishings. For example, downtowns seeking to reinforce their nineteenth-century roots might select Victorian-style streetlights and benches. Going a step further, some communities conduct historic research into the appearance of their nineteenth-century streetlights and replicate the original design, as did Allentown, Pennsylvania, when it redeveloped its downtown streetscapes. Likewise, downtowns or distinct downtown districts wanting to convey an artistic and hip image can do so through streetscape furnishings exhibiting a high level of artistry and uniqueness, although such an approach typically entails custom manufacturing and greater costs.

PARKING

It is rare for a planner to never hear of "parking problems" in the course of preparing a downtown plan. This fact is based upon the public's widespread expectation of being able to park directly adjacent to destinations, with only minimal walking involved. Unfortunately for downtowns, this expectation does not seem to be applied to suburban shopping centers, perhaps because the destination, while not necessarily close, is at least clearly visible across even the most expansive parking lot. There are no city blocks filled with buildings to obscure the view. With this competitive edge for the suburbs, parking must be given special attention by downtowns. There are five primary issues that a downtown plan should address for parking: supply, location, design, management, and promotion.

Supply

Although the overall science of planning for downtown parking is best left to the experts, the supply issue generally comes down to a series of simple mathematical equations. The key variables for making the necessary calculations include:

- the existing number of on- and off-street parking spaces;
- the existing level of demand;
- the potential new occupied building space; and
- future parking demand based on full downtown revitalization.

Inventorying the number of existing parking spaces is a time-consuming but straightforward process achieved through field surveys, although the use of aerial-photograph maps can reduce the amount of fieldwork needed. All spaces, public and private, should be inventoried. The current level of parking demand can be determined by a combination of hourly field checks and calculations based upon the current building occupancy levels for various land uses. For example, office space commonly generates demand for approximately one parking space per 300 square feet. Potential new occupied building space is determined by adding the existing vacant space that can still be leased to the plan's proposed infill development square footage. A downtown's future parking demand can be projected by considering all of these variables.

For many downtowns, despite the loud public complaints, more than enough parking already exists. To the surprise of many in Denton, Texas, a parking study conducted as part of their 2003 downtown master plan revealed that the downtown actually had a surplus of parking. According to the city's downtown master plan, only 2,600 spaces were in demand, yet 3,500 spaces already existed. In fact, even in a full "build out" scenario, many downtowns have sufficient existing parking, but it needs to be redesigned, managed, and marketed more effectively in order to meet the future demands. Nevertheless, in some instances, the supply of parking will indeed need to be increased, so the downtown plan must address that issue.

One important caveat: rarely is it advisable or truly necessary to demolish buildings, especially historic buildings, as a means to create parking. Regardless, the razing of historic structures to create surface parking has reached epidemic proportions for many downtowns across the country that lack sufficient regulatory protections. As an indirect strategy to break this unfortunate trend, some communities have enacted costly requirements for landscaping and other improvements to new parking lots as a means of discouraging demolitions. Others have eliminated parking as a permitted primary land use, instead mandating that it be an ancillary use associated with a building on the same site.

Location

The most strategic location of parking will depend upon where in the downtown it is most needed. The issue of on-street parking has already been discussed in detail. However, to reiterate, on-street parking should be provided anywhere that it can be accommodated. Also, where sufficient street widths occur, angled parking should be provided rather than parallel parking, in order to yield more spaces.

Parking lots should be located closest to where the demands are greatest, particularly near retail, restaurant, and institutional uses. However, they should be located internal to blocks when possible, so they do not create unattractive dead spaces on the streetscape. In the case of housing, market demands usually dictate that its parking be located directly adjacent to the building, as remote parking is not a viable alternative.

One of the benefits of the mixed use nature of downtowns is the potential feasibility for "shared parking." For example, a parking lot for ground-floor commercial space can also be used for upper-floor residential space, assuming there are no significant time overlaps of their peak demand hours. Likewise, church parking lots heavily used on the weekends by their congregations can serve other parking needs during the balance of the week. The concept of shared parking does not apply merely to parking lots but to individual parking spaces as well. Because of the compact and mixed use nature of downtowns, a single parking space can serve multiple trips for a driver, such as a trip to the post office, shopping, and a meal. In order to avoid unnecessary financial barriers to developing and redeveloping in downtowns, it is critical that municipal ordinances recognize the shared parking potential for downtowns and, thus, not require the same amount of parking as for suburban sites. Because the parking standards of many communities are based upon suburban models requiring more parking than urban areas, standards as applied to the downtown should be closely scrutinized.

Design

Careful design of parking lots can dramatically increase their level of use. Many parking lots are designed to be inefficient, failing to maximize the potential number of parking spaces. In fact, some downtown parking lots are not really designed at all. Instead, they consist merely of a paved area with no delineation of driving aisles or parking bays. In contrast, a well-designed parking lot should include the following features:

- Access driveways that have a minimal width and are located on secondary streets, to avoid disrupting a primary streetscape and exacerbating traffic congestion
- Driving aisles that do not exceed approximately 24 feet in width when accessing 90-degree stalls
- Parking stalls clearly delineated with paint striping
- Parking stalls with adequate but not excessive dimensions, typically ranging between nine and 10 feet in width
- Peripheral year-round screening comprising landscaping, fencing, or a masonry wall along any street frontage
- Internal landscaping to consist of curbed and landscaped islands with shade trees
- Human-scaled and attractive lighting

Other design challenges faced by many parking lots include utility poles, overhead wiring, and Dumpsters. With the exception of putting them underground, not much can be done about overhead wiring and its accompanying utility poles, as it is preferable that they be located in rear parking areas rather than within downtown streetscapes. One improvement, however, is to provide a curbed and landscaped island around utility poles in order to keep car bumpers away and to enhance their aesthetics. Dumpsters, on the other hand, are frequently blessed with more design options. They can be located in a discrete corner location and screened with an attractive enclosure architecturally compatible with adjacent buildings.

Sources for additional information on parking lot design include *The Aesthetics of Parking* (Smith 1988), *The Dimensions of Parking* (Blaesser 2000), and *The Parking Handbook for Small Communities* (Edwards 1994). The last source focuses on downtown parking in particular.

Management

In addition to physically enhancing parking lots, a parking management program can be an effective means of maximizing a downtown's limited available parking. While most downtown plans address the

Figure 3-15. The enthusiastic enforcement of parking regulations should not be a deterrent to downtown visitors—in fact, just the opposite if it ensures an adequate number of spaces by encouraging parking turnover. However, if downtown employees are parking in on-street spaces that should be reserved for the convenience of customers, that must be remedied for the economic survival of the downtown. Source: The Walker Collaborative

location and design of parking, management is frequently a neglected topic. Relative to off-street parking, on-street parking is typically in the greatest need of management because it is in the highest demand and the most frequently abused. Many downtowns are plagued by people parking on street for several hours, rather than having the spots rotate among short-term diners, shoppers, and office visitors. In particular, downtown employees tend to be offending parties, even though they may be harming their own businesses by monopolizing precious customer parking.

Some downtowns use parking meters to encourage turnover for both on-street and off-street parking, but there are other options for ensuring turnover without the negative side effects of meters, which include visual clutter and driver complaints of being "nickled and dimed." An increasingly popular high-tech alternative to meters is automated pay stations at which people buy tickets that can be displayed on their cars' dashboards. Many downtowns use individuals with law enforcement authority to monitor parking turnover by chalk-marking tires and issuing tickets. If the right personality is employed and portrayed more as a friendly downtown ambassador than a hassling bureaucrat, such an enforcement approach can be much more palatable to the public.

Like so many other communities, Americus, Georgia, had a downtown with a serious problem: employees and residents occupying on-street parking spaces that should have been left available to shoppers. To address the issue, the Downtown Development Authority lobbied the city to pass an ordinance requiring downtown business owners, employees, and residents to park in parking lots during the daytime. Parking fines were adopted at a steep $46 per violation and have since been raised to $48. However, as reported by the city's Main Street manager, a chorus of complaints has meant that the ordinance is not enforced unless a merchant reports a violator to the police. Unfortunately, this scenario is relatively common for measures to improve parking management. Citizen complaints to elected officials over increased enforcement, combined with a weakening of the enforcement entity's resolve, can give such programs a slow death.

Albany, Oregon, on the other hand, took an aggressive approach to parking management. In 1995, the Albany Downtown Association (ADA) and city representatives opted to grant parking enforcement authority to the ADA. Sponsoring a program called Park Wise, the ADA requires that all downtown employees either park outside of the main retail area or register for a parking permit. Many of the downtown lots are also managed by the ADA. A full-time Park Wise employee monitors parkers and issues tickets. Violators who are not downtown employees are issued a five-dollar ticket, while downtown employees are first given two "warning" tickets, then issued a $25 ticket for a first offense, and a $50 fine for subsequent offenses. Although the Park Wise program has been credited with solving downtown Albany's on-street parking problems, it was initially received so negatively by downtown employees that many boycotted downtown businesses in protest. While there are still some negative feelings toward the ADA's parking management program, they have reportedly subsided greatly since, and citizens have the right to appeal what they perceive to be unfair ticketing.

Promotion

Even the most ambitious strategy of parking development, redesign, and management will do little good if drivers are unaware of where and how to park. Consequently, there are three steps commonly taken to promote downtown parking. One is to give the downtown parking program a positive name and identifiable logo. Downtown Albany,

Figure 3-16. A positive name and distinctive logo are one means of promoting downtown parking programs. The Pensacola, Florida, Downtown Improvement Board adopted this logo in 1988 as a means of advertising its public parking lots and city-owned garage. Source: Pensacola Downtown Improvement Board

Oregon, calls its program Park Wise. The second step is to provide small but noticeable signs to guide people to parking lots and garages. Such signage can be particularly effective if a logo has been developed for the downtown's parking program, as the logo alone can suffice rather than illegible text on a small sign. The third common measure for promoting parking is the creation of a brochure mapping the downtown's parking facilities. Like so many downtown organizations, the parking committee of Main Street Denton, Texas, created and distributed downtown parking brochures to all downtown merchants who, in turn, handed them out to their customers. Although the brochures were eventually discontinued once the program was believed to have achieved its goal, such programs can be easily reinstated when needed. In addition to brochures, parking information can also be provided on the website of the downtown organization or local government. In short, by combining a positive logo, directional signage, and a parking brochure or website information, downtown parking options should no longer be a well-kept secret.

Garages

Parking garages are generally only an issue for downtowns serving a population of approximately 35,000 people or more, with the exception of those having a nearby university, strong tourism base, or similarly atypical circumstance. Even in the case of larger downtowns, garages are frequently recommended as part of a downtown parking strategy, but they are often not justified because the real estate economics and associated land values make surface parking more viable. Although development costs for parking vary from place to place, in many parts of the country the standard of $10,000 per structured parking space is used, compared with $1,000 per surface parking space.

Regardless of the specific costs, before a decision is made to develop a downtown parking garage, a parking demand study should be conducted, as well as a financial analysis. One common rule of thumb is that a parking structure should be considered only when the surface parking lots within the study area are at least 75 percent full during each hour from 8:00 a.m. to 5:00 p.m. Ideally, these results should be found during three different typical weekdays in nonconsecutive weeks. Given the expense of structured parking, it should always be understood that although a lack of parking can hamper downtown businesses, a parking surplus is never a business generator. People will visit a place only if there is a reason to go there, not just because the parking is free.

Designing Parking Garages

Parking garages are one of the most challenging types of structures to integrate comfortably into a downtown. The three major problems with most parking garages are: (1) their entrances disrupt the adjacent streetscape; (2) they create dead spaces at the street level; and (3) they are unattractive. In recent years, however, numerous well-designed garages have appeared around the nation to serve as models for the future. Below are design principles that some communities are now mandating for new downtown parking structures in order to combat their most common deficiencies and to be consistent with the downtown's needs:

• Limiting the width of the vehicular access points
• Requiring that a minimum percentage of ground-floor street frontage be designed for retail or service space
• Requiring flat floor plates with end ramps rather than continuously ramped floors
• Requiring massing, openings, exterior cladding, and architectural detailing to resemble a commercial building

With respect to the ground-floor retail requirements, a typical standard is that at least 50 percent of the street frontage must contain retail or service-business space. However, such standards should be applied only if the garage is located on a legitimate shopping street and if the demand for retail or service space will exist in the foreseeable future.

Although the concept of designing garages to look like buildings seems to be a growing trend, the merits of this approach are debatable.

a   *b*   *c*

Figure 3-17a–c. These garages represent three different approaches to designing parking structures. The garage at left is designed to look like a garage, but it includes ground-level retail and service space. The newly constructed garage at center attempts to blend into its historic streetscape by replicating a row of late-19th-century commercial buildings. The one at right goes a step further by duplicating a specific historic mill building that once stood in its place. Source: The Walker Collaborative

For those who believe that "form follows function," such garages are more difficult to identify than they should be. Many historic preservationists frown on building facsimiles, as they are inconsistent with a strict interpretation of the secretary of the interior's federal standards on which most local historic districts are based. It must also be understood that constructing parking garages that look like buildings will substantially increase their development costs.

When they are developed, public parking garages are typically constructed as either part of a larger public development, such as a new city hall or convention center, or as a stand-alone public project. One exception is a large-scale, private, mixed use development in which a garage is constructed through a public-private partnership, as was done in downtown Blacksburg, Virginia. In any circumstance, they should be located in close proximity to the downtown's area of greatest parking demand, and they should be large enough to satisfy as much of the downtown's total parking needs as possible. Potential funding approaches include municipal general obligation bonds, revenue bonds paid down by parking fees, and business improvement district revenues, although the viability of these funding tools are usually dictated by state enabling laws.

LOADING AREAS

First and foremost, loading zones should be located behind buildings so as to not functionally and visually interfere with the building's facade and associated streetscape. Loading areas must be accessible to large trucks, so alleys are crucial to sites located internal to a block and featuring rear loading. Because of their unattractive appearance, loading areas should be visually screened from streets. When located behind buildings, as they should be, no special screening is required because they are not visible from the street; loading areas that can be seen from a street, as in the case of corner lots, do indeed need screening. As with Dumpsters located in parking lots, screens should use a design and material compatible with the associated building. Although suburban sites often employ landscaping for loading area screening, more urban environments typically call for a building material in order to maximize limited space. It is not always necessary that the screening be completely opaque, but it should achieve some degree of visual obscuring of the loading area, as might be accomplished with lattice-work or a perforated brick wall.

TRANSPORTATION ALTERNATIVES

Vehicular traffic congestion can be crippling to some downtowns during peak hours, and it can strangle their long-term economic viability unless remedied. Furthermore, some people—including the very young, the very old, the accessibility impaired, and those who either cannot afford a vehicle or choose not to spend the money on a vehicle—simply do not drive. Therefore, alternative modes of transportation are needed to make a downtown accessible to the largest possible population.

Mass Transit

The forms of mass transit most commonly found in downtowns include commuter rail, light rail, and buses. Bus transportation is the most common form of transit for downtowns large and small. While a wide range of demographic groups will use buses in large cities, such as Boston and New York, bus service in smaller and less urban communities tends to primarily serve lower-income groups, teenagers, and the elderly because other market segments choose to drive. Also, parking costs are relatively inexpensive in smaller communities, so that is not a barrier to driving. These facts must be carefully considered when planning for bus service. When rethinking existing routes,

Figure 3-18. Many of the businesses surrounding the Gallivan Plaza light-rail stop on downtown Salt Lake City's South Main Street depend heavily upon the transit riders who use the city's light-rail system. Source: The Walker Collaborative

bus stops, and transfer stations, two key principles in planning are: (1) routes and stops should be located where they will do the most good, such as near dense housing, employment centers, shopping areas, and public facilities; and (2) bus stops and transfer stations should include shelters, maintenance programs, and security; without them, adjacent property owners and business operators might resist having transit stops located near their buildings.

A cousin to the conventional bus is the shuttle bus, including the "rubber-wheeled trolley." These vehicles are different from conventional buses in several ways. They are typically much smaller, often more attractive, and sometimes feature a nostalgic design imitating a historic trolley. Rubber-wheeled trolleys are also usually intended to target a different demographic group than conventional buses, especially tourists and downtown employees. For downtowns that lack the market demand to support regular shuttle bus service, they are frequently limited to special events and holiday shopping seasons, as well as lunchtime routes that target downtown employees. Despite their merits, operating costs are high, so rarely is there a sufficient market to make them worthwhile in all but the largest downtowns. Although Charleston, South Carolina, draws enough tourists to make them viable in their downtown, Natchez, Mississippi, discovered during the early 1990s that it lacked the market support except during special events. Regardless of the lessons offered by numerous communities, rubber-wheeled trolleys are still being recommended for many downtowns. Perhaps learning from the experience of others, Kalamazoo, Michigan, cautiously recommended in its 2004 downtown plan that the potential for rubber-wheeled trolleys be studied before proceeding with implementation.

Commuter rail typically brings people into a downtown from outlying areas, particularly satellite or "bedroom" communities within a 50-mile radius, depending upon the region. Downtowns that have commuter rail access are often thought of as only the largest cities, but numerous small downtowns surrounding such major cities grew up along rail lines and are often centered on the commuter rail station. Physically, the type of vehicles and tracks that constitute commuter rail are consistent with conventional passenger railroad service, such as Amtrak. While the rail lines for commuter transit are usually well established and not subject to change within the context of downtown planning, the function and design of commuter rail stops is not always so rigid. Cities such as Metuchen, New Jersey, and Schaumburg,

Illinois, have strategically leveraged their train stations in recent years to achieve economic benefits for their downtowns through station design improvements and careful tenant selection.

Light rail generally connects outlying neighborhoods with a downtown, as well as providing access throughout the downtown, and it tends to be limited to larger communities, such as Portland, Oregon. Physically, light rail vehicles are smaller in scale than commuter rail trains, their tracks are usually integrated more into the existing street system, and they are commonly powered by overhead electrical lines. As with commuter rail stations, light rail stops are often magnets for dense residential and commercial uses, even though their overall transportation role in the downtown may be relatively minor. Downtown plans should ensure that zoning encourages such uses and densities in order to leverage transit stops beyond the single purpose of transportation, which is known by the term "transit-oriented development" (TOD). Downtown Hayward, California, for example, built 750 units of housing for the area surrounding the downtown's existing Bay Area Rapid Transit (BART) station between 1992 and 2008. For more information on TOD, see *New Transit Town* (Dittmar and Ohland 2004) and Dunphy (2006). *New Transit Town* examines the lessons learned through case studies of several "first generation" TODs that will be applicable to many existing downtowns. A source on general transit options and their feasibility for downtowns is *Urban Transportation Systems* (Grava 2003).

Figure 3-19. Skagway, Alaska, strongly encourages cycling in its downtown by providing bicycle rentals and plenty of bike racks throughout the downtown. Given that many of its summer tourists arrive by cruise ships, automobiles are often not an option. Source: The Walker Collaborative

Downtown Expansions

Occasionally, a downtown has a rare opportunity to expand into adjacent contiguous property. This scenario occurs most often when a single use occupying a large land area is discontinued, giving the downtown a chance to physically grow beyond a previously existing boundary. Such abandoned uses are frequently institutional or publicly owned, including schools, hospitals, and public housing. In other instances, they are related to transportation or utility infrastructure, such as obsolete rail yards. Private-sector candidates to host downtown expansions include large car dealerships and industrial plants that have closed or relocated. In the case of Tupelo, Mississippi, the 40-acre former fairgrounds site located directly adjacent to the downtown became available for redevelopment.

When such uncommon opportunities arise, a serious planning effort should be initiated. The planning should be a very public affair, and it should include a broad look at the entire downtown. Unless the full downtown can be carefully considered, it is difficult to determine the most appropriate land uses, density, and design for the new expansion area. If the site has lost its original pattern of streets, blocks, and lots—or simply never had them—it is often logical to echo the downtown's development patterns. Abutting streets that run perpendicular to the site's boundary with the downtown and that terminate at the boundary can be extended into the site in order to continue the street pattern. Likewise, new city blocks can be sculpted in dimensions indigenous to the historic downtown.

Beyond the planning phase, one of the most critical points for this type of project is the implementation stage. A first step should be to adopt zoning and development regulations that will carry out the master plan's vision. Another important implementation issue is the site's ownership. If it is owned by multiple private parties, the typical avenue is to simply get the public policies in place, as well as any necessary infrastructure improvements, and let the real estate market do the rest. Some municipalities and redevelopment agencies elect to exercise their eminent domain powers in order to stimulate and control redevelopment if the current owners are incapable of doing so. Requests for proposals (RFPs) are frequently used to solicit developer interest in publicly owned properties. In the case of Tupelo's former fairgrounds site, after first commissioning a master plan the city adopted zoning and design standards that were tailored to the site and echoed the historic downtown. The next step was to identify and to contract with a master developer. He, in turn, negotiated several different individual developments, in addition to overseeing the creation of new streets and other infrastructure. At present, the 40-acre site consists of a new street network integrated with the balance of the downtown, various parking lots, a new city hall and associated park, and several mixed use and commercial buildings. This extension of downtown Tupelo is slowly becoming a seamless and organic outgrowth of the existing downtown, yet the former fairground's rich history has not been forgotten. Reportedly the site of Elvis Presley's first public performance, a small portion of the original fairgrounds has been preserved, and the city has provided interpretive exhibits to tell the story of its native son.

Figure 3-20. This new boulevard extends like a tentacle from historic downtown Tupelo, Mississippi, into the adjacent former fairgrounds site. The new structures fronting it at left borrow their design inspiration from the downtown's indigenous building stock. Source: The Walker Collaborative

Bicycles

In cities with little or no mass transit, bikes are often the third most common means of transportation after automobiles and walking. From the perspective of reducing automobile traffic, the relatively low numbers of cyclists rarely result in a measurable positive impact on congestion. However, their value for animating a downtown can be tremendous. Also, for downtowns fortunate enough to attract cycling group tours, 20 or 30 cyclists dropping in can provide restaurants with quick spikes in profits.

Regardless of whether cyclists come in trickles or waves, downtowns should be bicycle friendly by providing plenty of bike racks in appropriate locations. Downtown master plans should identify specific areas for public bike racks, and they should use bike rack designs favored by serious cyclists. As a supplement to the primary bike rack centers, occasional bike racks should be provided in other locations throughout the downtown where space allows. Also, if and when communities plan and develop bikeway networks, their downtowns need to be sure that they are part of the overall system.

BUILDINGS

The scale, location, and design of buildings can be the difference between a great downtown and a mediocre downtown. Most downtowns are blessed with enough historic buildings to set the template for positive infill development, although development regulations are usually needed to ensure that the historic pattern is indeed respected. Within the context of downtown planning, there are two key categories of buildings: existing buildings and proposed new "infill" buildings, and each warrants their fair share of attention.

Existing Buildings

Existing buildings in a downtown can be categorized into two groups: historic and nonhistoric. The National Register of Historic Places uses a 50-year threshold as one of its criteria to identify historic buildings. While there are plenty of aficionados of 1950s and 1960s architecture, the design features and level of architectural detail that most people tend to associate with "historic" buildings are largely missing from buildings of the post–World War II era. There are contrasting schools of thought, but most downtown planners are comfortable with the justified alteration or even demolition of many post–World War II buildings. On the other hand, buildings considered historic by both preservationist and nonpreservationists should clearly be preserved and enhanced in a manner that protects their architectural integrity and reinforces the overall historic character of the downtown.

Fortunately, many downtowns are blessed with a large stock of historic buildings still functional for today's needs. While the most immediate matters for their owners and managers tend to be keeping occupancy levels and rental rates at a high level, the building's maintenance is another important ongoing activity. Downtown plans should focus on those buildings in the greatest need of maintenance, physical rehabilitation, and adaptive use.

Building Rehabilitation

The physical rehabilitation of historic buildings is a key focus of many downtown plans. Buildings, in general, are important because they house the destinations that attract people to a downtown in the first place, in addition to housing employees and residents. Historic buildings are especially important because they provide the unique character that distinguishes the downtown from the balance of its community. In marketing terms, historic buildings help to differentiate the downtown from other "products" in the marketplace. In fact, preference surveys conducted as part of downtown master plans and market studies reveal, time after time, that it is the downtown's historic character that respondents most frequently identify as the downtown's greatest strength.

And it is not just shoppers and residents who are attracted to historic buildings. When the business management association for Seattle's Pioneer Square surveyed its businesses to find out why they chose Pioneer Square for their business location, the most frequently cited reason was that the area was a historic district. The ability of historic buildings to serve as a foundation for downtown revitalization is certainly no secret to the National Main Street Center, which uses historic preservation as the foundation of its revitalization approach. Donovan Rypkema, a nationally recognized leader in the economics of historic preservation, knows of no successful downtown revitalization programs in which historic preservation is not a key component: "I haven't seen it, I haven't read of it, I haven't heard of it." Without question, any effective downtown plan needs to pay particular attention to the potential role of historic buildings.

When rehabilitating historic buildings, federal preservation standards should be followed. The key objectives of the secretary of the interior's Standards for Rehabilitation are to retain as much of the original historic fabric as possible and to replace missing elements with historically appropriate elements. There are several reasons for following federal preservation standards. First, they help to avoid the glaring mistakes that seem to be repeated time after time, such as sandblasting

Federal Historic Preservation Standards

The secretary of the interior's Standards for Rehabilitation were first adopted in 1976 and expanded and revised in 1983 and 1992. Administered by the National Park Service's Heritage Preservation Services Division, this document defines "rehabilitation" as "the act or process of making possible an efficient compatible use for a property through repair, alterations and additions while preserving those portions or features that convey its historical, cultural or architectural values" (http://edocket.access.gpo.gov/cfr_2008/julqtr/36cfr68.2.htm). While the supporting guidelines are extensive and detailed, the 10 primary standards read as follows:

1. A property will be used as it was historically or be given a new use that requires minimal change to its distinctive materials, features, spaces and spatial relationships.

2. The historic character of a property will be retained and preserved. The removal of distinctive materials or alteration of features, spaces and spatial relationships that characterize a property will be avoided.

3. Each property will be recognized as a physical record of its time, place and use. Changes that create a false

sense of historical development, such as adding conjectural features or elements from other historic properties, will not be undertaken.

4. Changes to a property that have acquired historic significance in their own right will be retained and preserved.

5. Distinctive materials, features, finishes and construction techniques or examples of craftsmanship that characterize a property will be preserved.

6. Deteriorated historic features will be repaired rather than replaced. Where the severity of deterioration requires replacement of a distinctive feature, the new feature will match the old in design, color, texture and, where possible, materials. Replacement of missing features will be substantiated by documentary and physical evidence.

7. Chemical or physical treatments, if appropriate, will be undertaken using the gentlest means possible. Treatments that cause damage to historic materials will not be used.

8. Archeological resources will be protected and preserved in place. If such resources must be disturbed, mitigation measures will be undertaken.

9. New additions, exterior alterations or related new construction will not destroy historic materials, features and spatial relationships that characterize the property. The new work will be differentiated from the old and will be compatible with the historic materials, features, size, scale and proportion, and massing to protect the integrity of the property and its environment.

10. New additions and adjacent or related new construction will be undertaken in such a manner that, if removed in the future, the essential form and integrity of the historic property and its environment would be unimpaired.

a

b

Figure 3-21a–b. The average person has difficulty envisioning how a tired old building can be transformed into a beautiful jewel. Renderings can help the public appreciate the true potential of neglected historic structures and their surroundings. Source: The Walker Collaborative / Ben Johnson

brick exterior walls or adding a multipaned colonial-style storefront to a nineteenth-century commercial building. Second, following the federal standards is necessary for projects that intend to take advantage of the federal investment tax credit. For qualified projects, 20 percent of the eligible costs of the building's rehabilitation can be applied directly as a credit against federal income taxes. Often the credit is sold to investors to generate equity for the project. Sometimes it is used directly by the developer. Many rehabilitation projects would not occur without the use of this incentive. As just one of thousands of examples from around the country, this credit made feasible the rehabilitation of the 53-room Windsor Hotel in downtown Americus, Georgia, in 1983. That project, in turn, has been cited as playing a major role in redirecting the fortunes of downtown Americus in a positive direction. Some states that have income taxes also have their own version of the federal investment tax credit. Moreover, most local historic district design guidelines are based upon the federal standards. Thus, in those cases in which the downtown is part of a local historic district, the federal standards will be indirectly required anyway. If local historic district designation does not already exist but is a goal, the successful completion of some rehabilitation projects following the federal standards may be a selling tool for making local designation more palatable to downtown property owners. Furthermore, following the federal standards will help to elevate the downtown's architectural and historic integrity, increasing the odds it will meet the National Register criteria for future designation or maintain its status if already designated.

Adaptive Use of Buildings

Adaptive use, sometimes redundantly referred to as adaptive reuse, entails taking buildings originally constructed for one particular purpose and modifying them for a completely different use. Adaptive use can occur with either historic or nonhistoric buildings, although some adaptations of historic buildings can damage their historic integrity.

The practice of adaptive use is critical to keeping buildings relevant that might otherwise become obsolete. In some cases, obsolescence is caused by changes in technology. For example, the design and technological needs of hospitals have changed substantially since the 1920s, making hospitals constructed during that era functionally obsolete. However, some hospitals from that era have been successfully converted into apartments and condominiums, as was done in Natchez, Mississippi, during the 1990s. Another frequent occurrence is the end

Figure 3-22. This 19th-century warehouse complex on Main Street in Durham, North Carolina, was successfully adapted into the Brightleaf Square shopping mall. It now houses a variety of specialty retail shops, eateries, and small offices, and it serves as an important anchor for its surrounding district. Following this project's path to success, two other tobacco warehouses in downtown Durham have been adapted for condominiums, offices, and restaurants. Source: The Walker Collaborative

of a particular industry in a community, leaving an empty industrial or warehouse building. In other cases, a building's original purpose and design may no longer be relevant because of changes to its surrounding context. A common example is an urban church that has lost its congregation to the suburbs. In order to save such buildings from becoming victims of their obsolescence, a handful of innovative communities have adopted a Neighborhood Landmark designation for such properties to allow for a wider range of permitted land uses beyond their preexisting residential or institutional zoning.

When downtown Chippewa Falls, Wisconsin, faced the challenge of an empty historic shoe-manufacturing plant, a variety of local entities joined forces and found a capable developer. Through a combination of tax increment financing, Community Development Block Grant funds, the federal investment tax credit for historic rehabilitation, and a low-interest loan from the local Main Street program, the structure

Empowering "the" Downtown Developer

In Gallatin, Tennessee, his name is Mudd, Reggie Mudd. In Pensacola, Florida, his name is Clark Thompson. In Bryan, Texas, her name is Kay Conlee. Who are these people? They are "the" downtown developers, and almost every small to medium-size downtown is blessed with at least one. This is the person who periodically acquires a downtown building, restores it with painstaking care and attention toward detail, leases it to solid tenants that contribute to the downtown, and then does it all over again. Although their characteristics vary from town to town and person to person, they commonly include at least some of the following traits:

- They are often self-taught developers, rather than people with master's degrees in real estate development and a decade of corporate experience.
- They generally have little use for consultants, with the exception of architects and engineers when absolutely necessary.
- They like to avoid the government when possible, particularly the red tape that accompanies most financial incentive programs.
- They have good design instincts, which is another

reason they use design professionals only minimally.

- They often lack tenants prior to rehabilitating the building, which does not seem to worry them.
- They have a knack for picking quality tenants, even though they may judge them more on their character and business concepts than on their financial muscle, track records, or detailed business plans.
- They are blessed with an unusual level of common sense and a doit-yourself attitude.

Regardless of how closely "the" developer for any particular downtown fits this profile, the question is, How can the downtown harness this person's success and empower him or her to further expand their development achievements for the larger good of downtown?

There are many barriers, both legal and political, to simply handing over the keys of downtown to "the" developer. Realistically, there are two potential avenues to pursue, depending upon the particular community. One approach is to conduct a Request for Qualifications (RFQ) process that formally identifies this person and provides legitimacy to their anointment as "the chosen one." While some communities use this type of approach for individual multi-phased development projects by designating a "master developer," it would be politically difficult, and perhaps legally problematic, to go as far as exercising the condemnation of privately owned property so that "the" private developer could then develop the site. Also, given the fact that "the" developer typically avoids governmental red tape like the plague, they will likely be uninterested in such an opportunity. Rather than conducting a formal selection process or granting any formal status or rights to "the" developer, another alternative is to simply run interference for this person during their projects yet remain short of giving them an illegal level of preferential treatment.

Because every community has a different set of variables, there is no one-size-fits-all approach to empowering "the" downtown developer. Nevertheless, the important point is that he or she be recognized, appreciated, and empowered at some level for the benefit of downtown.

---

was adapted into 32 housing units. Including both affordable and market-rate units, the building continues to maintain high occupancy rates. Another Wisconsin community, Sheboygan Falls, achieved similar results when it adapted an 1879 woolen mill into affordable housing in 1992 through a variety of financing means. For its size, one of the country's uncontested leaders in adaptive use is the 27,000-person community of Burlington, Iowa. Among its many conversions are the fitting of the police station and county attorney's office into a former buggy factory in 1994, a doctor's office in a former Christian Science Reading Room, law offices in the Fraternal Order of Eagles building, and an art center and art guild in a historic church.

When engaging in downtown planning, it is always important to be alert to potential adaptive use opportunities. In fact, a plan's market analysis can be used to match potential uses to individual buildings. Identifying such opportunities often requires the planners to think creatively, helping downtowns to grow and to evolve.

Infill Development

A missing building on an urban streetscape is like a missing tooth in a beautiful smile. Downtowns need new buildings where former buildings have been lost and where existing buildings are beyond repair and must be razed. Some locations need new infill development sooner than others. For example, a downtown's primary retail street should be a top priority for infill development so the street can strengthen economically and spin off improvements to adjacent areas. Similarly, the high visibility of vacant corner lots makes them particularly important candidates for new buildings. When considering infill development as part of downtown planning, two architectural categories of such buildings commonly exist: background buildings and special buildings.

Background buildings. Background buildings do not stand out from their streetscape, but they fit the architectural and design context of the downtown. At a casual glance, a background building goes relatively unnoticed. By no means do background buildings have to be boring or unattractive, but they should follow the historical design vocabulary of their context with respect to the following urban and architectural design considerations:

- Building height and scale
- Building setback
- Building massing
- Roof form
- Ground-floor height
- Percentage of facade glazing

Figure 3-23. The Kid's Korner Pizza Building was built in downtown Rice Lake, Wisconsin, during the 1990s following the loss of its predecessor to a fire. It blends in nicely with its streetscape as an attractive yet subtle "background building." Source: Rice Main Street Associates

Collaborating on Infill

Having won the National Main Street Center's 1996 Great American Main Street Award, the Chippewa Falls, Wisconsin, Main Street program has clearly been doing something right. While the program has a long list of impressive victories, perhaps its greatest achievement to date has been the new Korger Building, completed in 2004. Replacing a historic building on the Cobban Block that was lost to a fire in 1992, this $1.6 million two-story infill building resulted from the collaboration of a wide range of entities and individuals:

- The Chippewa Falls Main Street, Inc. program served as a project catalyst and the coordinator of other resources for the project.
- The Main Street Cobban Block Development Task Force raised $5,000 from downtown business owners that was later used for engineering work on the site.
- The Main Street Design Committee's chairperson, a local architect, designed the building's exterior.
- The Korger family developed the building for their business, Korger's Decorating and Fine Furnitures, and designed the building's interior.
- Chippewa Falls purchased the property for $100,000 to ensure that it was not inappropriately developed, then sold the property to the Korger Family for $1. It also established a tax increment financing (TIF) district in 1994 that generated $70,000 in site improvement funds for the project and provided the developers a $475,000 loan at a 4 percent interest rate.
- The National Main Street Center provided consultants to help determine the most appropriate type of infill development.
- The Wisconsin Main Street program prepared a market analysis for the proposed new use, as well as a business and financing plan.
- Northwestern Bank provided a loan for some development costs and business inventory stock.
- The U.S. Small Business Administration helped secure the construction loan, taking a second position behind the bank and in front of the city.

Although the building footprint of this two-story, 17,000-squarefoot building is substantially larger than those typical of downtown Chippewa Falls, it incorporates a pair of historic columns salvaged from the town's former Carnegie library as a nod to the community's past. In addition to filling a void in the

Figure 3-24. The Korger Building's development in 2004 involved the direct participation of seven different entities. Located in downtown Chippewa Falls, Wisconsin, it represents the combined efforts of a variety of local, state, and federal governmental organizations, in addition to the private sector. Source: Chippewa Falls Main Street, Inc.

streetscape, the business inside is flourishing, as its sales volumes have exceeded expectations, and customers are coming from as far away as Chicago, more than 250 miles away. Former Main Street director, Jim Schuh, stated regarding downtown's 12-year wait for the perfect fit, "It is difficult for people to have patience and wait for the right project. Instead they tend to settle for something that is less than perfect. Luckily, Chippewa Falls took the right approach from the beginning and had the patience to stick with it until we found the right one—a 'patience and perseverance' approach."

- Orientation of windows and doors
- Building materials

In fact, this list of issues could serve as a template for a set of design guidelines for a downtown historic district. Another consideration for infill buildings is referred to as "tripartite building articulation." This esoteric term refers to the concept of structures being designed in accordance with the classical column, including a base, shaft, and capital. Most urban buildings constructed prior to 1950 used this design principle to some degree. Often, the "base" is defined by the bulkhead or water-table level of a commercial storefront, the "capital" is defined by the cornice, and the "shaft" is the main portion of the facade in between. Tripartite building articulation is more defined in some buildings than others.

An excellent example of an infill background building that meets all of these design considerations is the Kid's Korner Pizza Building in downtown Rice Lake, Wisconsin, a community of 8,300 people. Built during the mid-1990s to replace a structure that burned, the local Main Street Association's design advice led to a modern yet attractive one-story brick commercial building that blends seamlessly into the block. Completing the project's success is the fact that the pizzeria inhabiting it is one of downtown Lake Rice's most thriving businesses today.

While it is appropriate in a historic downtown to design buildings compatible with their neighbors, most historic preservationists frown on new buildings that slavishly copy historic buildings. In particular, the imitation of architectural detailing begins to cross the line between compatibility and forgery. Because deception is considered undesirable, the secretary of the interior's Standards for Rehabilitation discourage new buildings that imitate historic buildings. Given that the majority of locally designated historic districts are based upon those same federal standards, the guidelines for most local districts also discourage imitations of historic buildings.

Special buildings and sites. Buildings that might be considered "special" to a downtown are typically institutional or civic buildings. Examples include city halls, county courthouses, libraries, religious buildings, sports arenas, and convention centers. A building intended for a unique use should have a design that gives it prominence and underscores its significance to the downtown and the community. Designing a new building with a classical architectural style, such as Beaux Arts, is one effective means for reinforcing its institutional identity, and this approach has been used by countless downtowns in recent years. But contemporary and abstract designs can be equally successful in lending prominence.

Even if the building's design is not extraordinary, its specific location within its site can be. For example, key governmental buildings often have generous front setbacks in order to give them a formal front lawn that intentionally breaks the rhythm of the street's building setback patterns. In fact, most design standards adopted by local governments for design review within special districts encourage public and institutional buildings to deviate from the front setback standards in order to help distinguish them from their neighboring background buildings.

Figure 3-25. This new library proposed in the 2005 downtown master plan for Gallatin, Tennessee, uses two techniques to give the building prominence and underscore its civic function: the main portion of the structure is set back from the street wall with a formal plaza in the foreground, and its architecture echoes the Beaux Arts style of the historic courthouse located across the street. Source: The Walker Collaborative / Ben Johnson

Figure 3-26. This new commercial building uses a tower to emphasize its corner location and to provide an orienting landmark for the surrounding area. Source: The Walker Collaborative

The resulting lawns and plazas can eventually become some of the most important public spaces in a downtown.

In addition to buildings considered special because of their use, some buildings are special simply because their design takes advantage of a special site. Special sites include highly visible corner lots, referred to as "100 percent locations" in real estate terminology. Corner buildings often feature distinctive architectural elements, such as clock towers, clipped corner entrances, and upper-floor turrets to underscore their prominent location. These treatments create landmarks that help orient downtown visitors. Likewise, sites that anchor a "T" street intersection or otherwise terminate an urban vista may warrant a special design treatment, such as a cupola or some other vertical element. As in the case of institutional and public buildings, the adopted design guidelines of some communities account for the need to allow buildings at special locations, regardless of their use, to deviate from the norm.

SIGNAGE

Downtown signage can be classified into three basic groups: Business identification signs, product or service signs, and directional signs.

Business Identification Signs

Business identification signs, typically located on or near the front of the building, serve two functions. First and foremost, they allow customers to find their business. Second, they serve as advertising much in the way that a storefront window display does. Because most downtown buildings have little or no front setback, their signage is generally attached to the front facade in the form of a perpendicular projecting sign, a flush facade-mounted sign, a painted window sign, or an awning sign. An "object sign" is occasionally used to replicate an item strongly associated with the business, such as an oversized teakettle for a tea shop. Freestanding signs are sometimes used for buildings that have a substantial front setback from the street. Whether they are building mounted or freestanding, such signs are typically regulated by sign standards that control their location, size, materials, method of illumination, and similar design considerations. Unlike signage found on a highway, downtown business signs should be scaled for pedestrians and slow-moving vehicular traffic. Many municipal sign standards limit the size of signs to a percentage of the building's facade area rather than a one-size-fits-all approach. Placement should be done in a manner that does not obscure significant architectural components, such as window elements and architectural detailing. Material and illumination standards usually depend upon how historic or otherwise controlled of a character is sought for the downtown. For example, some communities will permit only wooden signs with external spot lighting shielded to avoid glare. Others are less stringent and might allow synthetic materials, such as internally illuminated plastic.

Product and Service Signs

Product or service signs advertise some particular product or service of a downtown business, such as a beer sign in a restaurant or bar window. Such signs are often neon, and because they are not considered to be as necessary as business identification signs they are not permitted in all downtowns. If allowed, their type and quantity should be tightly controlled in order to avoid scenarios such as numerous flyer-type paper signs obscuring a storefront window.

Directional Signs

While business identification signs and product or service signs are associated with the private sector, directional signs are typically part of the public realm and provide a wayfinding function. Directional signs guide downtown visitors to public parking, sports arenas, performance halls, museums, schools, parks, governmental buildings, historic sites, and similar destinations. They also tend to use a common color, such as brown, to indicate a cultural facility. Although some downtowns use directional signs located on their primary streets to advertise less visible businesses located on side streets, this approach is not recommended in most instances because it adds to visual clutter and can be difficult to limit in terms of which businesses are included.

PUBLIC SPACES, ART, AND INTERPRETATION

If absolutely necessary, most downtowns could find a way to survive in the absence of public spaces, art, and interpretation. These particular elements, however, give downtowns an intangible soul. They make a downtown come to life and seem more interesting and special. Some might successfully argue that public spaces, unlike public art and interpretation, are indeed essential and not a dispensable option. Within the context of downtown planning, "public spaces" most commonly refers not to streets (though they are important public spaces) but to parks, plazas, amphitheaters, greenways, and similar spaces. Art can be many things to many people, but most will agree that "interpretation" is the art of telling a story. While the majority of downtown plans address public spaces, most do not address art or interpretation because these issues are generally not considered to be as critical as other downtown issues. For those communities with the resources to go into such detail in their plans, and particularly those with strong tourism or destination potential, art and interpretation are indeed worthy of greater consideration.

Public Spaces: Function, Location, Size, and Enclosure

While it is easy to become prematurely engrossed in the details of designing individual public spaces, sound downtown planning calls first for a much larger perspective. What public spaces already exist in the downtown, what are their functions, and how effective are they in fulfilling their roles? What are their potentials for improvements? Once those questions are answered, new spaces might be contemplated. Many downtown plans propose too much public space, which can result in financial challenges for ongoing maintenance, as well as a lack of sufficient market demand, leaving them desolate, uninviting, and perhaps even dangerous. Therefore, downtown public spaces should be applied sparingly and thoughtfully.

There are many interdependent considerations with respect to the function, location, and size of public spaces. For example, a relatively small, "hardscaped," and formal plaza might be appropriate near a public building as a venue for civic ceremonies and speeches, but a large grassy park might be located where it can strategically accommodate multiple uses, hold large numbers of people, and leverage economic activity for adjacent businesses. Regardless of the intended use and audience, public spaces lacking good access, such as adjacent streets, will often go underused.

Planners have various standards available to them to help determine the optimal size for a given public space. Going back to the Spanish Colonial era, the Law of the Indies stipulated that "the size of the plaza shall be proportioned to the number of inhabitants . . . thus the plaza

a   b

Figures 3-27a–b. This rotary park proposed for a strategic location in downtown Normal, Illinois, embodies all of the characteristics of a popular public space: direct sunlight, sufficient shade, ample seating, landscaped groundcover, paved surfaces, and a water feature. Source: Bruce Bondy / Hoerr Schaudt Landscape Architects

should be decided upon taking into consideration the growth the town may experience." For the main plaza of the community, the smallest size recommended was 200 feet by 300 feet, while the largest size was 532 feet by 800 feet. Regardless of the size, it was always recommended that the plaza be rectilinear and at least one and a half times as long as it is wide. While most of today's authorities on the subject avoid being so prescriptive about dimensional standards, groups such as the National Park and Recreation Association (NPRA) still have definitive ideas on appropriate sizes tied to the space's user populations.

Also consider that actual size and perceived size are two different matters, as the design and surrounding enclosure, or lack thereof, can affect the perceived size of a public space. As advocated by Christopher Alexander in *A Pattern Language: Towns, Buildings, Construction*, "An outdoor space is positive when it has a distinct and definitive shape, as definite as the shape of a room, and when its shape is as important as the shapes of the buildings which surround it" (1977, 518). He goes on to cite a study conducted by the San Francisco City Planning Department in 1969 that found that "people seek areas which are partially enclosed and partly open—not too open, not too enclosed" (521). Also weighing in on the subject is Jane Jacobs in *The Death and Life of Great American Cities* (1961). Jacobs states that "the presence of buildings around a park is important in design. They enclose it. They make a definite shape out of the space, so it appears as an important event in the city scene, a positive feature, rather than a no-account left-over" (106). Planners Gary Hack and Kevin Lynch (1984, 157–58) are quick to point out that buildings have been the traditional definers of urban space, but "space definers may be visual suggestions rather than visual stops: colonnades, bollards, even changes in ground pattern or the imaginary extensions of things. . . . More often now, enclosure is achieved with trees and hedges, supported by the shaping of the ground." They further suggest that "an external enclosure is most comfortable when its walls are one-half to one-third as high as the width of the space enclosed, while, if the ratio falls below one-fourth, the space begins to lack a sense of enclosure." While there is clearly no lack of opinions when it comes to the need to enclose downtown public spaces, it must be understood that such spaces also need to be bound on one or more sides by a public right-of-way rather than being buried within a private context.

The Greening of Downtown

The unveiling of a downtown master plan is generally met with great anticipation, as well as a dose of scrutiny. A response from the public that has certainly occurred more than once is the question, Can't you make the plan greener? People often want to see more trees, shrubs, lawn areas, parks, greenways, and other landscaping features, and this sentiment is not always limited to the general public. The planning team's landscape architects sometimes need to be restrained from becoming a downtown's Johnny Appleseeds. Given that many of us have been taught by the writings of Transcendentalists, such as Ralph Waldo Emerson and Henry Thoreau, that cities are evil and pastoral landscapes are good, this phenomenon should be no surprise. There is no question that a little landscaping and the occasional park can go far in softening the hard edges of a downtown, beautifying it, and making it more livable. However, it is also the responsibility of downtown planners to persuade the public to embrace, rather than fight, the urbanity of a downtown. Rather than attempting to dilute a downtown with green space in an ill-advised attempt to make it more like the suburbs, downtowns should be celebrated for what they are, and urban design should be used to reinforce its unique qualities rather than trying to obscure them with landscaping. While public open spaces are an essential ingredient for a livable downtown, there are usually more opportunities for smaller urban parks and hardscaped plazas than for expansive parks on the scale of Boston Common.

What Makes for a Good Public Space?

Over the years, some well-know entities and individuals have dedicated themselves to the creation of great urban spaces. The Project for Public Spaces (PPS) is a nonprofit organization engaged in research, planning, and advocacy for the enhancement of existing urban spaces and the creation of new ones. Frederick Law Olmsted is known for his design of parks during the nineteenth century, including New York City's Central Park, and William Whyte spent endless hours during the twentieth century studying New York City's parks and plazas using time-lapse photography to better understand how people used them. Prompted by New York's granting of density bonuses to developers in return for little-used public spaces, Whyte's findings revealed some important common denominators among the most popular parks and plazas:

- Direct sunlight
- Sufficient shade during warmer months
- Generous amounts of seating
- Landscaped groundcover
- Paved surfaces
- Water features
- Good public access and visibility

Although the physical characteristics of a public space are important, the adjacent lands uses can be equally important. The most successful public spaces are surrounded by active and vibrant uses, such as dining and retail. Conversely, spaces bound by streets designed and used more like highways are frequently underused because the associated traffic is both a physical barrier and a nuisance. Regular maintenance and event programming are also critical to the success of many urban public spaces. Attention to maintenance ensures that spaces are attractive and functional, while periodic special events will draw a continuous market to be reminded of the space's existence and merits.

Making Public Spaces "Places"

Physical plans must make a serious effort to go beyond merely assigning land uses and building types to particular areas. Instead, a plan should strive toward creating genuine "places," especially given the marketing power distinct places can lend a downtown. Creating places is more of an art than a science. While there are no foolproof step-by-step instructions, publications on this subject include *Making Places Special* (Bunnell 2002) and *Placemaking on a Budget* (Zelinka and Jackson 2005). The most useful exercise that a planner can follow is to simply study existing places as models and ask local citizens what makes a place special.

In addition to using design to meld together physical components that add up to a special place, other methods help create places. One sometimes effective means is to give proposed new places a name that has some meaning to the community's stakeholders. For example, a plan in 2004 for a portion of downtown Rocky Mount, North Carolina, named the proposed new amphitheater after a native of the community—jazz great Thelonious Monk. The plan's key stakeholders seemed to be as excited about the symbolism in the amphitheater's name as they were about its proposed physical form. Assigning names to otherwise lifeless places existing only on paper is akin to giving them a soul, yet this approach does not have to be limited to new public spaces. A 2006 plan for downtown Pleasant Grove, Utah, recommended renaming the existing so-called Downtown Park to Walker Park in honor of the community's original designer and first mayor. With a little historic research and creativity, this strategy can be applied to the benefit of many future and existing downtown public spaces, perhaps even helping to nudge some proposed public spaces across the implementation threshold.

Art

Performing arts, in the form of street performers, are relevant to downtowns, and that subject is addressed in Chapter 5. This discussion is limited to visual arts. Three separate issues related to visual art are particularly relevant to downtowns: artists, art galleries, and public art.

Artists seeking affordable space, lofts with high ceilings, and a unique environment have constituted the first wave of pioneers to settle many deteriorated downtown areas. They need cheap space to live, work, and interact with one another. Their existence in downtowns is primarily a market issue, as they represent a distinct market segment that can benefit downtowns, much like yuppies and empty nesters. Art galleries are a related but separate issue, and they can exist in a downtown regardless of whether the downtown actually has artists who live and work there. The presence of art galleries is a tenant mix and business development issue, like other specialty retail uses, and is rarely addressed distinctly by downtown plans. Public visual art, however, is sometimes addressed by planners.

Public art can come in many forms, ranging from traditional statues of historical figures to abstract colorful objects whose status as "art" might be debatable. Regardless of how conventional or unconventional it might be, art is beneficial to downtowns because it makes them more interesting and attractive, giving people yet another reason to spend time downtown. As with other urban design features, public art can be used to further specific marketing concepts and to reinforce a distinct identity and character for the downtown.

The key issue for planning is the physical placement of art, and it depends greatly upon the specific type of art. For example, murals are an excellent way to enliven a large blank wall and require no encroachment into a public right-of-way. Likewise, banners attached to streetlights are a form of public art that occupies no significant space when mounted above head level. In fact, the downtown Encinitas, California, Arts Alive banner program adorns streetlights with original works of art that are ultimately auctioned off to raise money for their 101 Artists' Colony, the town's downtown art gallery program.

Three-dimensional, ground-mounted art, however, requires sufficient space to not obstruct a streetscape's pedestrian flows. Therefore, such art tends to be located on very broad sidewalks, as well as in parks and plazas. Downtown plans that address public art should create a map illustrating appropriate locations or public art zones. A plan commissioned by the Vallejo Redevelopment Agency in California in 2000 did just that, proposing public art as a major component for the downtown waterfront.

In addition to its location, public art raises many other important questions: Will public art be a requirement or voluntary for new development? Who will determine which works of art are appropriate for public display? Should a program for maintenance be in place, and how long

a   *b*

Figures 3-28a–b. West Main Street in downtown Louisville, Kentucky, uses artistic horses as a means of reinforcing an important local theme. Ybor City, near downtown Tampa, Florida, enlivens its streetscape with casually posed statues of local historic figures accompanied by explanatory plaques, allowing it to double as both art and interpretation. Source: The Walker Collaborative

should various works of art be displayed? A downtown plan addressing public art will need to consider many or all of these questions.

While the answers to most of these questions will depend upon the particular community, the issue of mandatory art versus voluntary art is a straightforward one with a limited range of options. The most extreme approach is to require that public art be provided as part of any private-sector development of a certain magnitude, while a less heavy-handed option is to provide incentives, such as density bonuses, in return for the provision of public art. New York City, for example, has experimented with such incentives for years as a means of securing art, plazas, and similar public amenities. Some communities limit the requirement of public art to public buildings, often requiring that a minimum percentage of the entire construction budget go toward art. Nashville, Tennessee, has a "percent-for-art" ordinance requiring that 1 percent of the net proceeds of bonds issued to pay for construction projects approved in the metropolitan government's capital improvements budget go toward public art. It is then up to the Metropolitan Nashville Arts Commission to decide whether to commission art for the specific building sites or to set aside the funds for future projects. Most communities, however, rely on the altruistic spirit of the private sector to voluntarily raise funds for public art.

Interpretation

Most downtown plans fail to address the issue of interpretation because it is not viewed, understandably, as an essential plan component in light of limited plan funding. But for those downtowns that elect to address the issue, particularly those with an especially rich history or strong tourism potential, interpretation can be achieved in a variety ways. In short, interpretation is simply the act of telling a story. As with public art, it, too, can add interest to a downtown, perhaps persuading visitors to linger a bit longer. By conveying specific themes, interpretation can also be used to reinforce an overall marketing strategy for the downtown. The two key considerations to interpretation, whether it is being done within a downtown or elsewhere, are the story to be told and the method of conveying it.

A downtown plan that addresses interpretation must first decide on the overall theme or themes to interpret and then identify the specific stories. The most common topic of interpretation for most downtowns is history, including events that occurred in the downtown and its physical evolution over time. Historic photographs of the downtown and associated personalities can be especially fascinating to many people. Some communities, on the other hand, use their downtown as venues to interpret history that occurred elsewhere in the town. When the downtown organization of Gettysburg, Pennsylvania, conducted a survey of battlefield tourists in the 1990s, they discovered that only approximately 25 percent of the visitors ever made it to downtown Gettysburg. To capitalize on a huge opportunity to benefit the downtown economically, a concentrated effort was subsequently made to better interpret the role played by downtown Gettysburg during the famous Civil War battle.

The potential methods for interpreting stories are as diverse as the imagination will allow. The most basic approach is to provide

a

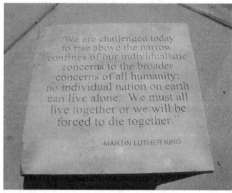

b

Figures 3-29a–b. Interpretive concrete stools are an innovative approach combining art with streetscape furnishings. Source: The Walker Collaborative

conventional wayside exhibits. Used extensively by organizations such as the National Park Service, today's wayside exhibits are much more interesting and colorful than the simple text-only plaques that were in vogue in previous decades. Usually in the physical form of a sign, these exhibits read much like a magazine, including a large heading, a smaller subheading with additional information, the main body of text, and perhaps even a sidebar story. Embellished with high-quality graphics, such exhibits provide a clear hierarchy of text layers so the reader can take in as much or as little information as desired. Beyond wayside exhibits, less conventional vehicles for interpretation include the integration of text or images into streetscape components, such as pavers, seating, and trash receptacles. Even audio recordings can provide interpretation at the push of a button, and living history demonstrations can employ people to converse with the public. However, such approaches come with a much higher price tag.

INFRASTRUCTURE AND UTILITIES

Like a home's bathroom plumbing, infrastructure and utilities are not glamorous, but they are important elements of any downtown. Nevertheless, astute planners recognize their importance within the context of downtown planning. Joey Dunn, who was involved with downtown planning for Bryan, Texas, states that although pretty pictures are extremely important in communicating the vision of what a downtown area can be, an effective downtown plan must also have "depth." The plan should provide practical guidance for improving infrastructure below the ground to support what happens above ground. And in most cases, this is where the bulk of the cost lies for improvement.

The three key questions related to infrastructure and utilities for any downtown plan include:

1. Do all of the necessary types of infrastructure and utilities exist in the downtown?
2. Are there specific areas of downtown where certain infrastructure and utilities still need to be extended?
3. Is there sufficient capacity for the existing infrastructure and utilities to accommodate all future infill development?

The primary downtown infrastructure and utility issues include stormwater drainage, sanitary sewer, water, gas, electricity, and telecommunications.

Stormwater Drainage

Urbanized areas feature vast amounts of impervious surface, such as buildings and pavement. That inherent condition results in tremendous volumes of stormwater runoff. The two key challenges to dealing with runoff are getting it off of the urban landscape and getting it into a drainage system. Keeping water from pooling on the surface is best achieved through a slight slope, whether it is a roof or a street surface, to channel water where it is intended to go. The destination of that water is typically the street gutter, which leads the water into a drain. Because some downtowns must endure rooftop drainage in which the downspouts empty directly onto the sidewalk, it is important that drainage be piped below the sidewalk level. Proper stormwater drainage systems for new development can be ensured through the construction plan review process overseen by local governments. Existing drainage problems, on the other hand, call for remedial work to achieve the proper slopes and drainage systems on a site-specific basis. Getting water into the drainage system is achieved by having sufficient and functional stormwater drains as part of the street system.

The two most common impediments to proper drainage are: (1) the clogging of drains; and (2) streets that have been paved so many times that gutter storage capacity is reduced and the drainage inlets are obstructed. Clogging is best avoided by screens that filter out debris and regular maintenance. The only way to mitigate paving obstructions is to periodically remove old layers of paving through milling to lower the overall grade level before the newest layer of pavement is applied.

Sanitary Sewer and Water

Underground sewer and water systems are designed much like a tree. They include the main "trunk" lines that connect sewage treatment plants and water reservoirs with numerous smaller branches. The branches continually split off into smaller pipes until reaching the end users, such as residences and businesses. Branch lines usually run within the public right-of-way parallel to streets, and individual lateral lines extend perpendicularly from the branches to serve each property. Gravity and pressure are used to move sewage and potable water through their respective pipes.

While most downtown plans do not focus much attention on the issue of sewer and water, they do often evaluate the overall existing capacity in light of future demands, including increased densities resulting from a future build-out scenario. Most plans that identify any upgrades recommend the replacement of failing lines, the extension of lateral lines to undeveloped sites, or the upgrade of line sizes for greater capacity. One constraint to increased sewage treatment capacity can be on the treatment end of the equation. Treatment plants occasionally reach their maximum capacity, often because the streams that receive the treated effluents are at their maximum environmental capacity. This limitation is more common for development peripheral to urban areas, as most downtowns are close enough to a significant body of water, such as a river, to avoid such problems.

Heating Things up in Downtown Holland

Founded in the 1840s by Dutch settlers, Holland, Michigan, is now a town of 34,000 people located just west of Grand Rapids and only a few miles from Lake Michigan. Its downtown revitalization efforts began in earnest in 1984 with the adoption of a Main Street program. It is no secret that downtowns located in colder northern climates, similar to their hot-climate counterparts to the south, must find ways to compete with the controlled environments of enclosed shopping malls during the more extreme seasons. The overhead pedestrian tubes ("skywalks") of downtown Minneapolis are just one manifestation of where such issues can lead a community. However, Holland chose a more creative alternative for its downtown. Rather than diluting the many merits of a genuine outdoor urban shopping district,

Holland elected in 1988 to take a different path as part of a comprehensive streetscape upgrade for a five-block area. Thinking outside of the proverbial box, the city installed a network of underground pipes that emit radiant heat to keep the streets free of snow and ice during the winter months. It has since expanded this heating network beyond the five-block area. This welcome enhancement has given Holland's residents one less reason to avoid their beloved downtown during inclement weather, while heating up the competition with suburban retail adversaries (Broberg 2005, 4). The experience of Holland is proof that even the most mundane downtown issue, when treated with thoughtfulness and creativity, can be transformed into an opportunity to provide yet another competitive edge for the downtown.

Fort Collins's Battle to Beautify

Fort Collins, Colorado, is a poster child for burying overhead lines, and its story of perseverance should provide inspiration to other communities. For years, community leaders had recognized the visual blight that overhead lines were causing for their picturesque college town nestled in the Rockies. Finally, in the early 1990s the city began gaining momentum with a comprehensive program to bury its overhead lines and utility boxes. Approximately 15 years later, it had reached their goal of relocating all electrical lines and utility boxes underground.

The town's decade-and-a-half journey to success was initiated with conservative baby steps. It started with lines that were in need of replacement anyway, and it also targeted areas in which street construction and sidewalk development were already occurring. In an attempt to further these efforts, Fort Collins's electric utility patented its own underground utility box, and it began sharing the costs of installing trenches with local cable and telephone companies.

Since the program was first initiated, the results have been dramatic. In addition to the community's improved aesthetics, the town has been able to severely reduce its tree-trimming budget, and storm-related power outages are a virtual nonoccurrence. In fact, the system's 99.997 percent reliability rate has now allowed the community to attract specific businesses that require such reliability. Although Fort Collins's program to bury overhead wiring and utility boxes was a citywide measure, numerous communities across the country could follow Fort Collins's lead and initiate their own such programs, perhaps starting with a pilot project in their downtowns.

Gas and Electricity

Although gas and electricity are the two prevalent forms of energy found in downtowns, their infrastructures have to be considered differently. Because gas is always piped underground and can be readily extended where needed, it is rarely an important issue for downtown plans. As with gas, availability and capacity are rarely an issue for electricity. However, when the existing lines are located overhead on utility poles, the negative appearance becomes a major issue, given the focus of most downtown plans on improving aesthetics. Computerized visual simulations were discussed previously as an effective means of communicating the potential of streetscape enhancements to the public. One of the most dramatic before-and-after comparisons that simulations can illustrate is the difference between having electrical lines overhead versus burying them. Although it can be costly and require considerable negotiations with the local electric company, burying overhead wires should be seriously considered by every downtown plan for which the issue exists. Another alternative, usually more cost-effective, is the relocation of overhead lines to alleys, if the downtown is blessed with an extensive alley system.

Telecommunications

Telecommunications, including telephone lines, cable, fiber optics, and wireless Internet service, will increasingly become a major issue for downtowns, particularly given the Internet's impact on both the business world and life in general. In order to be competitive with other office markets in a community, downtowns need to be equipped with state-of-the-art telecommunications infrastructure. Many downtowns are investing in wireless Internet capability, the most cutting-edge aspect of widely available telecommunications at the moment. The top telecommunications priority for a downtown plan should be to make sure that all forms of telecommunications are available to all parts of the downtown where they might be needed. The second priority relates to the same issue as overhead electrical lines: aesthetics. The downtown plan should offer suggestions for getting telecommunications off of the downtown's above-grade streetscapes and away from the public's eye.

Utility Tunnels and Appurtenances

One alternative for addressing the overhead wiring issues posed by electrical lines and telecommunications is the installation of utility tunnels. Whether they are prefabricated or created in the field, they consist of concrete conduits buried within the public right-of-way to accommodate all types of electrical lines, including telecommunications. Some of the prefabricated utility tunnels are designed to be integrated into the sidewalk system of a streetscape so that the concrete lids for accessing the utilities also function as the sidewalk surface.

An aspect of utilities usually overlooked during the planning process is "utility appurtenances," which are the various utilitarian devices required at the point where the utility line and the end user meet. Examples of such devices include gas meters, fire department connections (FDCs), traffic signal controllers, communications pedestals, electrical transformers, and electrical outlets. Some appurtenances, such as gas meters and FDCs, occur along building walls, so the key is to locate them along the least visible walls (e.g., along alleys, if available). Other appurtenances, such as traffic signal controllers and electrical transformers, are typically located within the streetscape area, so they need to be housed in a relatively attractive structure. Although they will need to be accessible for ongoing maintenance and sometimes well ventilated, screening options, such as fencing and landscaping, should be pursued to soften their appearance.

HARNESSING MOTHER NATURE

The topic of natural environmental features and their role in downtown planning is an irrelevant issue for many downtowns, but those playing host to waterfronts, streams, or diverse topography can find the issue a central focus of the plan. In fact, many of the hundreds of waterfront plans commissioned over the years are essentially downtown plans for the waterfront. Most downtown plans address natural features, whether as the central focus or as a secondary issue, and attempt to leverage those features.

Downtown Waterfronts

Once viewed as critical resources for transportation, water bodies and their waterfronts had been ignored by many downtowns across the country by the mid-twentieth century. This regrettable circumstance was especially prevalent among inland riverfronts (as opposed to coastal ones). Despite being the very reason that the community was established in the first place, many downtown waterfronts had become neglected sewage systems to be avoided by respectable people. Thankfully, that trend began reversing in recent decades through the extraordinary efforts of local governments, business leaders, and other downtown advocates, not to mention environmentalists. Many well-known examples of major cities that transformed segments of their waterfronts, or underutilized water resources, exist (e.g., Baltimore; San Antonio, Texas; Savannah, Georgia; and Providence, Rhode Island).

But ambitious downtown waterfront projects are certainly not limited to America's largest cities. Frederick, Maryland, transformed Carroll Creek from a major liability into a beloved asset. After a 1976 flood that inundated 100 acres of downtown Frederick and caused nearly $25 million in damages, the city implemented the $65 million

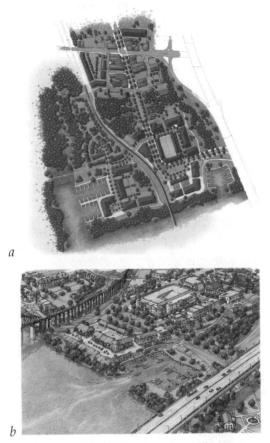

a

b

Figures 3-30a–b. This plan for the downtown riverfront in Northport, Alabama, exhibits all of the features of waterfront planning best practices, including the protection of environmentally sensitive lands and the provision of public access to the waterfront, formal public spaces, proactive recreational uses, and adjacent mixed use development capitalizing on waterfront views. On-street and structured parking avoid the need for surface lots that might create barriers to waterfront access. Source: The Walker Collaborative / Third Coast Development Studio (top); The Walker Collaborative / Urban Archism (bottom)

Carroll Creek Flood Control and Linear Park Project. By redirecting much of the stream's water to underground conduits while maintaining an above-grade meandering creek, downtown was removed from the FEMA-designated floodplain, eliminating the high flood insurance premiums for property owners and buttressing investor confidence. In 2006, an amphitheater, various water features, landscaping, and associated improvements were constructed along the creek. While a project of this scale is atypical, there are numerous other downtowns across the country that have focused their planning efforts on bayfronts, riverfronts, and creeks, ranging from formal esplanades to naturalistic meandering greenways. Case studies of such projects, as well as principles for ecologically sound waterfront development, can be found in Otto, McCormick, and Leccese (2004).

Every urban waterfront offers its own set of challenges, but the following planning principles have been applied to many successful downtown waterfronts:

- Permanent public access to and along the waterfront
- Development of a formal esplanade, an informal boardwalk, or similar improvements along the waterfront's edge
- Provision of docks and other nautical and recreational elements to the extent feasible
- Extension of the adjacent street system into the waterfront area
- Physical and economic linkages between the waterfront and the balance of the downtown
- Mixed use development maximizing views to the water
- Location and design of parking so as to avoid becoming a barrier to waterfront access
- Protection of water-dependent land uses, such as commercial fishing operations, to avoid their displacement
- Environmentally sensitive treatment of the aquatic and estuary resources

One key question associated with downtown waterfront development is, Who will be responsible for funding the publicly accessible waterfront improvements? In most cases, the local government will elect to fund the development of a waterfront esplanade, boardwalk, greenway, or similar linear improvements along the water's edge, even if it traverses private property. However, in areas where the real estate market is especially strong and the anticipated profit margins associated with private waterfront development are expected to be particularly high, such improvements are sometimes required of the developer as part of their project permitting. Casino developments, in particular, are often required to fully fund such improvements, even though they will be accessible to the general public rather than merely casino patrons. Other issues unique to waterfront planning beyond the course of a typical downtown plan include dealing with variable water levels, dredging for navigable waters, marina development permitting, and Army Corps of Engineers approvals, to name just a few. While waterfront planning can be a complex science often requiring more detailed and strategic thinking than usual downtown planning does, the benefits a waterfront or water resource can leverage to the broader downtown are unquestionably worth the extra effort.

Overcoming Topography

Dramatic topography can be leveraged for scenic views and the cost-effective construction of parking decks, but more often than not it is a challenge to be overcome. When the village of Ossining, New York, embarked on a downtown riverfront plan in 1994, it recognized from the outset that a key objective was to overcome the physical and

Figure 3-31. Although it was not implemented until several years after the adoption of the 1993 downtown riverfront plan, the construction of a stairway system in Troy, New York, connecting Rensselaer Polytechnic Institute with the downtown below it was a strategy intended to better link the two areas. With the most costly work completed, adjacent landscaping and maintenance would now make this connection more inviting. Source: The Walker Collaborative

psychological barrier that steep topography and a rail line created between its Hudson River frontage and the balance of downtown Ossining. Consequently, the plan proposed the creation of a greenway and infill development as two strategies to create a stronger linkage between the riverfront and the downtown core.

Similarly, when Troy, New York, prepared its downtown riverfront plan in 1993, one of the plan's objectives was to attract more students and employees from Rensselaer Polytechnic Institute (RPI). Crowning a steep hill looming over downtown Troy, the RPI campus represented an important target market to economically support the study area, but the topographic barrier between the two limited RPI's potential economic benefits, as there was no street to directly connect downtown and the university. Consequently, in addition to more aggressive marketing of the area to the RPI community, the plan proposed a stairway system to better connect the campus with downtown Troy. Although the stairway was not constructed until several years after the plan's adoption, it has since served as one more piece of the puzzle in strengthening the relationship—physically, economically and symbolically—between RPI and downtown Troy.

SUMMARY

In summary, the physical planning component of the downtown master plan must balance a broad range of issues, including historic preservation, infill development, public spaces, streetscapes, transportation, parking, utilities, and related concerns. Even the best downtown marketing strategy, as discussed in the following chapter, will have trouble overcoming a physical context lacking a "good bone structure." At the same time, however, many downtown plans of the past made an enormous blunder in addressing only the physical dimensions of the downtown. Physical planning concepts tend to be relatively straightforward, they are easily conveyed to the public, and they are highly visible. Regardless, they alone can rarely result in a downtown that enjoys sustainable success over time. Issues such as economics, marketing, and public policy must also be addressed and integrated into the physical plans because downtowns are complex and the issues that need to be addressed to ensure a downtown's success are broad and intertwined.

4

The Economic and Marketing Plan

For every complex problem, there is a solution that is simple, neat, and wrong.

—H. L. Mencken

Although the physical facets of downtown plans tend to receive the greatest attention and interest because they are so tangible and easily conveyed through graphics, the economic and market issues are equally important for most downtowns and more important for many. Economic and market issues are also strongly intertwined with physical planning issues, so they must all be thought of in unison. Countless downtown organizations have learned the hard way that a singular focus on physical enhancements is not the solution for long-term success. As Robin Taffler, the former Main Street manager for Murray, Kentucky, puts it: "It's not just about pretty; it's about a fundamental change in thinking. People get really hung up on the streetscape end of things and seem to forget or ignore the importance of the rest. . . . I wish in Murray's plan that we literally put 'Streetscape' at the back of the document and the other issues up front to reinforce their absolute importance."

While having an attractive and well-designed downtown is certainly an advantage, it is rarely the sole motivation for those drawn to it. There are numerous examples across the country of vibrant and prosperous downtowns featuring dull and worn concrete sidewalks and sparse streetscape furnishings. Two of the most important ingredients

The Lesson of Shreveport

Downtown Shreveport, Louisiana, stands as a testament to the notion that design alone will not achieve successful downtown revitalization. In the early 1990s, state legislation paved the way for riverboat gambling in Shreveport. Like other cities in the state that had the option to approve gambling, Shreveport negotiated a deal with the casino interests that resulted in substantial tax revenues. Much of those revenues were invested in infrastructure to accommodate the increased demands and opportunities that gambling patrons would bring. To

the city's credit, it first invested in downtown by commissioning a riverfront master plan, followed by the installation of high-quality streetscapes for several of the key streets. However, as the passage of time revealed, those measures did little to reinvigorate the downtown. Years later the beautiful streetscapes were still lined with countless vacant buildings featuring empty storefronts plastered with "For Lease" signs. According to Shreveport's Downtown Development Authority, the downtown still had 458,166 square feet of vacant office space alone in early 2005.

Shreveport is just one grain of sand in a mountain of evidence that successful downtown revitalization and ongoing management require a multifaceted approach. Design solutions alone will generally not succeed. Few people, if any, have ever visited a downtown just to walk down nicely paved and furnished streetscapes. Much deeper economic and market-based underpinnings must be addressed to make a downtown successful and to sustain that success. While new streetscapes are sometimes

Figure 4-1. Funded by tax proceeds from casino gambling during the early 1990s, new brick sidewalks and Victorian-style streetlights did little to improve the economic condition of downtown Shreveport. The city has since taken a more comprehensive approach to revitalization, including adopting a new plan in 2002 and extending the life of its downtown development authority. Source: The Walker Collaborative

advisable, they are only one piece of a complex puzzle.

More and more, communities are learning this important lesson, including Shreveport itself. In 2002, the city adopted its "Downtown 2010 Redevelopment Strategy," offering a comprehensive approach to downtown revitalization. In addition to addressing the typical physical planning issues, it also addresses organization, maintenance, marketing, and social issues. The same year that the new plan was adopted, Shreveport voters extended the life of the Downtown Development Authority from five to 25 years, another indication that Shreveport has made a new commitment to a balanced approach to urban revitalization. Other communities should follow its example and learn from the lesson of Shreveport.

---

in a downtown's success are a density of people and diversity of uses. In tandem, those two characteristics can result in dynamic places that will sustain themselves over time. Rather than competing in beauty contests, the biggest challenge for most downtowns is developing a rich diversity of destinations that will attract a critical mass of people to live, work, shop, and play. That challenge is the central focus of the following pages.

UNDERSTANDING THE MARKET

Defined most broadly, "the market" for a downtown is the realm of individuals who will experience, or have the likelihood to experience, some aspect of the downtown. The housing market, for example, includes those who might live downtown, the office market includes those that might work downtown, and the tourist and entertainment markets include those who might play downtown. The retail market consists of those who might purchase goods and services downtown. Sometimes, the term is used even more broadly to include the system in which the market functions, including places, pricing, competition, and related elements.

Market analysis, as described in Chapter 2, is the process of gathering and assessing market-related data, in addition to considering qualitative factors, to make projections for future market demands. Within the context of downtown planning, market analysis should be employed to answer each of journalism's proverbial five "Ws"—who, where, what, when, and why. Whom does the market comprise and what are their characteristics? Where does downtown fit into a community's broad market context? What type of goods, services, attractions, office space, or housing is the market seeking? When will sufficient market strength be available for specific uses? Why is the market not currently attracted to the downtown, if such is the case? To perform successful downtown planning, these questions should be known in advance through market analysis. Such analysis should consider the market "potentials" in terms of: (1) the existing pool of individuals using the downtown; (2) the potential users if a greater market share of the current pool could be captured by the downtown as it currently exists; and (3) additional potential users if certain improvements or marketing strategies were enacted.

Once a consultant has prepared a market analysis for a municipality or a downtown entity, it should be made available to the local business community, as it can be useful to the decision-making process of downtown retailers, developers, and other economic stakeholders. Of course, coaxing private-sector stakeholders to review the study may require some effort, including formatting and packaging it in an attractive manner. As Lee Harkness, the executive director of the Downtown Jamestown Development Corporation in New York, said about the 48-page color booklet it produced in 2005, "We wanted the results of the market analysis to be interesting and accessible so that people would actually read it." Unless a market analysis is promoted among a wide spectrum of the downtown's economic stakeholders, its full value cannot be realized.

Who Is the Market?

Understanding the most rudimentary facts about the potential downtown market is relatively simple for most communities. In addition to the U.S. Census Bureau, there are numerous organizations that regularly gather and update socioeconomic data on a communitywide and regional basis. This information is often broken down into smaller geographic areas, as well as by demographic characteristics, such as age, sex, race, income level, and education level. Because this data is usually tracked in accordance with standard time increments, such as annually or every 10 years, past trends can be identified, and, when combined with other market data and analysis, future trends can be projected. Although understanding the existing communitywide and regional market can be a relatively straightforward process, figuring out specifically downtown's current and potential market requires more work. While each community and downtown will differ, and there are numerous other smaller and more specific market segments, below are the five most common individual segments that a downtown market for retail and housing comprises.

Downtown employees. For downtowns that lack many residents and roll up the sidewalks by 5:00 or 6:00 p.m. each day, this can be the most significant retail market segment. If the majority of the downtown's restaurants keep only breakfast and lunch hours, employees are likely the current market focus. However, they should also be targeted for downtown housing in order to benefit all facets of the downtown, including retail. While often thought of as white-collar professionals, downtown workers who might be attracted to living in or near downtown can include a broad range of people, including store clerks, government workers, bank tellers, teachers, police officers, janitors, artists, and waiters, to name just a few. Developing affordable housing should, therefore, be part of the downtown plan .

Downtown residents. This market segment usually applies not only to people living in the downtown but also to residents of neighborhoods directly adjacent to the downtown. Regrettably, for many small and midsize city downtowns, few residents actually live there. If there are downtown residents, however, the goal is to retain them and attract new ones. And marketing downtown housing can go beyond the usual suspects (young people, retirees, etc.) to include those, as noted above, who work downtown and would like to cut their commutes or who are otherwise drawn to living downtown because of its amenities. According to Donovan Rypkema (2005), downtown residents typically spend three to four times as much money downtown as do downtown employees. And Randall Gross of Randall Gross/ Development Economics in Washington, D.C., reports that downtown residents, on an annual basis, spend more on downtown retail than do their downtown "destination shopper" counterparts, making them clearly a prized retail market segment.

Tourists. While not directly relevant to the downtown housing market, the benefits offered by tourists to the retail market are dependent upon the downtown's wealth of, or proximity to, tourist attractions, as well as the drawing power of those attractions. For example, a downtown that serves as the gateway to a ski resort area has much greater tourist potential than a downtown located far from any attractions, although downtowns that benefit from regional marketing efforts, such as in organized heritage tourism areas, can enjoy the advantages of tourism. Despite the many economic merits of tourism, the optimism of communities whose visions are clouded by unrealistic expectations for the drawing power of their local treasures should always be kept in check during the downtown planning process. Also, as a general rule, downtowns that can successfully attract their local market will also attract tourists, but downtowns that focus primarily on tourists are often limited primarily to tourists.

Students. This market segment depends upon the presence of a downtown or nearby college, university, high school, or training facility. With respect to dining and entertainment, students are often looking for interesting and hip places to hang out, and many prefer a unique urban environment to the atmosphere of the suburbs. College students, in particular, are easy to target for advertising via school newspapers and radio stations, and their student identification cards lend themselves to targeted discounts and specials. Not only are college students an important retail market segment for some downtowns, but they are a significant housing market as well. Even for downtowns with moderate- to high-price housing, students—particularly graduate students—can often pool their resources and share downtown apartments or condominiums. While they are not technically part of the student market, collegiate faculty and administrative staff can also be an important part of the downtown housing market.

The broader community. Given its size, this market segment often brings the greatest payoff but can be the toughest to attract. Downtown employees and residents are already a captive market, tourists have disposable time and money that makes them strong candidates for downtown shopping and dining, and students are easy to target through direct marketing vehicles. The broader community can be more difficult to attract, but the sheer numbers can reap huge benefits if successfully achieved. The potential pool of destination shoppers and diners within any given community can be tremendous, so capturing even a small percentage can benefit the downtown substantially. The same principle applies to the housing market, and, as noted above, the potential residential market should be viewed in broad terms with respect to various demographic segments.

Unlike the retail and housing market segments summarized above, the market for offices and other downtown uses is defined in completely different terms with different segments. The office market, for example, is defined by business type and office size needs. While every downtown is different, common office tenants include finance, insurance, and real estate (FIRE) offices, attorneys needing proximity to the courts, governmental workers, corporate offices seeking a particular image reinforced by a downtown location, and creative businesses wanting an interesting workspace and overall environment. With respect to space needs, many downtowns have attracted small businesses because they offer a full range of office sizes within existing buildings, as well as the occasional small business incubator allowing businesses to share resources and receive various forms of support. The National Business Incubation Association (NBIA) is a good source of information on establishing small business incubators, including their publications *A Comprehensive Guide to Business Incubation* (Hayhow 1995) and *Bricks and Mortar: How to Find and Design the Best Business Incubator Facilities* (NBIA 1992).

In addition to the most basic demographic segments, others that are often overlooked should not be, on account of their sheer retail market strength or their inclination to frequent downtowns for shopping and services. According to Jerry Hernandez, the former director of Main Street Watsonville, California, "Most Mexican- and other Latin Americans have a strong tradition of shopping downtown rather than in malls." Because Watsonville has experienced a dramatic demographic shift resulting in a large Mexican-American population, Main Street Watsonville adopted a regional Latino market strategy for its downtown.

Teenagers are another retail market segment attracted to urban environments. In recent decades, teenagers have proved to have surprisingly strong purchasing power, and annual surveys reveal that many teens are now opting for hip urban areas over suburban shopping malls. Even children with little spending power today cannot be completely overlooked. The Ardmore, Oklahoma, downtown program goes to great lengths to host children's activities. Not only do children's events attract parents with disposable income, but, as Bill Hightower of the Ardmore Main Street Authority has stated, "children are the shoppers of tomorrow. We want to get them in the habit of going downtown instead of the mall."

What Will the Market Support?

Asking, What will the market support? may seem similar to asking, What does the market want? but, in fact, they are quite different questions. Although 100 people in a consumer survey may tell you that they would like to see a bakery in their downtown, what they say and what they do may not be one and the same. Even if those 100 people can be

The Rise of the Creative Class

In 2002, *The Rise of the Creative Class* was published. Written by Carnegie Mellon University economics professor Richard Florida, its thesis is that cities making a concerted effort to create an environment that is hip, diverse, and interesting will attract the kinds of bright and talented young people that will add tremendous strength to the local economy. Instead of recruiting businesses in hopes that they will hire the community's existing residents, this approach focuses on attracting the workforce that will, in turn, attract businesses that want to hire them. A related paper coauthored by Florida and Gary Gates of the Urban Institute in 2001 concluded that cities with the most high-paying high-tech jobs also had disproportionately high populations of bohemians, immigrants, gays, and lesbians.

Many state and local governments are starting to catch on. Michigan governor Jennifer Granholm encouraged the mayors of 200 communities to establish "Cool Commissions" to retain and attract young and diverse people to the state. The nonprofit Live Baltimore Home Center, partly funded by the city, has targeted young professionals to move downtown and revitalize neighborhoods. Among other things, the city advertised in a gay newspaper in nearby Washington to attract young, professional "urban pioneers." In 2001, the group Mpact Memphis was established to brand Memphis in a light that will attract bright young people to bolster the economy. The group of 500 members is dominated by those in their 20s and 30s wanting to attract more people like them.

While Florida has his detractors, if his thesis is indeed correct and these various efforts across the country are not misguided, it bodes well for downtowns. While there are numerous stories of industries that located in a particular community because, in part, they were impressed by the revitalized downtown, this economic development strategy takes an entirely different

Figure 4-2. The nonprofit Live Baltimore Home Center has targeted young professionals to move downtown and revitalize Baltimore's urban neighborhoods, such as the Mount Vernon district. Bucking convention, they have advertised in a gay newspaper in Washington to attract young, professional "urban pioneers." Source: Shanan Peterson Wasielewski

tack. It is based upon first attracting the talented workforce that
will then attract the employers. For
cash-strapped communities wres-
tling with difficult choices between

spending limited funds on industrial recruitment or downtown
revitalization, Florida's work sheds
light on how the two issues may
not be so separate.

---

depended upon to follow through and walk the walk once a bakery opens
downtown, such a survey still tells you only what 100 people will do and
no more. Are 100 loyal customers enough to financially support the new
bakery? Probably not, unless they are buying $20 doughnuts and $30
sticky buns. The only reliable method to determine what the market
wants from its downtown—and will actually support—is to conduct
market analysis, and the results will differ among downtowns.

Although geographic regions and individual downtowns will vary,
experience across the country has resulted in clear trends regarding what the market wants for its downtowns and the types of businesses that most often succeed. While there is clearly no single list of
businesses that will work in every downtown, below are some of the
most common businesses with a proven track record in many small to
moderate-size downtowns.

Dining and Entertainment

- Fine "tablecloth" dining
- Family-style dining
- Ethnic restaurants
- Sports bars
- Wine bars
- Coffeehouses
- Microbreweries
- Dance clubs and music clubs
- Movie theaters (especially
  those that show artistic and
  foreign films)
- Live music

Retail and Services

- Men's and women's
  clothing
- Shoestores
- Bookstores

- Bakeries
- Gift shops and specialty stores
- Antiques stores
- Small grocery stores and markets
- Photocopying
- Laundries and dry cleaners
- Day-care centers
- Hotels
- Fitness centers
- DVD and video-rental stores
- Pharmacies
- Discount stores

Cultural and Recreational Facilities

- Amphitheaters
- Performance halls
- Museums
- Skateboarding parks
- Community centers

While business and tenant recruitment strategies often emphasize dining, entertainment, retail, services, and cultural facilities, other uses inherently beneficial to downtowns cannot be overlooked. Such uses include most institutional uses—city halls, county courthouses, post offices, libraries, and houses of worship, as well as venues for sporting events and concerts. Office uses are also a critical component of the downtown tenant mix, as are residences. While every community is different, many can support a variety of downtown housing types, including apartments, condominiums, and cooperatives, at a variety of price points.

People want a downtown that is clean and safe and that offers extended shopping hours with affordable and convenient parking. Furthermore, as the fast-growing industry of heritage tourism is proving all across the country, a robust market exists for places and objects unique to their locale. These very elements can be reinforced in downtowns in many ways, including physical design, tenant mix, services, product lines, and forms of entertainment.

IDENTITY DEVELOPMENT

Once the market for a downtown is fully understood through market analysis, work can begin on developing an identity. Too often, the image of a particular downtown has accumulated over many years and if it is negative will require effort to be reversed. As noted in Leinberger:

> There are many skeptics that will never see the point of bringing back an obsolete, forsaken downtown and give it little if no chance of succeeding. If there is one bromide heard by most people with experience working on downtown revitalization efforts, it is a suburban resident saying something to the effect of, "I haven't been downtown in 20 years and have no reason or desire to go there ever in the future." (2005, 4)

Like any product to be marketed, a specific identity should be developed for the downtown. Unless a distinct image is created, it is difficult to market the downtown as a product distinguished from other competing commercial centers and corridors in the trade area. With respect to larger downtowns, there may be multiple districts, each marketed with a distinct identity. The specific image deemed appropriate will depend upon the downtown's intrinsic qualities, as well as the targeted market segments for the downtown as determined by market analyses. However, the following image labels are often popular when trying to get decision makers to focus in on a distinct

How Many Surveys Are Enough?

Given the limited budgets of so many sponsors of downtown plans, surveys are understandably often viewed as a luxury. With the exception of website-based surveys for which the costs are relatively fixed regardless of the number of respondents, there is usually a direct relationship between the number of respondents surveyed and costs. Therefore, a natural tendency exists to want the fewest number of respondents while yielding optimal results.

So what is the magic minimum number of respondents necessary to make a survey statistically valid? According to Joshua Bloom, who authored an article, "Surveys," that appeared in the National Main Street Center's *Main Street News*, the correct answer is 400. James McQuivey, assistant professor at Boston University's College of Communications, suggests the analogy of a pile of sand. "You've got a big bucket—even a dump truck—filled with sand and you have a funnel. You're going to hold the funnel over the floor and pour some sand through the funnel. How much sand do you need to pour before you know with certainty the shape the sand will take on the floor? If you pour more sand, will the shape change? No. Statistics—and, by extension, surveys—allow you to pour a little bit of sand and draw reliable conclusions about what the pile would look like if you were to pour even more sand or survey an impractical number of people" (Bloom 2005). Thus, instead of a specific percentage of the surveyed population being the key for validity, perhaps it is more important to approach the threshold number of 400 respondents, regardless of whether the population being studied is one thousand or one million.

---

identity for marketing purposes: Small-Town USA, Historic District, Chic Shopping and Dining District, Hip Entertainment District, Arts District, and Bohemian District. (These are images to emulate, not names for the downtown.) Of course, each of these images may be interpreted differently by consumers. It may be a good idea to find images of existing downtowns or neighborhoods whose character clearly reflects the idea behind the image label.

While it is useful to consider a broad range of distinct identities as possibilities for a downtown, the image ultimately selected as the one to project usually includes elements of more than one image because most downtowns do not fit neatly within any one category. On the other hand, attempting to combine too many identities may confuse the public and result in a case of downtown schizophrenia or worse, absolutely no discernible identity. It should also be understood that crafting a single identity does not have to conflict with offering a variety of destinations and activities for a variety of market segments.

Regardless of the specific identity that a downtown might strive for, extreme caution should be used when employing the notion of identity development. As noted, there is strong market appeal to authenticity, and that is the one quality that generic and contrived suburban commercial centers cannot fabricate. Rather than attempting to shoehorn a downtown into some "off-the-shelf" image, it is generally advisable to identify and accentuate the intrinsic qualities of the downtown. Consequently, the term "identity development" is more applicable to downtown planning than is "image development" or "branding."

Figure 4-3. The marketing strategy for Skagway, Alaska, is clearly one of using the historic district downtown to capitalize on heritage tourism. Playing off of its colorful past as a mining town, Skagway's attributes include saloons, tourist-oriented shops, Victorian architecture with complementary signage, wooden boardwalks, and a National Park Service interpretive center that functions as a springboard for downtown walking tours. Source: The Walker Collaborative

CENTRALIZED RETAIL MANAGEMENT

Centralized Retail Management (CRM) is a technique used by thousands of shopping malls across the country in which the retailers are organized to function as a single unit. CRM includes coordinated days and hours of operation, common area maintenance, a tenant location strategy, merchandising, and customer service standards. Some of the other strategies often identified with CRM, such as joint advertising, are addressed below.

In a shopping mall, CRM is simple to execute because there is a single owner, and all tenants leasing space must follow the requirements of that owner as part of their lease agreement. In a downtown of multiple property owners and business operators, a high degree of organization and commitment is necessary in order for CRM to succeed. While plenty of prosperous downtowns do not employ CRM programs, those struggling often find CRM provides them with one more angle for competing with other areas.

Days and Hours of Operation

One competitive advantage enjoyed by suburban shopping malls is that the various tenants of the mall must comply with consistent days and hours of operation, and the community's shoppers are aware of those days and hours of operation. Downtown retailers need to use the same strategy. A challenge for many downtowns, especially smaller ones, is motivating retailers to maintain extended days and hours of operation beyond merely weekdays and 6:00 p.m. closing hours. Even in a downtown as large as that of Fort Wayne, Indiana, which serves a community of 250,000, the vast majority of its shops and restaurants are closed on weekends. Business operators explain that the low volume of business cannot justify enduring the costs of staying open on weekends and evenings. They are correct because as long as the market believes that downtown is closed on evenings and weekends, few people will venture downtown for shopping.

Instead, retailers must band together and agree on the specific days and hours of extended operations. A potential starting point is for all businesses to remain open every Friday and Saturday evening, as well as on weekdays until at least 7:00 p.m. to give shoppers a window of opportunity to make purchases after work. Many downtowns begin by targeting a regularly scheduled special event to extend business hours. In downtown Frederick, Maryland, the art district's First Saturday events prompt nearly three quarters of their retail and dining businesses to stay open at night. According to Kara Norman, the executive director of the Downtown Frederick Partnership, "Many businesses report that receipts rival, and sometimes exceed, their best holiday sales totals. It has been instrumental in convincing more than 25 storeowners to stay open until 9 p.m. every Friday night as well."

Some retailers will choose not to operate on certain days, such as Saturday or Sunday, for religious reasons, and that decision must be respected. Moreover, many businesses for which religion is not an issue would also like to close at least one day per week. In such cases, Monday is the day most frequently selected. This alternative is particularly popular in tourist-oriented communities where weekends are too lucrative to give up. With respect to weekday evenings, some downtowns select one or two days per week or month to keep shops open, and they make sure to get the word out through advertising. The growing pains can be difficult, and it may take up to six months of extended days and hours before the market catches on, but the long-term rewards for the downtown are often worth it.

Common Area Maintenance

As with many CRM concepts, Common Area Maintenance programs (CAMs) have their origins in suburban shopping malls. As part of their contract to lease space, mall tenants pay CAM fees so that the common areas are physically maintained and regularly cleaned. In shopping malls, common areas include all building space accessible to the public that is not part of a specific tenant space, such as atriums, food courts, and restrooms. Downtown's equivalent to a shopping mall's common area is the public right-of-way, including streetscapes, parks, and plazas. Technically, these areas are maintained by the local government. However, in many communities the level of maintenance provided by the local government is inadequate to compete with the level of maintenance seen in suburban shopping malls. Therefore, one of the greatest opportunities for individual downtown businesses to join forces in a constructive manner is to establish a CAM program. A downtown CAM program requires a management entity, a work program, and a stable funding source.

Management for a CAM program is typically provided by a downtown organization, although another option is to contract with the local government to provide a higher level of service than would normally be provided. Whoever provides the management needs personnel located in the downtown area to closely oversee the work of the

Figure 4-4. Common Area Maintenance (CAM) programs should include daily routines, such as picking up trash, sweeping, and emptying garbage cans, combined with less frequent but necessary chores, like pressure-cleaning paved surfaces. Source: The Walker Collaborative

maintenance employees. CAM program employees should be highly visible and identifiable both as a sign of progress for downtown and to make the employees more accountable, as they are being informally monitored by all downtown stakeholders. Many downtown organizations issue colorful jumpsuits containing the downtown logo to achieve high visibility.

The work program for CAM employees should be very specific and scheduled by days and times. In particular, landscape maintenance needs a seasonal schedule, especially when watering, weeding, and trimming are concerned. An example of a daily routine would be to pick up and sweep any noticeable trash within common areas, while chores that might be done every few days or weeks include scrubbing benches and paved surfaces. Repairs to streetscape elements will also be required as needed. Seasonal chores would include the installation of new streetlight banners for various holiday seasons, as well as the installation of Christmas decorations at the beginning of the holiday shopping season.

The greatest challenge for any downtown CAM program is securing an ongoing funding source, which is why downtowns should first
pressure their local government to provide better service before going it
alone. This issue is clearly the first to be resolved by the downtown plan
before the program can proceed. Most downtowns fund and organize
their CAM programs through Business Improvement Districts (BIDs),
which are known by other names in some states, including "special
improvement districts" and "special taxing districts." BIDs are most
commonly funded through an ad valorem property tax applied to all
properties within the designated BID district. The parameters for establishing a BID differ from state to state, depending upon state enabling
legislation. They are typically adopted by the local government's governing body following a referendum of the affected property owners.
Thousands of BIDs currently exist across the country. (See Chapter
5.) Another funding option is a periodic assessment based upon the
property frontage measurement, parcel size, or building floor area of
each property. CAM fees are typically assessed to property owners but
often passed on to tenants as part of their lease structure. Shoup (2005)
has suggested that a city could dedicate some or all of the parking revenue from a downtown district to support a CAM program or other
BID-authorized program. However, the negative aspects of charging
money for downtown parking must also be recognized. Downtowns
that have figured out a way to charge little or no money for parking
have found that they can compete, at least on that particular issue,
with their suburban counterparts that always feature free parking.

Before a CAM program is initiated, the downtown stakeholders
should first attempt to get a higher level of service from the local government so that the costs of running a CAM program can be avoided.
However, if such efforts are unsuccessful and a CAM program is
clearly needed, the city's current level of service should be carefully
documented. Many local governments tend to decrease their level
of service once a downtown CAM program is initiated because they
believe that the downtown stakeholders are now "taking care of things
on their own." Despite this common misconception, the local government should be held firmly to its original level of service, and it should
be emphasized that the downtown CAM program is intended to supplement, and not replace, the local government's basic services.

Tenant Location Strategy

The science of locating tenants is yet another CRM technique borrowed from shopping malls. In fact, however, the concept of clustering complementary businesses dates back thousands of years and can still be found in the market areas of numerous cities around the world. The location of tenants is easily controlled by malls through their design of certain spaces for particular locations, as well as their leasing practices, which match specific tenants to specific spaces. The typical mall approach is to disperse large department stores as the anchors, with small specialty retail stores serving as connections between the anchors. Food courts are often centrally located in the overall mall layout.

Achieving a coordinated tenant location strategy in a downtown is much more challenging given the fragmented property ownership patterns and the lack of a single controlling management entity with the legal authority to mandate business locations. However, as part of their CRM strategy, downtown organizations, working with property owners and leasing agents, can devise an overall strategy and make some effort to implement it through leasing practices. Because of the complexities involved, those downtowns that do attempt a strategy tend to keep it simple. In fact, the geographic clustering of mutually supporting uses is typically the only objective sought. Examples of uses that are frequently clustered include: (1) restaurants; (2) bookstores and coffeehouses; and (3) women's apparel.

In general, clustering downtown tenants into minidistricts is most applicable to larger downtowns having a critical mass of various types of mutually supporting tenants. It also requires a great amount of teamwork among downtown property owners and leasing agents, which can be seriously tested when being a team player means forgoing a sorely needed tenant. Because its success is so dependent upon strong ongoing management rather than being a more tangible one-time project, most downtown plans do not even attempt to address tenant location strategies, although more probably should.

Merchandising and Customer Service Standards

Merchandising is the activity of promoting merchandise to potential buyers, including the selection of specific product lines to sell. While most downtown master plans do not go into such detail to address this important retail issue, downtown retail strategies do. Merchandising is one of many areas in which conducting a thorough market analysis can pay off huge dividends. For example, the casual observer might conclude that a particular downtown needs no additional women's clothing stores because four already exist and all are financially struggling. However, an analysis might conclude that there is sufficient market demand to support 10 more women's clothing stores in the downtown and that the existing stores simply need to alter their product lines or make other changes in order to be successful. It is no secret that retail businesses that eventually fail after years of relative prosperity are often victims of their operators' lack of "remerchandising" to keep pace with constantly changing market tastes and demands.

Customer service is one topic that many downtown programs have focused on with measurable success. The quality of customer service typically varies greatly from store to store, yet it is an area in which a concentrated effort can allow downtown businesses to be more competitive with their suburban counterparts. The National Main Street Center advocates the application of "opening day standards" in everyday operations, which simply means applying a keen focus on customer service as if it were the business's first day of operations. Some local Main Street programs sponsor workshops with downtown business operators and employees on how to build strong customer loyalty. Seemingly small gestures—such as knowing a customer's name,

Figure 4-5. Although plenty of retail businesses survive despite themselves, many thrive because they continually evaluate their customers' changing preferences and respond with appropriate merchandise. Source: The Walker Collaborative

keeping his or her measurements and preferences on file, and contacting him or her when a certain product becomes available—can go a long way in selling downtown as the most customer-friendly place in town to shop.

BUSINESS DEVELOPMENT

Business development consists of three types of activities: retention, expansion, and recruitment. Although many downtown plans and revitalization programs focus more on recruitment than retention and expansion, retention and expansion should be the first priorities. It does little good to recruit one new business when two existing businesses close, assuming all things being equal with respect to their value to downtown. It is generally easier to keep an existing business in operation than it is to recruit and establish a new one.

Any business development strategy should be based upon the downtown's identified optimal tenant mix. Although it is worth fighting to retain most existing downtown businesses, those consistent with the optimal tenant mix deserve the highest level of attention. The optimal tenant mix should be determined through market analysis, including the consideration of competing commercial areas and the identification of market gaps that suggest future opportunities for downtown.

Many downtowns have elected to pursue a specific market niche. For example, the Rice Lake, Wisconsin, downtown program saw a market gap in the area's home furnishing offerings and decided to make that a market niche for downtown. The downtown already had several related businesses, so the town created a Home Improvement District and recruited additional complementary businesses. Rice Lake's six-block downtown now boasts more than a dozen home furnishing businesses, including ones offering furniture, antiques, custom cabinetry, appliances, carpet and vinyl flooring, repair, custom framing, and decorating. Furthermore, several of the original shops have expanded. Sheboygan Falls, Wisconsin, has pursued a very similar niche marketing focus on home furnishings. Its downtown has three home furnishing stores. Complementary businesses have been recruited since the Main Street program began in 1988, and Main Street now sponsors an annual promotion called Home and Hearth. Around 30 businesses have sales specials as part of this promotion, and approximately six to eight downtown businesses offer seminars and in-store demonstrations. Planners of the event note that they are moving away from the focus on home improvement to feature seasonal retail promotions, but clearly it was a successful niche during its nearly 20-year run.

It is noteworthy that a singular focus on a particular market niche can be carried too far, to the long-term detriment of the downtown. High Point, North Carolina, is rightfully recognized as the furniture capital of the world. Although much of the manufacturing has gravitated to foreign soils, High Point's downtown is still dominated by countless furniture showrooms, and the semi-annual furniture markets draw thousands of industry representatives from all over the world. However, the furniture showrooms have dominated downtown's ground-floor uses so dramatically in recent years that the downtown has ceased to function as a conventional downtown. There are now very few residents, services, restaurants, or conventional retail businesses. A local resident told the city when it was conducting its background study for the downtown, "One out-of-town visitor to my downtown office recently complained, 'I had to walk 10 blocks just to find a cup of coffee in this place.'" To the city's credit, it is now engaged in a major planning effort that will, in part, focus on reestablishing a better mix of downtown uses.

Another issue occasionally addressed by downtown plans is the ratio of locally owned businesses relative to regional and national chains and franchises. To the extent that a plan might address the topic, a balance is typically recommended, but one that is more heavily weighted toward locally owned businesses. Implementation measures for achieving a particular ratio are most commonly recommended as part of an overall business recruitment strategy, including incentives for locally owned businesses. Attempts to regulate the ratio of locally owned businesses and chains in a direct manner are essentially unheard-of. However, some communities have applied indirect measures. For example, Cambridge, Massachusetts, indirectly addressed the issue for commercial districts, such as Harvard Square, by adopting design standards with requirements intended to discourage chains and franchises. Nevertheless, many chains and franchises have learned to live with the standards, as evidenced by the current tenant mix.

The most successful small to moderate-size downtowns tend to be dominated by locally owned businesses. Just as downtowns, in general, have a much stronger identity and sense of character than suburban strip centers, the businesses that fill downtown buildings should reinforce those unique qualities. However, in order to remain vibrant and competitive with other commercial areas, it may be advantageous to supplement the base of locally owned businesses with at least a limited number of regional and national chains. A downtown's ability to land regional and national tenants is more contingent upon expenditure potentials identified through a market analysis than it is upon the population of its community. For example, downtown Princeton, New Jersey, long had a Woolworth's discount store and still has a CVS pharmacy. Located on Nassau Street, Princeton's main street, both businesses provided basic goods to sizable residential, employee, and student populations. Similarly, downtown Franklin, Tennessee, has landed in recent years a Starbucks coffee shop, a Chico's women's clothing store, a Ben and Jerry's ice cream parlor, and a Mellow Mushroom pizzeria to supplement the locally owned businesses. Although Franklin's population is only 46,000, its vibrant downtown is able to draw from a much larger market of day-trippers from the Nashville metropolitan area of 1.5 million people.

Can downtowns be too successful in landing national and regional chains? Nearly half of the downtown retailers in Westfield, New Jersey, are national chains, including The Gap, Banana Republic, Trader Joe's, and Williams-Sonoma. Most of those businesses have been established since 1993, when Westfield's Main Street program began and business recruitment efforts were initiated. The downtown occupancy rate is now at 95 percent, and annual sales climbed from $60 million in 1993 to nearly $200 million in 2003 (Dono and Glisson 2004, 14). King Street in Charleston, South Carolina, the downtown's primary shopping street, has experienced similar results from an influx of national chains. So far, the downtown economies of both Westfield and Charleston are quite robust. However, the more national and regional chains a downtown gains, the less uniqueness and authenticity it is likely to retain. Economically, an excessive percentage of national and regional tenants may not be harmful to the downtown—and, in fact, it might help it to thrive. Regardless, even if the downtown benefits, the broader local economy may not be so fortunate. Most economists agree that locally owned businesses tend to have a greater positive impact on their local economies than do regional and national chains because a portion of local business revenues are recycled within the community through salaries and investment, while those dollars leave town in the cases of regional and national chains.

Moreover, national tenants are not a guarantee of success. In fact, most downtowns 50 years ago featured a Walgreen's, a Ben Franklin "five and dime," or a similar chain, yet many of those same downtowns eventually witnessed their going-out-of-business sales. Downtown Nashville's Church Street Mall was constructed in the late 1980s and packed full of national chain stores, just like a conventional suburban mall. Regrettably, the tenants were, in fact, the same ones found in Nashville's other suburban malls, rather than being unique to the community. Although the mall's primary market was downtown employees, most chose to leave downtown after work and shop at their suburban counterparts rather than navigate downtown's rush-hour traffic to get to the Church Street Mall. As a result, the mall's short life ended when it was demolished in the late 1990s. Regardless of the pros and cons of national and regional chains, for many struggling downtowns lacking the necessary expenditure potentials required to recruit such tenants, this is a nonissue.

Business Retention and Expansion

Business retention and expansion activities can be grouped together because they are achieved in much the same way, which is quite different from business recruitment. Indirectly, the best way to keep existing businesses in operation and to increase their odds of expanding is to maintain a vibrant downtown that serves as a healthy environment for businesses to thrive. Of course, creating and maintaining a strong downtown is an extremely broad and ambitious goal. More specifically, effective business retention and expansion requires ongoing communications with business owners and operators. (See Moore, Meck, and Ebenhoh 2006 for more discussion.) Although most businesses are essentially on their own to either succeed or fail, downtown organization can help by, for example, pairing an operator with an experienced adviser, helping pave the way for a business loan or directing them to the Small Business Administration's closest office. With respect to business expansions, a downtown organization can help identify available building space or at least enlist the services of real estate professionals who can help. Because older structures do not always lend themselves to the space needs of today's tenants, the identification of available sites for new development might be part of the exercise.

While it is difficult for most downtown organizations to maintain a regular and direct dialogue with every business operator, events such as monthly breakfast meetings with business representatives can help to maintain communications in an efficient manner. Another approach is a small-business-mentoring program in which stable and well-established businesses are paired with upstarts. Main Street Corning, which oversees the revitalization of downtown Corning, Iowa, has a

The Hobby Merchant

The "hobby merchant" can be found in downtowns of all sizes but particularly in small downtowns with low rent costs. This is an individual who operates his or her business more as a hobby than a genuine profit-generating business. Often the person is either independently wealthy or has a high-income spouse, and he or she maintains a downtown business just for the fun of it. While there are undoubtedly some very business-minded and profitable antique dealers out there, antique shops seem to have a particularly high ratio of hobby merchants, as do gift shops and tearooms.

Although hobby merchant shops may be preferable to vacant ground-floor spaces, this type of business is certainly not part of the targeted tenant mix for most downtowns. The owners' greatest attribute is that they are often willing to volunteer to assist the downtown organization because they have the time. Also, since the owner is usually a native of the community, he or she may have a lot of local contacts, as well as a sincere desire to help the downtown. However, these virtues are generally outweighed by the drawbacks. For example, because hobby merchants are not driven by profits, they tend to keep limited days and hours of operation. Therefore, when a downtown plan recommends keeping businesses open on Saturdays and some evenings, the hobby merchant is often unwilling to put in that extra effort. For similar reasons, it is also difficult to sign them up for joint advertising, sales promotions, and other activities. Because a downtown is only as prosperous as its individual businesses, the hobby merchant can be a serious hindrance.

Hobby merchants are a sensitive issue rarely addressed by downtown plans, and the issue can be resolved only by the property owners who rent out retail space. Hobby merchants who own their buildings are tougher nuts to crack and are dissuaded from setting up shop only if the real estate market encourages them to lease space to a more profitable use. For downtowns in which hobby merchants are a particular barrier to progress, the downtown organization should periodically meet with property owners and leasing agents to encourage them to scrutinize their tenants with this issue in mind. In thriving downtowns, hobby merchants are economically weeded out because the rent levels climb above their slim profit margins, so outside intervention is often unnecessary. Whether it is an issue that can be formally addressed or not by a particular downtown, the concept of the hobby merchant should at least be recognized and accounted for by all downtown managers.

local population of only 1,800. Nevertheless, its small size did not hinder it from establishing the Business Visitation Program, intended to keep struggling downtown businesses afloat. Four teams of two people were formed, each consisting of one retailer and one service business owner. Maintaining strict confidentiality, the two-person teams initially made more than 70 business visits. Each visit entailed interviewing the owner with a variety of standard questions designed to gauge their current performance so that floundering businesses might be identified and helped. Since the initial wave of interviews was conducted, visits have been done only as needed, including welcoming new businesses to the downtown. However, those involved have cited the program's great success in maintaining a dialogue with downtown merchants and throwing a life preserver to struggling businesses before they sink. In downtown organizations with sufficient funding, some hire consultants to carry out the same function performed by volunteers in Corning.

Powell, Wyoming, is an exemplary model of proactive efforts in business retention—or in their specific case, business adaptation. When the downtown's only department store began to fade because of competition from big-box retail in the region, community residents adopted a do-it-yourself attitude. Approximately 500 citizens put up the money to establish Powell Mercantile, a store selling all kinds of clothing. Not only did Powell Mercantile's success serve as a catalyst to prompt several other businesses to open downtown, but the store has done so well that the citizens of Worland, Wyoming, 90 miles away, decided to follow Powell's lead and open their own store (Walljasper 2005).

Business Recruitment

Ideally, a formal business recruitment effort should not be initiated until the timing is right. Good timing includes adequate preparation for the recruitment process, as well as positive trends for the downtown that make it more appealing as a business location. The following components should already be in place before recruitment efforts begin:

- Identification of the optimal tenant mix
- Inventory of available building space or developable sites
- Business recruitment strategy
- Marketing package promoting the advantages of downtown

The process for identifying the optimal tenant mix was covered in Chapter 2. For those downtown plans that can go into such detail, the business recruitment strategy should answer the following questions:

- What specific businesses will be recruited?
- How will the initial contact be made?
- Where should the initial contact occur?
- Who should make the initial contact?
- What materials should be included in the marketing package?
- When and how should any follow-up occur after the initial contact?

In general terms, there are no right or wrong answers because they depend upon the specific circumstances of the downtown, the business being recruited, and the individuals involved. Obviously, any relationships with the owner of the business being recruited should be taken advantage of by the downtown organization, so the direct involvement of the organization's full membership should be encouraged. Rather than placing business recruitment responsibilities solely on the shoulders of their small staff, the Albany Downtown Association (ADA) in Oregon established a Business Recruitment Team in the first half of the 1990s. That group of volunteers, primarily merchants, combined their efforts to identify and recruit candidates for downtown Albany. However, the ADA took a new approach to recruitment. Rather than place the primary responsibility with a small designated group, the ADA trained all downtown business operators in recruitment in order to take advantage of any chance encounters that merchants might have with potential new downtown business owners. Although the team was disbanded in the mid-1990s, it will soon be reinstated with funding from the Main Street USA program.

Rather than relying on volunteers or downtown organization staff who may have only limited experience and expertise with business recruitment, some downtowns have hired consultants to perform the task, particularly if the consultant has already conducted a market analysis to identify the desired new businesses. Among the many advantages of using a consultant for such work are the following:

- Consultants can "speak the language" of the developer, broker, or business operator to explain the economics of the market and the likely market potentials.

- Consultants are independent of the city or downtown organization to the extent that they will likely not be perceived as a biased promoter of the particular downtown.
- Consultants are equipped with expertise that allows them to effectively glean from developers, brokers, and business operators their specific market and financial requirements.

Chippewa Falls Business Plan Contest

Chippewa Falls, Wisconsin, realized early into its revitalization efforts that a key focus needed to be on the development of more downtown businesses through business retention, expansion, and recruitment activities.

Using the economic development program of a nearby county government as inspiration, in 1995 the Chippewa Falls Main Street program established a creative way to attract start-up businesses to its downtown. It sponsored an annual contest whereby prospective new businesses submitted their business plans to compete with other proposed new businesses. A business specialist with the Wisconsin Department of Development helped applicants prepare their plans. A panel of six judges then evaluated the plans based upon their quality, as well as the ability of the proposed business to fill a market niche for downtown Chippewa Falls. The winner's prize consisted of a $5,000 grant and a $20,000 low-interest loan to help get his or her business started. The grant money was donated by downtown Chippewa Falls's five banks. The winner of the first contest in 1995 was Computer Systems & Services, and the 1996 winner was Little Professor Book Seller.

Like so many experimental programs, this one seemed promising when originated, but it failed to achieve long-term results. By the third year of the program, its financial sponsors lost interest, so the program was discontinued. A decade later, neither business was in operation. Nevertheless, this program can still serve as an innovative model for other downtowns to follow, as the success of such programs depends greatly upon their details and execution. Clearly, it would be worthwhile for other downtown organizations to research the details of the Chippewa Falls program, identify where its weaknesses existed, and determine how the same concept might be applied successfully to their own downtowns.

Regardless of who does the actual courting, the marketing package to promote the advantages of starting a business downtown should contain an inventory of available spaces, including information on their location, square footage, rental costs per square foot, parking availability, and contact information. For properties that will be rented on a "triple net" basis (i.e., lessee pays standard rent, as well as taxes, insurance, and maintenance costs), average monthly costs for insurance, utilities, and property taxes should also be included. Because some targeted businesses will be better served by new building space, available sites for development should be included, along with all relevant property information. Other materials in the package might include a map of downtown, information on the downtown organization, a list of governmental and similar contacts relevant to opening a business, downtown promotional brochures, information on existing incentive programs for businesses, and any positive articles on downtown. The Hannibal, Missouri, Main Street program went a step further and, with the help of the chamber of commerce and the regional development authority, produced a business recruitment video highlighting the benefits of locating a business there (National Main Street Center 1997, 22). Although their specific strategies may change over time based upon experience, some of the most successful downtowns have developed and persistently executed detailed business recruitment strategies.

MARKETING AND PROMOTION

Those in the field of downtown revitalization are necessarily in the marketing and promotion business. They are attempting to market dozens of retail and service businesses, as well as downtown housing, office space, and cultural facilities. Among the most effective methods of marketing and promoting downtowns are advertising, storefront window displays, brochures, newsletters, newspapers, sales promotions, special events, residential open houses, and, of course, the Internet. For those downtowns with sufficient resources to do so, their downtown plan should address all of these methods.

Advertising

Advertising usually comes with a price tag, but before downtown programs spend dollars on advertising, opportunities for free advertising should first be exhausted. The first step toward garnering free publicity is to develop strong relationships with local media professionals.

Those in journalism, television, and radio can be helpful in promoting downtown events and positive news stories, so those relationships should be cultivated. When newsworthy happenings occur or interesting issues arise in the downtown, a press release should be sent to the right people. When the media is helpful, the downtown organization's appreciation should be strongly conveyed.

When contemplating paid advertising as a means of marketing the downtown and its businesses, two key considerations include: (1) choosing the specific types of media to be used; and (2) identifying opportunities to stretch marketing dollars through joint advertising.

Advertising in electronic and print media can be an effective approach to marketing a downtown, although it can be expensive. Television advertising is generally the most costly form of media and often beyond the means of most downtown programs. An exception is very small communities in which television advertising is not cost-prohibitive. Radio advertising is usually less expensive than television but more costly than print media. For most downtown programs, electronic forms of media are reserved for key occasions, such as the promotion of special events. Newspaper advertising, on the other hand, is much more achievable and lends itself to the collaboration of multiple businesses through joint advertising.

Joint advertising is an effective way for small businesses to leverage their limited marketing funds by joining forces with like-minded downtown businesses. Joint advertising is often employed by businesses sharing some common theme, such as restaurants, clothing stores, and antique stores. In downtowns with a tenant location strategy, these businesses are typically clustered together geographically.

For a time, antique dealers in downtown Ardmore, Oklahoma, a community of 30,000, banded together to purchase joint advertising in the local newspaper and to share billboard space on the interstate. Likewise, the Albany, Oregon, Downtown Association coordinated advertisements in local media for many of its members for a number of years. The Berkeley, California, downtown group also purchases joint advertising and coordinates an advertising campaign to market the downtown as a destination. When the program originated, the group ran a monthly full-page advertisement in two different newspapers. The ad consisted of a series of individual ads funded by the featured businesses, and each ad featured a different banner heading, such as "shopping," "dining," "arts and entertainment," and "special events." Because of recent changes in their local media, as well as a statewide economic downturn, businesses are no longer taking advantage of the program to the extent that they did initially. However, the organization has adapted to these changing conditions by creating new tools.

Regardless of their program details, downtown organizations can play a key role in these joint advertising efforts by serving as the catalyst and coordinating the advertising. Such an effort is also an opportunity for the downtown organization to use its adopted logo within the ads in order to convey the image of a unified commercial entity, much as is done by suburban shopping malls.

Storefront Window Displays

Window displays are one of the most underrated opportunities for downtowns to really shine. Storefronts are essentially free advertisements that can run constantly. In conducting research for *Predatory Marketing* (1998), C. Britt Breemer concluded that 53 percent of shoppers decide whether to enter a store based upon its exterior appearance. Furthermore, a commonly cited rule of thumb in the retail industry is that a store, whether on a downtown street or in a shopping mall, has roughly eight seconds to attract the interest of passersby. This idea is based upon typical storefront widths and pedestrian speeds. Attractive and enticing storefront displays are not difficult or expensive to achieve when contrasted with the benefits derived for both the individual businesses and the downtown in general. There are experts

Figure 4-6. This window display creatively uses fans to blow garments in a manner that animates them and catches the eye of pedestrians. The display stays lit all evening, helping to enliven the downtown 24 hours a day.
Source: The Walker Collaborative

who spend their careers creating window displays, and their talents should be sought by more downtowns.

The five key principles for good storefront window design are quality, simplicity, creativity, illumination, and variation over time. Only the highest-quality merchandise should be used in the display, as quality will attract consumers. Although displays should not be boring, simplicity can be a virtue. Displays that are too cluttered and busy will confuse window shoppers and dampen their interest. Many window displays feature an opaque background. The intent is that, by not having objects in the background to distract the viewer, all eyes will be trained on the merchandise being highlighted in the foreground. Some displays do not use this approach for a number of reasons, including: to allow more daylight into the store; to provide an opportunity for window shoppers to peer into the store; and to avoid the cost of the display backing. While those are some of the benefits of not using a display backing, designing a display strong enough to compete with the backdrop of activity can be a challenge. Although creativity is easier said than done, efforts at being clever and different will usually pay off because window shoppers will remember creative displays even if they do not enter the store at that particular time.

Illumination is another critical factor. Lighting should be carefully directed onto the subjects of the display, but glare should be avoided. Illumination should be maintained 24 hours a day to keep downtown looking lively. Storefront lighting is also an important but often overlooked means of illuminating evening streetscapes.

In order to maintain interest, displays should be changed a minimum of once every three weeks. Appreciating the importance of window displays, The Gap clothing stores change their displays once a week.

Cross-marketing

Perhaps the strongest gesture toward teamwork among downtown merchants is the use of storefront window displays for cross-marketing. Here is an example of how cross-marketing might work: a men's clothing store decides to create a display in which a mannequin is sitting at a desk wearing a business suit carried by the store. As part of the display, a desk and chair are needed, so the clothing store borrows them from the furniture store down the street. A small placard crediting the furniture store is placed on the desk. The primary focus is still on the clothing store and its merchandise, but cross-marketing provides the opportunity to say, "By the way, there is a great furniture store down the street." For obvious reasons, businesses that compete with each other would

Bursting the Bubble of a Downtown Retailer

Situated among the many strong tenants on downtown's Main Street, a bath store in a community of 35,000 people was looking for a way to increase its visibility. After much thought, it finally hit upon a creative idea to draw some attention. Wanting to highlight the fact that soaps were its main product line, it installed a small machine on its storefront that blew soapy bubbles into the air.

For the first few years, the bubble machine was a major hit. It did not visually detract from the storefront, it made no discernible noise, and it churned out thousands of festive bubbles per day to help liven up the downtown. However, over time, problems began to arise. One of the complaints was that when the bubbles landed on an object and then burst, they left behind residue. Small soapy rings were reportedly appearing on parked cars and neighboring storefronts. A tenant downwind complained that when her door was propped open on nice days, bubbles were blowing into her store and landing on her merchandise. While those nuisance-based complaints might sound rather trivial, the real lightning rod was the safety issue. It was observed that children often relished the challenge of chasing the floating bubbles. Although no accidents had actually occurred, there was a concern that children or even adults might chase a bubble into the street and become another traffic accident statistic.

In reality, it is questionable just how tangible these concerns were. In fact, it has been suggested that the basis of the controversy was related to petty differences among downtown merchants rather than valid

Figure 4-7. The bubble machine is mounted just above the "open" banner.
Source: The Walker Collaborative

concerns over soapy residues and public safety. Regardless, the issue eventually made it to city council in the form of a proposed ordinance to outlaw all bubble-making contraptions and similar devices that might create a nuisance or hazard. To the amazement of many, the ordinance passed.

There is a lesson to be learned. For many downtowns, opportunities to animate the street are few and far between. In addition to the lack of destination businesses, one common complaint of many downtowns is that they are "boring."

Therefore, gimmicks for animating the street—whether they are street performers, public art, or bubble machines—should be valued. Rather than being admonished, merchants who take the initiative to be creative for the benefit of themselves and their downtown should be appreciated and encouraged. As this story points out, however, planning and gathering public and merchant input before the "bubble machine" is installed is a good idea and may defuse some of the potential later infighting.

---

not make good candidates to be paired for cross-marketing efforts. However, by simply keeping this approach in mind, many retailers can easily identify opportunities for cross-marketing their downtown colleagues.

In a similar vein, some downtown organizations sponsor a program in which merchandise from downtown businesses is displayed in the windows of vacant downtown storefronts. Willing property owners can often be convinced that not only will this approach enhance the appearance of their building, but by helping individual downtown businesses, they are helping the overall downtown and thus the marketing of their property. Although determining which businesses earn an opportunity to install off-site window displays can be difficult when interest levels are high, a politically neutral approach to filling vacant windows is to display art, whether created by professional artists or kindergarteners.

Brochures

Brochures promoting downtown have been a dependable standby for many years and are still relevant and effective today. The key issues for a downtown plan to consider in recommending the use of brochures include the specific subject matter, design, and method of distribution.

The selected brochure topic depends on how many different brochures will be created for the downtown. For example, a small downtown, or one with a very limited budget, may choose to have only a single all-encompassing brochure that addresses retail options, dining, entertainment, and parking. It might even include a profile of the downtown's history and architecture. However, it is difficult for larger and more complex downtowns to fit all of those subjects within a single brochure. Here is a list of potential brochure topics:

- History and architecture
- Dining and shopping
- Parking locations
- Antiquing
- Entertainment
- Special events
- Parks and greenways

Brochures on a downtown's history and architecture are typically intended to guide the user on a walking tour. Therefore, this type of brochure includes a map to identify specific sites, as well as a brief description of each site being interpreted. When Dodgeville, Wisconsin, a town of just over 4,000 people, decided to create a historic walking tour booklet for its downtown, it started by getting a series of articles into the local newspaper and soliciting historic photographs. The result was a booklet created in 1995 with more than 60 historic photographs, put together through hundreds of hours of volunteer time. With regard to brochures that list specific businesses, it must be kept in mind that not all of them will necessarily still exist a year later. Therefore, if a brochure will be listing individual businesses, periodic updates will be necessary.

Brochure design has traditionally been left to the expertise of marketing and graphic design professionals. Although there are now software packages available that allow novices to create attractive brochures, it is still wise to involve a design professional at some level whenever possible. If the expense of professional help is an issue, sometimes a marketing firm located in the downtown will be willing to donate or discount its services in exchange for a credit in the brochure.

All of the attention paid to content and design will be of little value if the brochure never makes it into the hands of consumers. The creation of a brochure should not be initiated until a dependable funding source is first identified for production and distribution. Geographically,

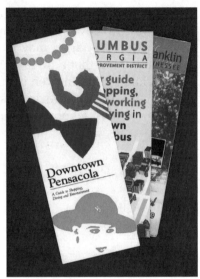

Figure 4-8. Even with the Internet and other media, simple brochures can serve as effective tools for marketing a downtown, especially to tourists who encounter brochure racks. Source: The Walker Collaborative

the area of distribution should be broad. It should include the very downtown being marketed, the downtown's outlying community, and neighboring communities. If the community has good accessibility to major highways and interstates, brochures might be provided as far away as a couple of hundred miles so that travelers have plenty of time to adapt their plans. The specific types of locations that should be stocked with brochures include:

- Rest stops and visitor information centers
- Tourist attractions
- Hotels and other types of lodging
- Restaurants
- Chamber of commerce offices
- Convention and visitors bureau offices

Many of these types of locations have brochure racks intended for promoting regional attractions, including historic downtowns. Once acceptable locations are determined and an initial supply of brochures is provided, a systematic process should be established to monitor supplies and replenish brochures as needed. In addition to placement in racks, direct mailings are another approach to be considered, depending upon the particular downtown and the market being targeted.

Newsletters and Newspapers

Newsletters are a common means for organizations to stay in touch with their members and are used by many downtown groups to communicate with their key stakeholders. Newspapers published specifically for a particular downtown, on the other hand, are targeting a much broader market of people who live, work, or visit the downtown or who have the potential to do so.

Newsletters are typically mailed out monthly, quarterly, or semi-annually. For an organization with a small staff, production and distribution can consume time and effort, so any downtown plan that addresses the issue must first determine if the benefits justify the costs. One way to ease the burden of production is to solicit articles from members, although coordination and editing will still be required. If an organization determines that a newsletter is indeed needed, it must decide on the frequency of editions. Most groups that produce newsletters are now using the Internet as either an option or the only means of distribution. While that approach will be problematic for people without Internet access or who simply prefer a paper version, digital newsletters save time and money compared to mass mailings.

Some downtown programs have gone so far as to create their own newspapers. They can range in frequency from once a week to once a month, are supported primarily through advertising, and tend to target downtown employees and residents to create a feeling of camaraderie among downtown stakeholders. The intent is also to inform people regarding downtown events, to develop a greater appreciation for downtown, and to promote downtown businesses. When the Pensacola, Florida, Downtown Improvement Board embarked on a major marketing campaign in 1987, it created a monthly newspaper, *The Downtown Crowd*, which played off of a tongue-in-check phrase for Pensacola's clique of political and business insiders. Much like newspapers created by other downtown organizations across the county, standard components of each edition included the following:

- Calendar of downtown events
- Progress update for the downtown organization
- News articles relevant to downtown
- Guest editorial
- "A Face in the Crowd"—profiling a downtown personality

- Advertising—primarily by downtown businesses
- Occasional public opinion surveys related to downtown

Most of the same considerations that apply to newsletters apply equally to downtown newspapers, such as whether to offer a digital version as either an option or as the sole format. Likewise, the costs and benefits need to be examined to conclude whether a downtown newspaper is a valid idea. One of the key determinants will be whether sufficient advertising can be sold to make the newspaper financially viable.

Internet Websites

Given the Internet's influence on all facets of life today, websites can be an important means of marketing and promoting downtowns. Since even the smallest businesses and nonprofit organizations now have websites, a website is a necessity for any downtown organization. At a minimum, a downtown organization's website should contain the following components:

- Overview of the organization
- Explanation of various services provided
- Map of downtown
- Description of downtown offerings by theme—shopping, entertainment, dining, housing, parking, history, and architecture
- Calendar of downtown events
- Progress update for the downtown organization
- List of available properties
- Occasional public opinion surveys related to downtown
- Contact information for the organization

The content on a downtown's website should combine the themed information found in brochures with the propaganda and current events information of a newsletter. Although do-it-yourself software packages are available for creating websites, a professional will develop a website for a few thousand dollars so long as the text and graphics are provided by the organization. As in the case of brochure design, website design for a downtown organization might be performed for little or no cost by a website designer located downtown in return for a credit for the designer's business on the website.

Residential Open Houses

Open houses are one method of piquing the interest of potential new downtown residents who might lack sufficient interest to work with a real estate agent but who might be persuaded otherwise once they "kick a few tires." Because prospects can casually come and go, they tend to feel insulated from the pressure of real estate professionals to make a decision on a particular unit. Residential open houses are commonly sponsored by the community's downtown organization and conducted on a weekend to accommodate the schedule of the prospects. However, some real estate companies representing multiple downtown properties will organize their own open house tours in which they guide groups of interested people through a variety of properties. Even if the open house participants are not prepared to make an immediate move to the downtown, the event can at least expand their understanding of available housing types and plant the seed for a future move downtown.

Other Promotional Activities

Other activities that should be considered within the context of downtown planning to promote and animate the downtown include sales promotions, special events, and street performers. Sales promotions and special events are important to any downtown for both short-term and long-term benefits. In the short term, these activities grab people's attention and draw them to the downtown. While they are there, they might also contribute to the downtown economy by spending money. Over the long term, promotions and special events are opportunities for people who may not normally frequent the downtown to spend time there and have a positive experience. They may tell their friends and neighbors about their experience and will likely return to downtown for future dining and shopping. While sales promotions and special events can be hosted by even the smallest downtown, street performers tend to be limited to larger downtowns. Some communities attempt to regulate them.

Street vendors. Street vendors are one important means for enlivening any downtown, as they add interest and activity to the street. To survive economically, they need a high level of foot traffic. Also, unless regulated, they can have negative aspects. Some downtown merchants will complain that street vendors have the advantage of not paying property taxes, but limiting their goods and services to those that do not compete directly with existing merchants is one way of avoiding such complaints. A regulatory program should also require them to operate only in designated locations that are not disruptive to pedestrian traffic, and design standards should ensure that their vendor carts maintain a minimum level of appearance to reflect positively upon the downtown. A license and fee system should also be required supplement the costs of regulating vendors. For more information on this subject, see Ball (2002).

Sales promotions. Sales promotions occur when multiple retailers join forces to plan, market, and host a sales event. The retailers typically hold the sales promotion event on a weekend or toward the end of the week, and they often use joint advertising in the local newspaper to promote it. Sales promotions sometimes involve extended business hours, the outdoor display of merchandise in front of stores, food vendors, small-scale entertainment, and pricing discounts. They are sometimes associated with a particular holiday, but not always. Because of the logistics and coordination involved, sales events generally require an entity, such as a merchants association or a Main Street program, to serve as host.

Downtowns sponsoring sales promotions need to follow two important rules: (1) do not hold them too frequently, and (2) maintain a high level of quality. They should occur infrequently not only because of the effort required to organize them but because too many sales promotions will cause their novelty to wear off, resulting in lower sales volumes. Maintaining a high level of quality is critical to the long-term image of downtown. If, for example, card tables without attractive skirting are set up on the sidewalks to display junky trinkets, the downtown will develop a bargain basement image that will be difficult to overcome. Therefore, some downtowns adopt some general design standards to address the appearance issue.

Special events. Special events can be an extremely effective means of bringing people downtown who may otherwise never visit. While merchants often complain that few sales occur during such events, the long-term benefit of enhancing the downtown's image is more important. If people come to the downtown and feel safe and have a positive experience, the odds are greatly increased that they will return at some future point in time to shop and dine.

The same type of market analysis that forecasts the potential for new retail, office, and housing in the downtown can be used to project the potential for existing and new special events, as was done by Smithfield, Virginia, for an event associated with its world-famous Smithfield Hams. Particularly important issues to be addressed include the likely attendance levels, who the market is, how best to promote the event

Figure 4-9. Special events are an effective way of attracting people to downtown who rarely venture there otherwise. The odds that these people will later return for shopping or dining are greatly enhanced if they have a positive downtown experience. Source: The Walker Collaborative

with the market, who will organize the event, and how costs might compare with revenues. As a general rule, the principles applied to sales promotions apply equally to special events: limit their frequency and maintain standards of quality. Within the context of downtown planning, special events can be categorized into three groups: (1) existing events currently held within the downtown; (2) existing events currently held outside of the downtown; and (3) new events.

The key questions related to existing downtown events are: Are they worth continuing downtown and, if so, are there ways to enhance them? With respect to potential new downtown events, it is usually easier to relocate an existing event to downtown than to start a new one. In many communities, an event such as the Fourth of July parade traditionally occurred downtown but was moved to the suburbs at some point for a reason that seemed valid at the time. The strongest cases for returning such events downtown are that (1) downtown is the community's most unique and special place, making it most appropriate for special events; and (2) if the event previously functioned well downtown, it can probably work there again. Sometimes an effort to relocate the special event downtown can encounter stiff opposition from suburban interests, particularly the management of the suburban mall if it currently hosts the event.

With respect to starting a new special event for downtown, the costs and benefits must first be considered thoroughly, as with any marketing and promotional activities for downtowns. The event's organizers

Watsonville's Balanced Approach to Events

When hosting special events, downtowns should think in terms of two different types: frequent smaller events or programming that bring regular traffic to the downtown, and less frequent large-scale events that expose many people to downtown who might not otherwise ever visit it. Watsonville, California, a community of 51,700, has a downtown organization that has used both small-scale programming and less frequent large-scale special events. Among the regular events is the Watsonville Farmer's Market, held every Friday downtown. By offering locally grown produce, as well as crafts and musical entertainment, the downtown has become a regional destination. As part of its strategy for larger occasional events, Main Street Watsonville established the annual Spring Strawberry Dessert Festival. Taking advantage of its location in one of the largest strawberry-producing regions in the world, this event was held the Sunday of Memorial Day weekend. It attracted thousands of people to downtown Watsonville to enjoy food, live musical performances, and children's games and entertainment. The Memorial Day festival has recently been replaced by a Monterey Bay Strawberry Festival in Watsonville on the first weekend in August.

Watsonville's two-pronged strategy for events achieves two distinct but important objectives. On the one hand, the small-scale frequent programming animates the downtown for its regular users, helps build a sense of camaraderie among downtown employees, and attracts a substantial number of people who do not live or work there. The less frequent large-scale events, on the other hand, draw substantial numbers of people who might not otherwise ever visit the downtown, providing a widespread buzz within the region. Watsonville's balanced approach to events is an excellent model for other downtowns across the country.

must also have a clear understanding of why they are holding a special event. One of the greatest motivations for many downtown groups is to simply draw attention to downtown and expose visitors to a positive downtown experience. Some mature special events can also raise considerable funds, but expectations should be low during the early years of an event because many do not become profitable until at least three or four years into their existence.

It is noteworthy that some types of small-scale special events can be held regularly and with relative frequency with great success, despite warnings otherwise. This type of event or programming is typically part of a monthly or weekly series, such as "Shakespeare in the Park" or "Lunchtime Jazz." Programmed event series are much easier to organize and execute than larger annual events because they are typically smaller in scale and their organization can be standardized for efficiency. Numerous downtowns across the country have found farmers markets to serve as highly effective weekend draws during the growing season. As one among numerous examples, a new farmers market was a key recommendation for the Hayward, California, downtown plan. Even if a farmers market already occurs elsewhere in town, many downtown plans will recommend relocating it to the downtown, as was recommended in the Denton, Texas, 2003 downtown plan. Although downtown Gallatin, Tennessee, already had a small farmers market in a low-profile parking lot, its 2005 downtown master plan recommended a new multiuse pavilion to house the event. The city recently secured grant funding to build it, and the design phase is under way.

Street performers. Street performers can add a great deal of energy to any downtown. They are typically found in only the largest downtowns because they rely on tips from spectators, so they need a large population to earn enough to make their efforts worthwhile. However, smaller tourist towns are an exception. Eureka, California, has a population of only 26,128, according to the 2000 Census, but Highway 101 brings plenty of tourists and through traffic. Consequently, its downtown has enjoyed a flourishing street performer scene for several years. Shortly after adopting a municipal ordinance to regulate street performers, the Main Street Artists and Performers Association was established in 1996 to audition and license street performers. Eureka's street performers—musicians and actors—were permitted to pass around a tip jar after each performance so long as they had a license. Although the program was terminated in 1999 because of the labor intensity of the auditioning process, as well as freedom of speech questions regarding the legality of regulating performers in public spaces, street performers are still prevalent and encouraged in downtown Eureka. While it is likely that Eureka's problems attempting to regulate street performers would occur in most communities, such entertainment should still be nurtured and promoted as a means of animating downtowns. In fact, more downtowns should follow the example set by St. Louis's Washington Avenue Loft District, which gave specific consideration to accommodating street performances as part of a master plan for the district's public spaces.

SOCIAL ISSUES

Even if a downtown plan thoroughly addresses the key economic and marketing issues, ultimate success may never occur if serious social issues are neglected. In particular, social issues can have a direct impact upon a downtown's image, which, in turn, can greatly affect its economic prosperity. Social issues such as crime, homelessness, and gentrification apply to nearly every downtown in America, from the largest cities to the smallest towns, including affluent communities. However, the issues are much more pronounced in some downtowns than others. Similarly, some cities and downtown organizations have admirably elected to acknowledge the problems and address them in a proactive manner, while others simply turn their heads. Even those communities lacking a spirit of social benevolence and choosing not to deal with the fundamental roots of these issues often reach the conclusion that they must address them at some level if they want to be able to market the downtown as a pleasant place to visit and shop. For example, the homeless are usually more visible in downtowns that host the resources that support them, such as shelters and soup kitchens. In such instances, the downtown organization might view homelessness as more of a marketing issue for their downtown than a social issue that they should truly care about. Similarly, because perception is reality, crime is often viewed by downtowns as primarily a marketing issue, especially in those downtowns that experience very little violent crime.

Crime

Within the context of downtown planning, strategies to address crime typically focus on violent crime. Although crime occurs throughout most communities, downtowns often have an image of crime tacked onto them, rightly or wrongly. Part of this perception stems from a deep-seated American belief that urban areas are somehow sinister.

Addressing crime within a downtown plan must be done carefully. On the one hand, battling crime effectively requires a concerted effort, including a strategy and an implementing organization. On the other hand, unless crime is already a widely recognized problem for the downtown, it needs to be addressed in a low-profile manner to avoid drawing too much public attention to the issue and perpetuating the image of a dangerous downtown. Philosophies about how to achieve long-term solutions for reducing crime vary. Because crime often occurs where there is a deficiency of "eyes on the street," as the great urban writer Jane Jacobs observed, an increased population density would seem to be the answer. On the other hand, the more people come into contact with one another, the greater the chances for conflicts to occur. Regardless of your school of thought, the following are approaches commonly recommended by downtown plans to address crime and the perception of crime.

Additional security. Added law enforcement, particularly those on the ground walking, pedaling, or riding a beat on horseback, can extend a feeling of greater security. If additional security is provided, efforts should be made to portray the officers as ambassadors of good will who are friendly and available for giving directions and the like, in addition to enforcing the law. If on-duty police officers cannot be used, off-duty officers should be hired for the job, as their qualifications, training, and equipment will be superior to those of most private security employees. For those downtowns that adopt a business improvement district (BID), additional security is a common service provided through it.

Crime watch programs. Most communities already have a crime watch program in which interested citizens and business operators are coached by the police on how to identify and report criminal activity. The key to successful crime watch programs is the active involvement and coordinated efforts of a network of people. Downtown organizations can develop a committee to focus solely on the issue of crime, and they can be a conduit for the local police department to recruit and train volunteers. Berkeley, California, had uniformed "Berkeley Guides" downtown to supplement the police patrols and to serve as friendly ambassadors. The city cut the program in July 2005 because of statewide fiscal problems. In 2008, the Downtown Berkeley Association began to help manage a new program for dealing with the homeless, the "Berkeley Host Program." The program is funded by parking meter revenue. It is similar to the "Berkeley Guides" program inasmuch as citizens assist homeless people with their problems and report things like aggressive panhandling to the authorities.

Improved lighting. This approach to combating crime is simple and relatively inexpensive but effective. Many crimes, particularly burglaries and vandalism, occur at night. By improving the lighting, criminals are often discouraged by the increased visibility and elect either not to commit crimes or to do so elsewhere. Good lighting for streetscapes, public spaces, and parking areas is also important for increasing the public perception of safety. If more people feel safer and frequent downtown at night, that added population can result in increased safety, so that the perception of safety helps create the reality. It is important, however, that the lights used are at human scale and attractive. Inappropriately tall fixtures with excessive light levels can actually decrease the perception of safety, much as do security grates, chain-link fences, or burglar bars on doors and window. Also, the importance of storefront windows remaining lit 24 hours per day as a means of animating a downtown is widely recognized, but the security benefits should also not be overlooked.

Electronic surveillance. Surveillance cameras have already become a common crime-fighting feature in many big-city downtowns, and even smaller communities now use them in key locations, such as stairwells of parking garages. There are two main elements to such a system: the cameras and the individuals to monitor what the cameras are capturing on video. The purchase and installation of cameras is a one-time cost until they have to be replaced, while their maintenance and staffing to conduct the surveillance are ongoing costs. Some communities, such as High Point, North Carolina, with a population of 94,000, already have sophisticated camera systems for monitoring traffic at key intersections throughout the community. It also doubles as a crime prevention tool within the community's downtown area.

Graffiti eradication programs. Although graffiti writing is certainly not a violent crime, it can add to the negative image of a downtown and increase perceptions of more serious crimes. Many communities have found that graffiti attracts more graffiti, so the sooner it is eliminated, the better. California's Downtown Berkeley Association (DBA) has experimented with a variety of approaches to the problem. The DBA originally provided businesses with a "DBA Graffiti Kit" that included a paintbrush, a quart of paint matching their building, and a brochure that explained how to apply protective coatings that make graffiti easy to remove. While the kits are no longer distributed because of the costs, the city has since passed an ordinance requiring property owners to eliminate graffiti within a specified time after it appears.

Another approach used by some communities has been to establish programs that transform graffiti criminals into "street artists" by channeling their energy and creativity in more positive directions, such as painting approved murals onto selected blank walls. The Eureka Mural Project was established in 1993 in Eureka, California, to do just that. Cosponsored by the Eureka Arts and Culture Commission, Eureka Main Street, and a local arts group, the program is led by an experienced muralist and was initially funded by the city and the California Arts Council. Although the arts council is no longer supporting it because of the state's financial challenges, the private sector has filled the void.

While the ideas above are short-term solutions to urban crime that make their way into some downtown plans, the long-term answer is to attract more people to downtowns. In addition to the need for plenty of daytime workers and shoppers to enhance security, downtowns especially need residents to provide more eyes on the street 24 hours a day.

Homelessness

When addressed through downtown planning, homelessness is an issue that must be dealt with delicately. While most would agree that the homeless deserve compassion and humane treatment, the efforts of many downtown organizations to address the negative impacts of homelessness on their downtowns are often viewed, understandably, as insensitive because they frequently focus more on reducing the visibility of street people rather than the root causes of homelessness. Clearly, the presence of the homeless increases the perception that downtown is unsafe or an unpleasant place to be, even if the vast majority of them do not pose a legitimate threat to public safety.

Homelessness is a complex issue, with a variety of causes. A large percentage of the homeless are mentally ill. Some have been deinstitutionalized and simply need medication and assistance with employment and housing. Many have addictions to drugs or alcohol, which have resulted in the loss of their jobs and family support systems. The answer for this homeless population is substance-abuse counseling, as well as help with housing and employment. Another subset of the homeless is made up of teenage "runaways" who sometimes get caught up in vices, such as prostitution and drugs. Perhaps the most surprising segment of the homeless to many is the working homeless. Randall Gross of Randall Gross/Development Economics in Washington, D.C., mentions that in Charles County, Maryland, for example, a housing study revealed that some people sleep in their automobiles, commute to Washington, D.C., or its suburbs, work a full day at a legitimate job, and then return to Charles County, where they cannot afford to reside in proper housing. He noted that housing in downtown Waldorf, in particular, has become unaffordable for most, and many people believe that much of the blame can be placed on the county's zoning, which

Dealing Aggressively with Aggressive Panhandlers

Berkeley, California, a suburb of San Francisco, is reportedly home to some of America's most aggressive panhandlers. They have a reputation for generally hostile and disorderly behavior that has chased away many shoppers and diners in downtown Berkeley. To mitigate the problem, Berkeley's citizens passed Measure O, a ballot initiative that combines social services to help the homeless with powers giving the police greater authority to deal with aggressive panhandlers and those otherwise disturbing the peace. The social services package included a detoxification center, a full-service shelter, a mobile crisis team, and a homeless outreach team. In return, the ordinance regulating public behavior includes the following standards:

- No panhandling after dark, near ATMs, or within a certain distance of business entrances
- No fighting or lewd language
- No sitting or lying on sidewalks between 6:00 a.m. and 12:00 a.m.

Even though the ordinance was initially tied up in the courts by the American Civil Liberties Union, the Berkeley police immediately felt empowered by the public mandate to deal with aggressive panhandling and other types of undesirable behavior in a firmer manner.

Another program devised to deal with the panhandling issue was the Berkeley Cares Voucher and Donation Program, sponsored by Berkeley Cares. This nonprofit organization established a program during the 1980s whereby people could purchase 25-cent vouchers in many of downtown businesses and give them to panhandlers instead of money. The vouchers were redeemable for food and certain services but not for alcohol and tobacco. Upon the program's initiation, a noticeable decrease in panhandling occurred. The program was discontinued in 2000. Nevertheless, Berkeley continues to combine policing with a strong program of social services to address the panhandling problem.

---

mandates minimum housing unit sizes and prohibits the development of town houses and apartments.

In addition to being a complex and frequently misunderstood topic, homelessness is a NIMBY ("Not in My Back Yard") issue for many involved with downtown revitalization, as those looking out for their particular downtown often strive to get the homeless out of their "backyard." Their efforts might include discouraging downtown locations for the support system of the homeless, such as homeless shelters, soup kitchens, day labor offices, plasma centers, and low-end liquor stores. If such resources remain downtown despite efforts to relocate them, an alternative strategy is to move them to less visible locations within the downtown, away from the key shopping streets and tourism venues. Another approach employed by some downtown groups is to identify locations where the homeless seem to congregate and to make them less comfortable. As mean-spirited as it may sound, plazas can be well lit and benches can be provided with an extra armrest in the middle, both measures that make sleeping more difficult.

Clearly, these are all just quick-fix approaches for the selfish good of a particular downtown. The humane and long-term solution will entail getting these people the help they sorely need. While most downtown organizations do not have the resources or adopted mission to get into the social services business, opportunities for partnering with social service providers in some manner may exist. More downtown plans need to address the issue of homelessness, rather than turn a blind eye.

Gentrification

As in the case of homelessness, gentrification—the economic displacement of lower-income people by higher-income people—is an emotionally charged issue. Gentrification can affect both residents and businesses. In the case of residential renters, as an area improves and property values increase, they can no longer afford the rent and must move on. In some cases, renting is no longer even an option, as rental units are converted to for-purchase properties. Even property owners can be similarly affected if they can no longer afford to pay their property taxes, although they typically enjoy the benefits of the increased value when they sell. Businesses can suffer a similar fate. As a commercial district becomes more vibrant and lucrative, the rents increase and some businesses will have to relocate. This phenomenon is particularly common when relatively low-end commercial areas providing conventional goods and services take on more of a specialty retail, dining, and entertainment flavor.

So is gentrification really a problem? It clearly is for the people forced to relocate. With respect to a downtown's retail sector, it is problematic if too many national and regional chains begin replacing locally owned "mom and pop" businesses. While some chains can be desirable, too many will dilute the unique character that gives downtowns their senses of character and identity, as well as their competitive edges. To the extent that the goal of a downtown or urban neighborhood revitalization program is to enhance the physical and economic condition of the area, gentrification would seem to be a benchmark for success. However, given that truly successful downtowns also have a positive social dimension and feature a high quality of life for all of its inhabitants, gentrification is unquestionably undesirable.

There are many options for reacting to gentrification, but they can be categorized into three general approaches. One is simply to not improve an area, which is not an acceptable choice for most communities. Another alternative is to enact legal constraints that dampen the natural dynamics of the real estate market, such as the residential rent controls that have been used by Boston and New York. Studies of residential rent control have found that housing costs tend to increase for those not fortunate enough to have rent-controlled units because rent control discourages the development of new housing, thereby causing demand to exceed supply. Either of these two alternatives has its own set of problems that, for most people, would overshadow the gentrification problem altogether. The third alternative for addressing residential gentrification is the provision of affordable housing and ownership programs. Affordable housing can either be developed by the public sector or, with sufficient requirements or incentives, by the private sector. In fact, public-private partnerships are often the optimal approach to maximizing investments into affordable housing. Ownership programs are driven by various levels of government, as well as financial institutions. While they are typically thought of solely for housing, commercial property ownership programs are a tool that can help to avoid the displacement of small businesses that would otherwise be pushed out because of increasing rent levels. In short, this approach of assistance with affordable housing and ownership is the most viable option for most downtowns, and a detailed strategy for establishing such programs can be accommodated within downtown plans.

Donovan Rypkema, an expert on downtowns and the economics of historic preservation, has a thought-provoking perspective on the subject of gentrification: "The word gentrification has outlived its usefulness. Too many connotations no longer apply. Perhaps 'economic integration' is a better description. . . . Except for those who, for their own reasons, want to see the poor continue to be isolated, economic integration is a concept that new and old residents alike can support" (Rypkema 1994, 65).

5

Implementation Strategy

Is not civilization, with all it has accomplished, the result of man's not letting things alone, and of his not letting nature take its course?

—Lester Ward

A downtown plan without an implementation strategy is like written directions to an important destination in which the critical last paragraph is missing. Without an implementation strategy, those seeking to breathe life into a downtown plan are left stranded. The key issues to be addressed by a downtown plan's implementation strategy include:

- Organizational structure
- Public policies
- Funding and financing
- Prioritizing, assigning, and phasing

ORGANIZATIONAL STRUCTURE

Any chore as complex as managing and revitalizing a downtown requires a high level of organization. Downtown redevelopment does not just happen, even if a solid game plan is in place. Plans are not self-implementing. In order to achieve success, one or more entities must exist for the express purpose of carrying out the downtown strategy, and the downtown plan should explore all reasonable organizational possibilities.

Organizational Options

Successful downtown programs are implemented by either a single downtown organization or multiple organizations working together.

What follows is an overview of how downtown entities operate, as well as the role of local governments and community development corporations (CDCs) in reviving and sustaining downtowns.

A downtown organization. No matter how involved a local government might become in the downtown redevelopment process, it is best to have a single organization charged solely with the responsibility of downtown. Many downtown organizations across the country are affiliated with the National Main Street Center of the National Trust for Historic Preservation. Even downtowns not formally associated with that organization often use the Main Street program's four point approach: organization, design, economic restructuring, and promotion.

Franklin Downtown Development (FDD) of Franklin, Virginia, is one example of an organization offering the typical services of a downtown organization:

- Organize periodic meetings among downtown stakeholders
- Serve as a liaison between the city and new businesses trying to open
- Assist with business grand openings and ribbon cuttings
- Coordinate joint advertising campaigns, promotions, and special events
- Provide clerical services to downtown businesses, such as copying and faxing
- Assist in the creation of signs, flyers, posters, and gift certificates for businesses
- Provide publicity for new businesses, products, services, and other business news
- Assist in marketing downtown real estate
- Offer design assistance for building rehabilitations
- Provide grants and low-interest loans for building improvements

Regardless of their specific services, one of the most important functions a downtown entity can provide is an organizational framework for an otherwise fragmented assortment of private businesses. As explained by Deborah Badhia, the executive director of California's Downtown Berkeley Association (DBA), "We're playing a role of unifying all downtown businesses. We help to put an umbrella over the district. The DBA creates both identity and synergy."

By virtue of their singular purpose of enhancing downtown, downtown entities do not have the distraction of serving other functions and constituencies that might compete for attention with the implementation of the downtown plan. Local governments and chambers of commerce, for example, must serve much broader constituencies beyond the borders of downtown. Even the smallest communities that lack sufficient funding for a full-time Main Street manager have found creative ways to secure such services, such as the sharing of a manager among multiple small communities within the same region.

Local government. With the exception of the smallest communities having few options, local governments are usually not the ideal organization to lead downtown revitalization efforts. Nevertheless, they almost always play an extremely important role in the overall process. Not only do they provide basic services to downtowns, such as garbage pickup and general maintenance, they often contribute operational funding to the downtown organization, construct costly new streetscape improvements, and serve as the conduit for funding programs, such as special assessment districts and tax increment financing. Some independent downtown organizations are created through legislation of the local government, with board members being appointed by the municipality's governing body, as is the case for the Pensacola, Florida, Downtown Improvement Board. Another important role for local governments is city planning. Most downtown organizations do not attempt to perform that function in place of their local municipal planning department. In fact, the local government's planning director is often an ex officio member of the downtown organization's board of directors to ensure a strong relationship between the organization and the local planning department.

Many downtown entities have taken advantage of available office space in city halls and county courthouses, but this practice is accompanied by a caveat for two reasons. First, the downtown organization may need to periodically lobby the local government, sometimes even butting heads, in order to look out for the best interests of downtown. Sometimes the issue may relate to the municipality's services to downtown, while other times it might relate to ordinances that need changing for the betterment of downtown. Whatever the issues, the downtown organization will have greater autonomy to deal with the local government if it is not physically attached to it, although receiving funding from the local government might negate that issue to some extent. Second, there is an important perception issue. The most successful downtown groups tend to have a strong entrepreneurial spirit and need to be viewed in that light in order to gain widespread support. Most downtown businesses and property owners are uninterested in supporting "just another government program." Downtown organizations based in municipal buildings are often viewed, rightly or wrongly, as being regulatory and bureaucratic.

Despite those considerations, it is still critical that the downtown group have a strong and positive working relationship with the local government, including its financial support. At the same time, however, many downtown organizations attempt to maintain an arm's-length distance in the eyes of the public. In fact, Virginia's statewide Main Street organization has in recent years discouraged its local programs from locating in municipal offices. In response, the Franklin, Virginia, program, like many others, relocated from city hall. Franklin's Main Street manager believes it was generally a good idea and has seen no measurable changes in his positive working relationship with the city.

Community development corporations. Community Development in the 1990s describes CDCs as

> self-help organizations, governed by residents, businesspeople, and other leaders of the communities they serve. They plan improvements to solve local problems, building on neighborhood assets. The number of CDCs has grown steadily over the past 20 years, and CDCs are now located in every large and medium-sized city in the country. (Walker and Weinheimer 1998, 2)

Although CDCs are best known for their work in creating affordable housing for low-income people, many are also involved in commercial, office, and industrial development. CDCs are not typically known for sponsoring master plans for entire downtowns, although they are sometimes involved in planning for specific low-income areas within downtowns. Often armed with private foundation and federal Community Development Block Grant (CDBG) funding, their role in downtown planning tends to be more significant on the implementation end of the project, particularly with respect to urban housing development. Regardless, because of their potential to be important players in the downtown's future, CDCs should be involved early and directly in the downtown planning process.

Organizational Composition

The four main components of a downtown organization include the governing board, the staff, committees, and volunteers. Any downtown plan that addresses the issue of organization should attempt to strike the right balance between those four elements as a vital step in creating and sustaining an effective downtown organization. Also, in those cases in which a downtown organization already exists and the plan addresses ways to enhance it, the planners must tread lightly, particularly if the organization is also the plan sponsor.

Governing board. The board provides the policy-making leadership at the very top of the organization's hierarchy. It can range in size from as small as three members to as large as 30 or more, although boards having between approximately five and 12 members seem to be most manageable and work most effectively. The number and qualifications for board members should be stipulated in the organization's establishing legislation or bylaws, but they typically include downtown stakeholders representing property owners, business owners, residents, and institutions. Whether stipulated in writing or not, it is useful to include representatives of financial institutions, major industries, and others who can help bring funding to the organization and its efforts. A small number of nonvoting, ex officio board members are also common. They are typically representatives of local and regional

Figure 5-1. Boards that lead downtown organizations can range from as small as three members to as large as 30 members, but boards of between five and 12 members tend to be the most manageable and effective. Source: The Walker Collaborative / Betsy Kane

governments, such as the city planning director and economic development authority director.

Depending on the size and qualifications of the staff, certain professions can add tremendously to the board's depth of expertise and ability to function, including attorneys, accountants, marketing professionals, and real estate brokers. Within the board, there should also be officers responsible for specific duties, including a chairperson, vice chairperson, treasurer, and secretary.

Some downtown organizations have experimented with their board composition over time and allowed it to evolve as it gains experience. In the early days of the Eureka, California, Main Street Program, the 11-member board was heavily represented by the heads of communitywide entities, including the executive directors of the regional economic development center, the convention and visitors center, and a local arts center, as well as a representative of the city's redevelopment agency. Given that these individuals would not normally be considered legitimate downtown stakeholders, they would serve as ex officio members for most downtown organizations. Not surprisingly, over time, Eureka's program recognized that more direct stakeholders needed representation, so the board composition has since evolved to include more downtown property owners and merchants.

Staffing. The smallest downtown organizations either have no staff or merely a part-time project manager, while larger entities serving large downtowns might have a dozen staff members or more. Key determinants of staff size are obviously the size of the community and the financial resources available. The majority of truly successful downtown groups have, at a bare minimum, at least one full-time manager supported by one or two staff members. The manager is responsible for the day-to-day operations of the organization and answers directly to the board, while the supporting staff members answer to the manager.

Because of the wide range of activities related to downtown revitalization, the manager needs to be versatile in all relevant areas—a jack of all trades. In the case of the smallest downtown groups, the managers tend to fall into one of two general categories: (1) young and relatively inexperienced professionals, usually from outside of the community, with a college degree in a field such as urban planning, economics, marketing, business, or historic preservation; or (2) older and more seasoned professionals who grew up in the community and have no specific training for the job but who are well connected through their previous experience with a downtown business, chamber of commerce, or local government.

Obvious exceptions to this rule exist. In communities with larger and more established downtown programs and correspondingly larger salaries, the managers are often downtown redevelopment professionals who are climbing the ladder toward larger downtowns with higher-profile and higher-paying positions. Consequently, their life span at any one particular job is often limited to only a few years until they move on toward their personal professional goal. Furthermore, the highly political nature of the job and the pressure to perform often results in high turnover rates. There is no model résumé for success, as the effectiveness of the manager will depend much upon personality, determination, resourcefulness, and energy level. If any particular characteristics can be said to be essential to the job, they are strong organizational skills, good marketing instincts, and political savvy.

Committees. Committees are created by the board and serve at its pleasure. Some are standing committees that exist on an ongoing basis and meet regularly, while others are ad hoc committees that function only as needed to address a particular issue. Downtown organizations affiliated with the National Main Street program typically have at least four standing committees consistent with the Main Street four-point approach: organization, design, economic restructuring, and promotion.

For some organizations, committees and subcommittees are viewed as a subunit of the board and are supported by the staff. In other organizations, they function more as a supplement and support system for the staff. A word of warning: committees, regardless of what model they fit, can generate a great deal of work for staff. As an example, the Chippewa Falls, Wisconsin, Main Street program uses approximately 300 volunteers serving on nine standing committees and several additional ad hoc committees. Given the numerous awards and national recognition that Chippewa Falls's downtown program has received over the years, it is difficult to argue its high level of achievement. Perhaps the numerous individuals having a strong sense of ownership in downtown Chippewa Falls are a factor in their success. Regardless, maintaining such a large number of committees and subcommittees is certainly not recommended for every downtown because of the tremendous workload it can cause for staff.

Volunteers. Downtown organizations vary greatly with respect to the number of volunteers they use in their programs. As noted, Chippewa

Falls, a community of only 13,000, enjoys the efforts of approximately 300 volunteers. At more than 2 percent of the population, that is an unusual level of support. Similarly, Sigourney, Iowa, a town of only 2,200, has documented more than 35,000 hours of volunteer work since Sigourney Main Street's inception in 1990. On the other end of the spectrum, many downtown entities, including those of some of the largest downtowns, use very few volunteers. Clearly, volunteers are a tremendous asset as both free labor and active promoters of the cause. The main determinants of the practicability of using volunteers are the ability of the staff to manage them, the specific activities of the downtown organization, and whether those activities lend themselves to the use of volunteers.

PUBLIC POLICY

Given the ever-changing nature of public policy, it is futile to inventory all of the current public policies that might relate to the contents and implementation of a downtown master plan. Instead, it is more useful to illustrate how public policy can be used to forge and implement downtown plans and to highlight specific examples at the federal, state, and local levels of government. Public funding sources are covered separately following this section on policy.

Federal and State Policy

Among the federal and state policies that have the greatest impact on downtowns are those related to historic resources, transportation, the location of governmental facilities, and cultural programs.

Historic resources. Federal policies protecting historic resources have existed since the adoption of the National Historic Preservation Act in 1966, and those protections are not likely to be eliminated anytime in the foreseeable future. In short, properties listed on, or deemed eligible for, the National Register of Historic Places receive special treatment when federally funded or licensed projects might negatively affect those historic resources. Many states have also adopted State Register programs for historic resources that are modeled after the federal program. While there are clearly no guarantees the resources in question will ultimately be saved, a review process known as Section 106 Review must examine potential impacts and consider alternatives and mitigating actions. The review process is typically carried out by State Historic Preservation Officers (SHPOs) on behalf of the federal Advisory Council on Historic Preservation. Examples of downtown projects potentially affecting historic resources that would trigger the federal Section 106 Review process include federally funded transportation improvements, riverfront development requiring an Army Corps of Engineers permit, and demolitions to clear land for the development of federally funded buildings, including public housing. Those supportive of historic preservation would obviously view these federal protections in a positive light, although downtown redevelopment professionals will also recognize the potential hindrances they pose. The other advantage of National Register designation is the eligibility it extends to individual properties for the federal 20 percent investment tax credit for qualified historic rehabilitations. That incentive can often be the difference between a financially viable historic building rehabilitation and one that is not. Whether it is ultimately determined that National Register district designation would be advantageous or detrimental for a particular downtown, a recommendation one way or the other should be included in its associated downtown plan.

Transportation. The most common transportation scenario affecting downtowns is the proposed widening of a state-designated road traversing a downtown. Many state departments of transportation (DOTs) have made great strides in recent years in becoming more sensitive to the design needs of urban streets, rather than focusing solely on the efficient movement of traffic. While street standards will vary from state to state, as will the attitudes of DOTs, the most important virtue for addressing the issue is patience. Downtown organizations and their planners must first gain a solid understanding of the design standards and practices being followed by their particular DOT, and they must then persistently negotiate on behalf of their downtown to ensure that the subject street is not transformed into a barrier that splits downtown in half. When such issues arise, the services of a qualified traffic engineer should be secured in order to communicate with the DOT on a technical level and to lobby on behalf of the downtown. Having an adopted downtown plan that specifically addresses the street's preferred design also helps build the case for context-sensitive street design, allowing downtown advocates to be proactive rather than reactive. Moreover, downtown plans do not always have to be limited to merely a defensive mechanism when dealing with DOTs. Rather than simply reacting to proposed transportation changes, opportunities to change streets for the benefit of a downtown, such as traffic calming measures, should be identified and pursued vigorously.

Governmental facilities. Town halls, post offices, and courthouses are important to the economic well-being of downtowns because they generate downtown employees and visitors. Public buildings also hold a symbolic significance for most downtowns, underscoring the fact that the downtown, as a civic hub, is the most important place in the community. Downtown proponents need to be aware of all existing policies that encourage federal and state governments to keep their facilities downtown. In fact, Executive Order 13006 requires all federal agencies to "utilize and maintain, wherever operationally appropriate and economically prudent, historic properties and districts, especially those located in our central business districts." The two key federal entities involved with implementation of this policy are the General Services Administration and the Advisory Council on Historic Preservation.

When the main post office in New Bern, North Carolina, made plans in the early 1990s to relocate outside of the downtown, Swiss Bear Downtown Development Corporation, the Main Street program, lobbied the U.S. Postal Service to hold a public meeting to obtain community input. Following an outpouring of support for the post office to remain downtown, the postal service compromised by placing a branch post office in an office building restored in the mid-1980s. The former post office building has since landed a federal court as its key tenant, another important activity-generating use.

The Franklin, Tennessee, downtown group faced a similar challenge during the early 1990s when it was proposed that its 1924 downtown post office be vacated for a new suburban facility. The Downtown Franklin Association quickly sprung into action and collected more than 9,000 signatures on a petition to keep the facility downtown. It also gained the support of the state's U.S. senators and managed to get the post office building listed on the National Trust's Eleven Most Endangered Places list. Although the proposed suburban post office was still built, the downtown post office was allowed to continue its service, and today it experiences brisk business as an important anchor for downtown Franklin. The National Trust now lists the post office as "saved."

Cultural programs. In order to remain relevant, downtowns should serve as the primary cultural centers for their communities. Fortunately, many federal and state programs encourage cultural programs for the public. At the federal level, the National Endowment for the Arts (NEA) and the National Endowment for the Humanities (NEH) fund

Figure 5-2. The main interpretive center of Rivers Park in Troy, New York, is housed in the ground floor of the historic building at left. This riverfront facility generates substantial foot traffic for nearby businesses. As a result, Troy's 1993 downtown riverfront plan advocated the programmatic expansion of the facility. Source: The Walker Collaborative

various cultural programs, many of which can benefit downtowns by making them more vibrant and vital places. Although some states are more progressive than others in this regard, many, such as New York and Maryland, fund such programs. A New York State Parks program, the "Heritage Area System" (http://nysparks.state.ny.us/heritage/herit_area.asp), works with local entities to establish downtown parks and museums that interpret local history and sponsor cultural activities, such as educational classes and special events. Likewise, the Maryland Department of Business and Economic Development designates Arts and Entertainment Districts for meritorious communities seeking to establish or expand such districts. As an example, in 2003 the state appointed the Downtown Frederick Partnership (DFP) along with the Frederick Arts Council as comanaging entities for its A & E district, making it responsible for promoting tax credits and other incentives to attract and retain artists and art-related businesses within the district. DFP's First Saturdays have been successful in encouraging nearly three-quarters of the downtown's retail and dining businesses to stay open at night, and many have reported sales exceeding peak holiday figures (Dono and Glisson 2005). To the extent that a downtown plan includes recommendations for cultural programs, as well as an implementation section, federal and state programs that support such activities should be considered.

Local Policy

Public policies enacted by local governments have been used to shape downtowns for centuries. Most of today's Americans who flock to Europe by the thousands each year to enjoy the beauty of medieval towns and villages are completely oblivious to the fact that many of these picturesque places evolved according to a set of rigid governmental standards. Likewise, communities established in the New World by Spain during the sixteenth century slavishly followed the Law of the Indies with respect to the most fundamental considerations of how they were laid out. And after the Great Fire of 1666, London took regulation to a new level by not only dictating construction materials but even stipulating that two-story buildings be located on "bylanes," four-story buildings be located on "high and principal streets," and so forth (Kostof 1992, 200).

Today, local policies have the greatest impact on a downtown. Fortunately, they are also the easiest to change if that needs to happen. Numerous types of local policies directly effect downtowns, including

Figure 5-3. Some downtowns have found that a totally unrestrained real estate market will result in the domination of ground-floor uses that can kill the vitality of urban streets. In order to encourage more retail and dining, Blacksburg, Virginia, adopted zoning regulations severely limiting the amount of ground-floor office space and residences in its downtown. Source: The Walker Collaborative / Land Planning & Design Associates

land-use zoning, design review districts, sign standards, building codes, and parking requirements, to name a few. A review of their public policy considerations follows.

Zoning. As already emphasized, successful downtowns play host to a rich mixture of physically integrated land uses, including retail, services, housing, offices, institutional, and sometimes industrial uses. Although the existing zoning of most downtowns allows such a mix, some do not. Some zoning ordinances, for example, limit or prohibit housing within their downtowns. When a downtown strategy was prepared for Pleasant Grove, Utah, in 2006, the consultant team discovered the city prohibited more than two residential units per building. Consequently, loosening up that zoning provision became a key policy recommendation.

Another important downtown zoning issue relates to parking. Some ordinances treat parking as a distinct land-use classification, rather than as an ancillary use associated with a primary use. This approach to zoning can encourage the demolition of buildings, including historic buildings worthy of preservation, for the development of parking facilities not directly associated with any particular building. Specific uses, even if accompanied by stringent design standards, can also inherently conflict with a downtown. For instance, automobile dealerships that result in parking lots fronting onto downtown streets will negatively affect both the aesthetics and pedestrian vitality of an urban streetscape.

While most communities refrain from going so far as to regulate which specific land uses may occur on which floors of a building, some have found that too many ground-floor offices have transformed their downtowns into virtual office parks. Pinehurst, North Carolina, for example, has such a predominance of offices on the ground level of its historic downtown that it eventually decided to adopt provisions substantially limiting them beyond those already grandfathered in. In addition to prohibiting medical and dental offices altogether and limiting offices to those accessory to the principal building, the village commercial zoning regulations stipulate that "no office shall be located on the ground floor unless the ground floor of the principal building is occupied by at least 50 percent retail uses in frontage and area." The ordinance is currently under review. The village government is considering making the regulations stricter to limit even more the number of ground-level offices downtown.

These are but a few of the many zoning hurdles that can stand in the way of a good downtown plan. Not only must the plan identify these types of roadblocks and recommend how they be treated, but it should also proactively recognize new zoning opportunities to revitalize the downtown, such as incentives for redevelopment.

Design standards and form-based zoning. Even though most communities permit a broad range of land uses in their downtowns, the development or bulk standards for downtown zoning districts are frequently at odds with the historic urban context. In particular, zoning dating from the 1950s, 1960s, and 1970s often stipulates suburban design characteristics, such as allowing or requiring excessive front building setbacks, parking lots fronting onto streets, and vehicular access points at streets rather than rear alleys. In fact, if a particular downtown was to completely redevelop in accordance with such standards, it would be wholly replaced by a suburban shopping center. Although this undesirable scenario is rare in actual practice, the negative consequences of such zoning are indeed apparent on the edges of many downtowns in which the original urban fabric has been chipped away by suburban-style strip commercial development, which now serves as an ominous gateway to the downtown.

Not all existing zoning challenges are so thorough and comprehensive as to require a complete rewrite of a downtown's development standards. When the New Iberia, Louisiana, Main Street program made a push in 2000 to encourage the conversion of upper-floor vacant space into residences, it soon encountered a major obstacle: a city ordinance prohibiting the construction of anything over a public sidewalk, including balconies. In light of the importance of balconies to downtown New Iberia, both as a trademark of its vernacular architecture and as a vital residential amenity, a "balcony ordinance" was quickly adopted to permit them in the downtown area. Since the new ordinance's adoption, several upper-floor rehabilitations with balconies have been completed, and more are planned (Dono and Glisson 2005, 9).

While a quick fix of development standards worked for downtown New Iberia, the design standard deficiencies for many downtowns are so extensive that such an approach would yield an unworkable patchwork of regulations. Without question, a downtown planning process is the best opportunity to rethink existing development standards and to suggest wholesale change.

Within the context of downtown plans, design standards are typically included in the form of general principles, as opposed to a level of detail that can be implemented as public policy. Although the preparation of detailed design standards is commonly a separate and subsequent project intended to implement the downtown plan, there are exceptions. Depending upon the local jurisdiction's enabling legislation, some communities can use general design principals contained in a plan as the basis of a design review process enacted through historic zoning or some other special design review district. Another option is for more detailed design standards to be prepared as part of the overall downtown planning process when sufficient project funding is available. When Northport, Alabama, commissioned a downtown and riverfront master plan in 2007, the scope of services included the complete rewriting of existing zoning, as well as drafting detailed design standards. The plan, zoning, and design standards have since been completed and formally adopted. Regardless of their specific regulatory context, urban and architectural design guidelines for downtowns should address the following types of issues:

Figure 5-4. This corner infill building illustrates how some key urban design standards can be met yet still yield unsatisfactory results because others are missed. This structure would comply with the design standards of many communities with respect to building setback, overall height, roof form, exterior materials, and orientation of windows. However, it also underscores the need for standards to address issues such as a minimum ground-floor heights, canopy design, minimum storefront glazing ratios, and window designs. Source: The Walker Collaborative

- Block size and configuration
- Lot size and orientation to the street
- Building setbacks and massing
- Overall building height and ground floor height
- Facade design: rhythm and orientation of openings, balconies, canopies, and detailing
- Canopy design
- Roof forms
- Building materials
- Parking lot location and design
- Streetscapes: on-street parking, sidewalks, landscaping, lighting, street furnishings
- Signage

Well-written standards will distinguish between existing older buildings and new infill development. If applied to a locally designated or National Register historic district, standards should be consistent with the federal standards and guidelines, with a heavy emphasis on maintenance and historically accurate restoration, in order to ensure that high-quality preservation results and to meet the requirements for historic rehabilitation projects attempting to secure the federal investment tax credit. With respect to new development, infill standards should attempt to reinforce the general urban design characteristics of the downtown, such as building heights, front setbacks, massing, roof forms, and materials. In most cases, however, they should stop short of requiring facsimiles of historic buildings and instead should seek general compatibility without deceiving the public regarding their age.

When developing design standards, the manner in which they will be implemented is an important determinant for how they are drafted. In communities with only marginal political support for design standards, the prudent approach might be to make them voluntary and encourage their adherence through incentives such as facade restoration grants, low-interest loans, or property tax breaks. Even when design guidelines are mandated, two extreme approaches can be used to implement them, with many variations in between. At one end of the spectrum is the community that uses relatively broad design principles or guidelines providing a fair amount of flexibility and discretion for a design review body to interpret through a design review process. When these review bodies use design experts, they can often arrive at design solutions that truly are win-wins for the downtown and the applicants. On the other hand, some communities are looking for very prescriptive standards that can be implemented by a single staff person. In such instances, the approval is often quicker than going through a design review process, but the black-and-white nature of the standards frequently preclude the optimal design solution. An alternative approach is to require a design review process for all but the most minor applications, with clear standards being applied by a staff person for less significant applications, such as those for certain types of signs.

Another important subject the downtown plan should address is the legal context for implementing design standards. The most common approach over the past few decades has been to adopt a special "design overlay district" applied to a downtown without affecting the underlying "base zoning." This approach does not affect permitted land uses or densities of the base zoning, but the design standards of the overlay district supersede the bulk standards of the base zoning district. Decisions about the design aspects of a development application are made by the overlay zone's affiliated design review body in accordance with the adopted design standards. In some communities, the design review body's decisions are mandatory, and in some cases only advisory, as in the case of Blacksburg, Virginia. In order

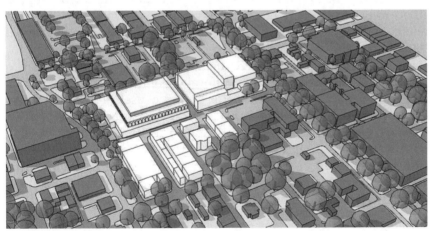

Figure 5-5. Downtown design standards focused less on historic preservation and more on new infill development often address only the most basic urban design considerations. When the greatest concern is to reinforce the urban and pedestrian nature of the downtown, key issues include building setbacks, height, massing, and facade glazing. Source: Russ Stephenson, AIA, CNU

to encourage more technically sound decisions and to avoid politics, making the design review body's decisions binding is preferable, a stipulation the downtown plan should recommend.

A more recent but growing tool now used to achieve the same end results as special overlay zoning is form-based zoning. Rather than relying on a cumbersome system of overlay zones and underlying base zones, form-based zones combine land-use and design standards, although more emphasis is placed on design than on land uses. The "green field" Traditional Neighborhood Development (TND) projects of the 1980s were the originators of form-based codes, but these codes are now being applied to downtowns. With an emphasis on design, they are firmly rooted in the new urbanism movement.

In 2003, Saratoga Springs, New York, adopted a form-based code after struggling for years to achieve compatible infill development in and near its downtown. According to Geoff Bornemann, former city planning director, "the key mandated items are that buildings must be close to the street, must occupy most of the frontage of their property, and must be two real stories but less than 70 feet high." Although some communities have made form-based zoning an option and tied it to incentives, such as fast-tracking approvals and density bonuses, Saratoga Springs's strong real estate market has not required such inducements. In the first two to three years after the town adopted its form-based zoning, 12 major developments worth $182 million and containing 850,000 square feet of building space were approved. Although some states lack enabling legislation to pave the way for form-based zoning, many have already adjusted their legislation to explicitly permit it, including California, Connecticut, Pennsylvania, and Wisconsin. Form-based zoning is being used in Mississippi to guide rebuilding along the hurricane-ravaged coast of the Gulf of Mexico (Langdon 2006, 29). With respect to its nationwide appeal, some communities will be reluctant to deviate so dramatically from their existing zoning structure, but form-based zoning is an implementation tool worthy of consideration. It is also likely to be the country's dominant downtown zoning tool in future decades.

Building codes. The content and application of local building codes can greatly influence the degree of successful building rehabilitation. Although most local governments adopt a nationally recognized set of standards, their rigid interpretation can make building rehabilitations cost-prohibitive or even impossible. Electing to take a more proactive approach to that dilemma, the Design Committee of Downtown

Partners in Burlington, Iowa, researched and drafted a conservation building code. It was adopted by Burlington to accommodate the sensitive rehabilitation of historic buildings without subjecting them to modern requirements that might preclude their future reuse. The same group then drafted a dangerous-buildings ordinance, also adopted by Burlington, so as to ensure that demolition is a last resort for historic buildings. Many other communities across the country are adopting similar building codes, and many have used New Jersey's pioneering historic building code as a model.

Not all policy approaches to encourage the rehabilitation of older buildings entail code amendments. In 1986, the metropolitan government of Nashville, Tennessee, established the Metro Rehab Committee. Comprising four individuals representing the code administration department and the fire marshal's office, its objective is to interpret existing building codes. According to an article in *The Tennesseean*, while the adoption of new codes was considered prior to the committee's creation, this special review body was chosen as the most effective tool. The hundreds of upper-floor residential units carved out of downtown Nashville's historic building stock in recent years stand as testimony to the committee's value. In other communities, particularly smaller ones, new codes or a special committee have not been the remedy of choice. Instead, simply making a concerted effort to accommodate historic buildings via an informal mandate from the community's top elected officials, known otherwise as a change of attitude, has worked in many towns across America.

An important step in preparing any downtown plan is to talk firsthand with developers who are active in local building rehabilitation projects. Depending upon the results of those discussions, recommendations should then be made to either revise the existing building codes as needed or to administer them in a manner sympathetic toward the reuse of historic buildings. When making the case for building code solutions, it must be stressed that historic buildings are critical to giving the downtown its unique character and, consequently, its competitive edge with other mixed use areas. For audiences persuaded more by environmental sustainability ideals, a frequently referenced quote of preservationists is "the greenest building is the one that's already built."

Parking requirements. Issues related to parking requirements can vary widely depending upon whether the topic is on-site or on-street parking. Recognizing the unique challenges that downtowns face with on-site parking, many communities leave the issue up to market forces.

In other words, if a new shop, office, or housing development wants to succeed, its operators will figure out a solution to meeting parking demands. On the other hand, some outdated ordinances require suburban-type parking standards citywide without consideration for the shared parking opportunities that high density, mixed use areas can create. Such requirements are typically based upon the provision of one parking space per specific amount of building square footage by use. Given their potential for discouraging building rehabilitations and new development, such policies must be amended for the economic survival of the downtown.

On-street parking regulations are an entirely different matter because on-street parking is intended to serve short-term rather than long-term parkers. (See Chapter 3.) The need for regulation comes into play when long-term parkers tie up spaces intended for short-term parkers. Regardless of what approach to regulating parking a downtown plan may advocate, it can be a hotly contested issue, and genuine attention should be paid to the opinions and concerns of those stakeholders most directly affected.

Other local policy considerations. Most downtown plans intentionally avoid taking on the issue of communitywide land-use planning and zoning, such as the strategy of reducing the amount of commercial and mixed use zoning outside of the downtown in an attempt to redirect

Public Policy's Unintended Consequences

Natchez, Mississippi, has an international reputation for its collection of antebellum mansions. Thousands of people travel annually to Natchez to tour the homes and to visit the historic downtown and the Mississippi riverfront known as Under the Hill. The combination of a strong tourism market and numerous historic buildings has resulted in a proliferation of bed and breakfast establishments. Most of the B&Bs have been established in the historic residential areas

surrounding the downtown and, not surprisingly, conflicts between residents and B&B establishments have surfaced from time to time.

Consequently, in 1992 the city decided to be proactive and crafted a special ordinance that would allow B&Bs to prosper, but in limited numbers and in harmony with surrounding residential areas. A key requirement of the ordinance was to permit only one B&B per block face on a first-come first-served basis. At the time of the

Figure 5-6. Bed and breakfasts in Natchez, Mississippi, such as the Wensel House, are regulated by a special ordinance adopted by the city in 1992. Like so many pioneering regulations that address issues previously overlooked, the city's initial B&B ordinance had to be tweaked after its implementation revealed loopholes resulting in unintended consequences. Source: Mary W. Miller

ordinance's adoption, most people on both sides of the issue praised it as a reasonable compromise that balanced the interests of all parties. However, over time, an unintended consequence of the ordinance began to surface. To prevent neighbors on the same block face from establishing a B&B that might become a nuisance, some property owners appeared before the Board of Zoning Appeals to gain their own B&B approval first, although they had no intention of actually running a B&B operation. Once this trend became evident, the city modified the ordinance to require B&B applicants to meet minimum operational

standards to ensure they are serious about their enterprise, including advertising the B&B in one or more tourism publications.

Many regulatory tools that are pioneering and not based upon a model borrowed from another city will require testing and tweaking during their first year or two in order to arrive at a solid regulation that can ultimately withstand the test of time. Rather than viewing the need for subsequent amendments as an initial public policy blunder, such revisions should be anticipated and seen as a normal exercise in the adoption of new regulations.

future growth downtown. One exception is High Point, North Carolina, which employed a citywide visioning process and crafted a vision statement for the overall community's future growth as a lead-in to their Core City master plan. Although some downtowns are best served by focusing primarily on their immediate study area, many could greatly benefit from policy changes outside of the downtown. In addition to land-use and zoning issues, communitywide policies related to transportation and public facilities can also directly affect the downtown. Sadly, many public utilities have absolutely no involvement with their community's long-range planning process, which often results in a blueprint for sprawl. Such autonomy can be a detriment to the future of the community in general and the downtown in particular.

Undoubtedly, all downtown plans should include a review of the existing local policies and suggest any revisions necessary to accommodate the plan's recommendations. It is imperative that local governments then formally adopt the plans and follow through with the suggested amendments in order for the downtown plan to be fully realized. As Susan Moffat-Thomas, director of the New Bern, North Carolina, downtown development organization, notes, "The city has to embrace the downtown plan and incorporate it into its policies in order for it to mean anything."

FUNDING AND FINANCING

Like so many things in life, successful downtown reclamation is difficult to achieve without money. A certain level of public-sector funding is always necessary, particularly during the early stages of revitalization. However, experience has shown that, for every dollar of public funding invested in most downtown enhancement efforts, approximately $10 to $15 of private-sector funding has accompanied it (Leinberger 2005, 4).

In current public policy, funding sources are fluid and subject to change, particularly public-sector sources. Therefore, the focus here is on funding approaches, rather than specific funding sources, and on providing examples of how these approaches have been used by various downtowns. The two general categories of funding for downtown programs are those for the ongoing operations of a downtown organization and those for individual redevelopment projects. Any downtown plan that addresses funding should address both types. An argument can be made that a third important funding category also exists for all downtowns—the operating funding for the many businesses and institutions that the downtown comprises, although that topic is clearly beyond the scope of most downtown plans.

Operational Funding

Most downtown organizations are faced with cobbling together an assortment of funding sources in order to stay afloat. The most rudimentary source is membership dues. Although dues alone rarely generate enough money to keep the doors open, they can certainly help if the membership base is substantial. One community that has gone beyond the typical approaches to expanding membership is Denton, Texas. Rather than focus solely on those who would be considered direct downtown stakeholders, such as downtown property owners and merchants, Denton's downtown organization looks beyond downtown. Through aggressive membership drives, Main Street Denton has now reached a point at which approximately 50 percent of its members are not among those considered to be traditional downtown stakeholders but instead are citizens of the community at large. An even more novel approach to membership generation is applied one state over. In Oklahoma, Durant Main Street (DMS) offers group health insurance to its members. By organizing its members as a group, the DMS Economic Restructuring Committee was able to negotiate favorable health insurance rates for member businesses and their employees (VanBellingham 2006, 3). This major coup has made membership in DMS considerably more attractive.

In addition to membership dues, local governments are often a key source of operational funding. Like many other states, Virginia's Main Street program requires the local governments of its Main Street communities to help fund the program for a minimum of three years. Most of those local governments recognize the value of the programs and continue to help fund them beyond that time frame. While not all municipalities elect to be so generous, even relatively small amounts of funding are important. For instance, the annual $30,000 that the city of Albany, Oregon, gives the Albany Downtown Association represents $30,000 that will not have to be secured through more time-consuming means that distract from the organization's mission. It also conveys the city's support for the program.

The Chippewa Falls, Wisconsin, Main Street program offers one example of a diverse funding approach. Of the revenues that contribute toward their $140,000 annual budget, 33 percent comes from their Business Improvement District (BID) taxes, 32 percent is from private-sector contributions, 20 percent comes from special events and projects, and 15 percent is from an annual appropriation from the city. Because of the program's tremendous success as a catalyst for downtown revitalization, in which every dollar invested in their operations has translated into $18 invested in downtown redevelopment and businesses, it likes to refer to its private-sector contributions as "investments."

Downtown groups that lack a stable funding source often struggle to achieve measurable progress for their downtown because their staffs are forced to spend too much time trying to raise money for their own salaries. One of the most stable funding sources allowing downtown organizations to avoid this dilemma is a BID. As noted previously, BIDs are most commonly funded through an extra ad valorem property tax applied to all properties within the designated district. The parameters for establishing a BID differ from state to state, depending upon state enabling legislation. They are typically adopted by the local government following a referendum of the affected property owners.

Communities of all sizes and in all corners of the country have found BIDs to be an effective funding tool. New York City alone has more than 60 BIDs for the numerous commercial districts that make up that city. On the other end of the spectrum is Burlington, Iowa, a town of only 26,500. The many early successes of Burlington's downtown program were sufficient to give property owners the confidence necessary to approve the adoption of a downtown BID in 1996, and it has since reaped great benefits. Referred to in Iowa as a Self-Supporting Municipal Improvement District, it raises approximately $64,000 annually through an additional 3 percent property tax—enough to give Downtown Partners a stable operating source so it can focus its attention on important projects to enhance downtown Burlington.

By the early 1980s, it had become clear that the downtown of Franklin, Virginia, was in need of some serious help in order to become the dynamic commercial district it was in the past. Consequently, a referendum was held and passed to establish a BID, referred to as a Special Taxing District in Virginia, to help fund Franklin's downtown organization. That funding source of approximately $45,000 annually, combined with an annual appropriation of $50,000 from the city as well as occasional special event fund-raisers, provided their downtown organization with the financial stability necessary to make downtown Franklin a strong success. In 1999, however, Franklin was hit by a severe flood that resulted in the downtown remaining essentially closed for an entire year. The special tax was halted shortly after

Voting to Tax Themselves

The downtown of Pensacola, Florida, had hit rock bottom by 1970, as evidenced by physical deterioration, empty ground-floor spaces, and a lack of pedestrians on the street. In response to this gloomy picture, the Pensacola Downtown Improvement Board was established through a referendum. The ad valorem property taxes to support the BID generated approximately $100,000 annually for the organization's small staff to engage in "brick and mortar" activities in collaboration with the city.

Although there were some victories along the way, including aesthetic improvements and the construction of a public parking garage, it had become clear by the mid-1980s that a one-dimensional strategy focused on streetscapes and parking facilities was insufficient to turn around downtown Pensacola. In response, a second referendum was held to determine whether the ad valorem tax would be doubled, with the understanding that the extra funds would be earmarked solely for marketing purposes. After much politicking by the organization's board members, the referendum passed overwhelmingly.

With the newfound funding in hand, a request for proposals (RFP) was issued to hire a marketing firm and a special marketing council was appointed by the board of directors. Given much free rein by the board, the marketing council, the hired marketing firm, and the staff formulated a creative and detailed marketing plan, with plenty of funds left over to actually implement much of it. Although downtown Pensacola will always have the unenviable task of competing with beautiful white-sand beaches for the attentions of both local residents and tourists, the more balanced approach to revitalization afforded by the expanded BID funding brought measurable improvements to it.

the flood in order to provide some temporary financial relief to the property owners, but it was reinstated in 2001 when it was clear that downtown was on its way to recovery. As at least partial evidence that the program continues to succeed, Franklin's downtown in 2008 had an occupancy level of approximately 82 percent.

When it comes to generating funds for downtown organizations, a tremendous amount of ideas are shared among communities, so most approaches have already been tested by someone. Cutting-edge funding strategies quickly become either experiments gone awry or widely used tools. However, one of the more creative examples of raising funds for downtown revitalization operational expenses is CityScape, the Main Street program for Cookeville, Tennessee. In 2005, it succeeded in getting state legislators to authorize, specifically for it, the right to hold a charitable raffle. Following requirements of the secretary of state's Charitable Gaming Division, CityScape sold 3,000 raffle tickets at $10 each. By awarding a single winner the $10,000 prize, it was able to keep the additional $20,000 for their organization's operating needs.

Project Funding

Once the challenge of keeping a downtown organization financially afloat has been met, the next task is to find funding for individual redevelopment projects. Project funding sources exist at a variety of government levels, and private sources can provide equity financing and loans.

Federal and state funding programs. Although subject to change with the shifting of political winds, several federal programs critical to the financial viability of countless downtown redevelopment projects exist. While dozens of programs may have a relevance to downtown planning and revitalization, the following programs are among the most significant:

- *Community Development Block Grants.* CDBG funds are available through the federal Department of Housing and Urban Development (HUD) for specific program categories, including community revitalization, scattered site housing, infrastructure, economic development, housing development, urgent needs, and capacity building. Entitlement cities that meet minimum population requirements are guaranteed funds each year based upon a specific formula, and those funds must benefit low- and moderate-income persons.
- *Historic Rehabilitation Investment Tax Credits.* These 20 percent federal income tax credits are given for the rehabilitation of National Register eligible buildings that are income producing and that follow federal preservation standards.
- *New Markets Tax Credits.* The New Markets Tax Credit (NMTC) Program permits taxpayers to receive a credit against federal income taxes for making qualified equity investments in designated Community Development Entities (CDEs). The qualified equity investment must, in turn, be used by the CDE to provide

investments for improvements targeted at low-income areas.

- *Low- and Moderate-income Housing Tax Credits*. This HUD program provides a federal income tax credit of approximately 70 percent of the eligible costs of a housing development, which are primarily the hard costs of rehabilitation or new construction. The tax credits are competitively allocated by the state, and they go toward housing available to those earning no more than 60 percent of the area median income (AMI).

Other important federal funding sources for downtown projects include the U.S. Department of Agriculture (USDA), the Economic Development Administration (EDA), and the Small Business Administration (SBA). Given that there are 50 states and each has numerous ever-changing programs, a succinct and current list of state programs is not possible. However, it is noteworthy that many state funding programs applicable to downtowns mirror their federal counterparts.

Financial packaging examples. The Ardmore, Oklahoma, Main Street Authority serves as one praiseworthy model for how to fund projects. To implement a $1.2 million, five-block streetscape redevelopment, the city provided 60 percent of the funds, and the property owners voted to tax themselves for the rest. The Main Street program then raised an additional $200,000 for streetscape furnishings through the sale of engraved bricks and commemorative plaques to be placed on the furnishings. To encourage private-sector projects, the Ardmore Main Street Authority adopted a grant program providing property owners up to $1,000 for qualified facade renovations and $100 for facade paint. For more substantial building rehabilitation projects, it organized a consortium of local banks to establish a $600,000 low-interest loan pool for qualified projects (National Main Street Center 1997, 21–22). Similarly, the Danville, Kentucky, downtown organization—the Heart of Danville—coordinated a $1 million low-interest loan program involving five local banks. Loans through this program were available for the qualified purchase of property, business inventory, and equipment, up until a few years ago. Interest rates were at 1 percent below prime (National Main Street Center 1997, 49). Currently, the city operates a "Central Alban Revitalization Area," which uses TIF funds to give property owners who can provide matching funds access to grants and low-interest funds. Likewise, California's Downtown Encinitas MainStreet Association (DEMA) grants successful applicants up to $2,000 for facade improvements, in addition to granting them up to $1,000 for the services of design professionals. To date, close to 100

Banking on Future Success

Tax increment financing (TIF) is a financial tool used by thousands of communities across the country to stimulate urban redevelopment. In brief, it allows infrastructure and related improvements associated with specific private-sector developments to be funded by future additional tax revenues generated by the improvements. A loan for such improvements is typically first secured, and the "incremental" tax revenues above the predevelopment levels are later used to pay off the loan. State enabling legislation sets the parameters for how TIF is used in each state, but it is generally sequenced as follows:

- A city government first designates the TIF district based upon specific criteria.
- A developer then applies for TIF support for a proposed development project within the TIF district.
- The projected increase in the property's postdevelopment assessed value is calculated.
- Bonds equivalent to the incremental increase in the property's tax-revenue-generating potential are issued as the basis of the TIF funding.
- TIF funds are made available to the developer for the project.
- The bonds issued for the TIF are paid off by the tax revenue

increment over the next several years.

While it varies from state to state, TIF can usually be applied to a variety of activities, including property acquisition, relocation of displaced residents, demolition for site preparation, and on-site improvements, such as utilities, lighting, streets, and similar work. TIF funds are typically backed by revenue bonds, in which case, if the development project should fail, the city's taxpayers will be responsible for paying them off. In some states, the TIF funds can be used to pay off qualified private loans from financial institutions rather than governmental bonds. Although most areas of a community fall under multiple taxing jurisdictions, such as the city, county, school district, and other entities, some of those taxing jurisdictions may not be subject to forgoing the tax revenue increase of a TIF program.

In Texas TIF districts are referred to as Tax Increment Reinvestment Zones (TIRZs). The Denton, Texas, 2003 downtown master plan acknowledges that it "depends largely on the TIRZ to develop funds for ongoing improvements. The TIRZ also creates an institutional downtown structure that is important to sustain downtown activities over time" (Fregonese Calthorpe Associates 2003, 43).

Most downtown plans are not so willing to go out on a limb with any single financing tool. Nevertheless, TIF is a powerful tool for funding downtown development projects without spending existing municipal funds or increasing the tax rates of property owners. Instead of spending existing municipal funds, it relies on future municipal funds. Likewise, instead of increasing the tax rate of property owners, it relies on future increased tax revenues raised through future increased property values and assessments. TIF is a valuable financing tool because it essentially allows development to pay for itself, and it is politically expedient because it requires no tax increases in order to fund the necessary improvements.

---

business and property owners have taken advantage of the program, and more than $84 million of improvements have occurred (Dono and Glisson 2004, 5).

Property tax abatements are another popular tool to encourage the private sector to rehabilitate historic buildings. In states where tax abatements are permitted, most programs have very specific requirements to qualify. They often mirror the federal investment tax credit for historic rehabilitation by requiring a minimum investment in the building rehabilitation costs and a specific set of design standards to ensure historic integrity. Denton, Texas, has established two optional tax-abatement programs. One is intended to encourage owners of historic buildings to get them designated as local landmarks in return for a tax reduction over a 15-year period when the property is taxed at only 50 percent of its assessed value. Although the owner is not required to make any property improvements, he or she must follow the city's design standards if improvements are made. The other abatement program is designed as an incentive to rehabilitate historic buildings. It provides a 10-year freeze on the preimprovement assessed value when an approved rehabilitation exceeds $20,000 or 25 percent of the property's assessed value, whichever is less. As a result of Denton's abatement programs, more than 100 historic buildings in the downtown have undergone some form of improvement.

One shining example of a funding redevelopment project in the Midwest is Sigourney, Iowa. Main Street Sigourney wanted to restore their beautiful 1883 fountain that had deteriorated into a state of complete disrepair. To fund the $30,000 project, they held ice cream socials, sold Christmas cookies, sold commemorative merchandise, sponsored a sandwich stand at the weekly farmers market, and raised thousands of dollars in donations from individuals, businesses, and organizations. It is that type of resourcefulness and teamwork that is so often needed to win major downtown victories.

Despite the countless successes nationwide, examples of failed public funding programs are numerous, and they can be equally instructive for other downtowns. A fiscal structure assessment for Newark, Ohio, revealed that, despite the intent of state laws, property tax abatements were being misdirected to low-income housing rather than toward leveraging economic development. The result of political connections among city council members and slumlords, this unfortunate example proves that funding tools are only as effective as the people charged with applying them.

PRIORITIES, ASSIGNMENTS, AND PHASING

The level of detail that can go into a downtown master plan depends primarily upon the amount of money and human resources available to create the plan. Regardless of the limitations in funding and manpower, plans having the highest odds of successful implementation generally address the priority level, responsible parties, and phasing sequence of their key recommendations.

Which Plan Recommendations Get Priority?

Almost any type of plan must acknowledge that sufficient funding may not be available for implementing every recommendation of the plan. Downtown plans, in particular, often include ideas many years and many dollars away. Therefore, it is beneficial to give priority to certain recommendations so that, even if very limited funds are available for implementation, wise decisions can be made on how they are expended.

Some ways of giving priority to plan recommendations have a better track record than others. One approach taken by some communities is to spread the funding around geographically in order to please multiple stakeholders. In practice, examples might include making random minor streetscape enhancements spread throughout the downtown or establishing a facade rehabilitation program that allows qualified property owners anywhere downtown to apply for funding. While this approach might score short-term political points among some of the downtown's stakeholders, the long-term benefits to the downtown may be less tangible. Relatively small physical enhancements dispersed over a broad area rarely have long-term positive impacts, and such approaches are more likely to be advocated by shortsighted politicians than by urban planners focused on the next 20 years.

On the other hand, many downtowns wisely choose to target a small area within the downtown that has the greatest existing strengths and future potential to build upon. This approach is founded upon the idea that if a downtown can create a one- or two-block area that features great design and extremely strong tenants, market forces will enable that good fortune to spread to adjacent areas. While exceptions exist, downtown revitalization successes generally tend to spread contiguously from block to block rather than leapfrogging from area to area. An analogy sometimes used to defend this strategy is that the first step to a healthy human body is a healthy heart. Also, no matter how planning recommendations are set geographically within the downtown, they should always be strongly tied to economic opportunities identified in the plan's market analysis.

Regardless of the overarching philosophy employed in giving priority to some plan recommendations, most plans will rank recommendations in two to five levels, such as high, moderate, and low priority. Any method of giving priority to recommendations needs to be accompanied by text to emphasize that the priorities are all relative to one another. For example, a recommendation to provide pedestrian crosswalks at a specific intersection might be deemed low priority in the grand scheme of the downtown plan, yet it may still be an important idea worthy of implementation at some point in time. Even with such qualifying language, the chance always exists that labels such as "low priority" will later be used to the advantage of those against the idea. Consequently, some plans deliberately avoid ranking recommendations. However, without stated priorities, decision making about the use of limited funds becomes difficult and arbitrary.

When priorities are set, it is important to keep in mind that, as portions of the plan are implemented and as circumstances change, the priorities will need to be reevaluated periodically and modified as necessary. In fact, priority rankings are one of the easiest and most appropriate aspects of a downtown plan to revise, and they can be done without compromising the recommendations themselves.

Assigning Responsibilities

Some plan recommendations will clearly be the responsibility of one specific group, while responsible parties for other aspects of plan implementation are less obvious, and even multiple parties may be needed to implement some plan recommendations. As a case in point, streetscape improvements are almost always the responsibility of the local government, while centralized retail management (CRM) is usually the responsibility of the downtown organization or a merchants association. Because most downtown plans also propose private-sector development, real estate developers, collectively, should not be left off the list for new office, housing and retail development.

Delegating the responsibility for carrying out the plan's many ideas should be approached delicately in order to not alienate a key player in the plan's implementation. One option is for the initial draft of this plan section (e.g., a section describing "implementation assignments" or "responsible parties") to be prepared either by a third party, such as a consultant who may or may not have prepared the plan, or jointly by all of the key stakeholders. Either approach will help avoid the perception, or reality, that one group is using the opportunity to delegate the workload to their advantage. Also, the assignment of responsibilities should be realistic with respect to the resources available. For example, a proposed streetscape redevelopment costing hundreds of thousands of dollars should not be assigned to a merchants association composed solely of volunteers and having no financial or legislative muscle.

Phasing of Plan Actions

Phasing of plan actions and giving priority to plan recommendations are related yet different processes. Instituting some recommendations might be considered to be a low priority, but because of their ease or low cost of implementation, they might be recommended as a "phase one" action. Public policy recommendations, such as zoning revisions, frequently fit this description. Conversely, a high-priority recommendation might be implemented later because the available funding or projected market strength needed for project viability will be insufficient until later. Below is a discussion of various types of plan recommendations and how they might be treated within a strategy for implementing the plan.

Low-hanging fruit. This term applies to plan recommendations that are relatively easy to implement with respect to costs, time, and effort. As noted above, public policy revisions, such as relaxing on-site downtown parking requirements, are an example of this. Although a few public policy tweaks here and there might be very attainable early in the implementation process, policy revisions, such as the creation of new zoning classifications and detailed design guidelines for a design review overlay district, are not typically considered low-hanging fruit because they can cost tens of thousands of dollars in consultant fees. Regardless, if several of these types of projects can be identified for early implementation, the costs of preparing a downtown master plan can be quickly justified.

Highly visible projects. Downtown projects that have a high degree of public visibility can be tremendously valuable in generating confidence, enthusiasm, and momentum for plan implementation. Most such projects are physical in nature, such as the restoration of a key downtown building, streetscape improvements, or the installation of public art. Some downtown plans feature a so-called quick-victory project designed for just such a purpose—to score quick points with the public early in the game. When specifically included within the downtown plan, the quick-victory project often includes more detail than other plan recommendations in order to facilitate successful implementation. As in the case of the low-hanging fruit projects, highly visible projects are often given priority and implemented soon after the plan is put in place. However, because such projects can also be costly, such as streetscape redevelopments, the timing may depend more on funding availability than any other factors.

Sequencing. Implementation of some downtown recommendations must occur before others. For example, it would undoubtedly be foolhardy to install a brand new streetscape only to follow it months later with the burying of overhead electrical lines within the street rights-of-way. Other sequencing issues are less obvious but equally as important. The timing of major marketing campaigns for downtowns warrants particular thought. Because most downtowns will always be somewhat works in progress, no ideal time exists to begin aggressive marketing, but it cannot be held off forever. In some cases, however, it is wise to save major marketing campaigns for the later stages of a downtown revitalization effort. This principle applies especially toward progress in landing strong tenants, as opposed to physical enhancements to the downtown. With respect to the market segment that has not traditionally visited downtown, the downtown has only one opportunity to make a first impression, so the curtains should not come up prematurely. Luring visitors to a downtown in which they are underwhelmed can do irreparable damage to future marketing efforts. Nevertheless, it must also be recognized that most downtown marketing strategies are multiphased, and "soft programming" is perfectly reasonable for some downtowns early in the revitalization process.

With respect to streetscape improvements, regardless of their overall sequencing in plan implementation, the seasonal timing can be critical. Given that more than 25 percent of the annual sales for many retailers occur during the two months prior to the December holidays, streetscape projects should avoid those months to the extent possible. If they do not, special arrangements must be made to retain access to store entrances, and extra marketing will be required to dispel the notion that downtown should be avoided because it is under construction. In short, both the timing and sequencing of plan actions must be carefully thought out before they are committed to the plan.

Conclusion

What Is Really Important?

There is an enormous need, a crying need, in our cities for new life, new struc-
ture, new institutions, new ways of doing things.
    —James W. Rouse, *Rebuilding America's Cities: Roads to Recovery*

The preceding pages have covered a great deal of material on the methods and concepts behind creating an effective downtown plan. Far
beyond this book, there is so much information available on various
aspects of downtown planning that it can be difficult to sift through
the multitude of ideas and home in on what is really important. Given
that most downtown advocates and professionals have a limited supply of staffing and funding to expend, it is critical to understand the
most central ideas for the successful creation and implementation of a
downtown plan. Consequently, the following ideas, above all others,
should be remembered.

ORGANIZATION

Without some entity in charge and held accountable, most struggling
downtowns would never improve unless sufficient market forces
smile fortuitously upon them. A downtown organization or municipal
government is usually necessary in order for a downtown plan to ever
be instigated, and that entity is typically the primary party responsible
for plan implementation. In fact, if confronted with the difficult choice
between funding a downtown revitalization organization and a downtown master plan, most downtowns would be better served by opting

for the organization. Organization is a key to the long-term success of downtowns, and the vast majority of effective downtown entities can eventually figure out a way to fund a downtown plan.

INFORMATION

One of the first and most critical steps of any downtown planning process is the gathering and analysis of information relating to the study area's many facets. Examples of information to be assembled and evaluated include demographic data, market statistics, traffic data, and information about the area's physical form, public policy, economic trends, and parking statistics. A plan cannot be truly valid unless the downtown's past trends, existing conditions, and future potential are fully understood. Although the collection and analysis of information can be overdone, sometimes even shortchanging the subsequent planning process, asking the right questions and finding the answers is a critical first step. Not only is research and analysis important for practical reasons, but without it the ultimate plan's credibility is at stake, thereby jeopardizing public support and its successful implementation.

PUBLIC INVOLVEMENT

Experience has shown that there is a direct correlation between the level of public involvement in planning projects and the odds for successful plan implementation. Planning processes that build public trust through their transparency and solicit public involvement in a meaningful way tend to generate strong support and a sense of ownership by downtown stakeholders. Creative ways of soliciting public involvement should be employed from the very outset of any downtown planning project. One of the most proven methods for doing so is the charrette process, which deputizes citizens as planners so they can have hands-on involvement in formulating the plan. Many other equally successful public input tools are available. The most capable supporters that surface during public involvement sessions should then be recruited as implementation committee members to help rally the troops for subsequent plan implementation. In addition to identifying leadership for plan implementation, the downtown's various stakeholder groups must also continue to be engaged. For example, to effectively implement the plan's economic strategies, the full involvement of downtown business owners will be critical. Similarly, to implement the physical planning recommendations, such as streetscape redevelopment, municipal officials must remain supportive and engaged.

A CLEAR VISION

Any effective downtown plan must paint a clear picture for the downtown's future, both figuratively and quite literally. At the broadest level, the plan document as a whole should convey a discernible picture of what the downtown can potentially become within the next 10 or 20 years. More specifically, the plan should include graphics that powerfully capture the public's imagination and generate enthusiasm. Most people have difficulty envisioning physical change, especially if it involves an area that they know well and for which they have long-held perceptions and biases. Consequently, high-quality graphics, such as artist renderings and computerized visual simulations, can be critical to creating the vision that provides a tangible target for the future, thereby helping to sell the plan.

RESPECT FOR THE PAST

Market surveys conducted to gauge consumer preferences for downtowns reveal time after time that "historic character" is the number-one attribute identified for most downtowns. Savvy developers understand the power of historic buildings to offer a unique backdrop for dining and entertainment venues. The highly successful National Main Street program uses historic preservation as the foundation of its nationwide downtown revitalization program for these very reasons. To take advantage of the competitive edge history has provided, every downtown plan should make a concerted effort to capitalize on the downtown's history and historic character, including measures to preserve and restore historic buildings. Including historic photographs of the downtown within the plan document can even go far in striking an emotional chord with the reader that might trigger a desire to help return the downtown to its former glory.

EVOLUTION

While downtowns should preserve what is important, they must evolve. Species that fail to adapt to changing conditions and evolve eventually become extinct, and the same can happen to downtowns. Many uses cannot be readily accommodated in historic buildings, so new development must occur. Such development might be on vacant or underused parcels within the downtown's core or on the downtown's periphery in a manner that allows the downtown to physically expand. New development should be thought of as an important marketing tool to attract tenants who are vital to the downtown's future. New buildings should be molded by design standards that reinforce the downtown's unique qualities. Nevertheless, it must also be remembered that Victorian-era commercial structures were radical new additions to their downtowns more than a century ago, and today's new contemporary structures might be equally treasured in another hundred years.

URBAN FORM

One of the most visible downfalls of many downtowns is the slow but steady erosion of their traditional urban form, particularly at the downtown's edges. Even the smallest downtowns historically have a distinctly urban form comprising buildings located close to the street, storefronts featuring generous amounts of window area, parking lots located behind buildings, and on-street parking. Buildings are located on pedestrian-scale blocks, generally not exceeding a length of approximately 500 feet, and those blocks are woven together by interconnected streets. This pattern has been diluted in many downtowns during the past 50 years by suburban-type development. Such inappropriate development divorces buildings from their streets by imposing front parking lots, introducing driveways that disrupt the urban streetscape, and yielding building facades with reflective glass, heavily tinted glass, or very little glass. One of the greatest victories a downtown plan can achieve is a clear set of development policies to ensure that the traditional urban form of a downtown is protected and reinforced by future development.

REASONS TO BE DOWNTOWN

No matter how functional or attractive a downtown may be with respect to its streetscapes, buildings, and public spaces, people will visit only if drawn there. Countless downtowns have spent considerable dollars on beautiful new streetscapes built of the highest quality materials, only to continue seeing them flanked by empty storefronts. Assuming that a vibrant and economically healthy downtown is the ultimate goal for most downtown plans, as opposed to simply an aesthetically pleasing one, a strong focus must be placed on the creation of destinations for both visitors and everyday users. This principle is based upon having not one or two major anchors to attract people but rather a multitude of uses and activities. Although achieving success can require a great deal of work, the formula for getting there is rather straightforward. It simply requires: (1) identifying the optimal mix of retail, offices, housing, institutions, and other uses; (2) developing a strategy for retaining, expanding, and recruiting uses consistent with that mix; and (3) putting that strategy into action. Planners and others must address numerous details in implementing this approach, including: the performance of a market analysis; the production of marketing materials; the adoption of incentives; the cultivation of property owners, developers, and leasing agents; and similar measures. The primary goal of attracting more people to the downtown—both temporary visitors and year-round inhabitants—should never be overlooked.

EXPERIENCE

Experience is important to downtown planning and implementation at multiple levels. First, the individuals responsible for formulating a downtown plan should be experienced in doing so. Numerous professionals with experience relevant to downtown planning in one form or another exist, and many spend substantial time observing and thinking about downtowns. Downtown stakeholders and planners run a great risk hiring someone to help create the plan who does not have actual experience in planning specific to the creation of a successful downtown. Moreover, the ideas proposed in a downtown plan should be tested by experience. Given that thousands of downtown master plans have been created and implemented across the country during the past few decades, it is rare when a downtown plan advocates some concept not already tried elsewhere. Reinventing the wheel is rarely advisable in any context, and particularly in downtown planning. Although such plans need to be tailored to a particular downtown, too many proven models are available for pioneering to be considered a reasonable path in downtown revitalization, especially with the cost of failure high and the necessary resources so precious.

INCREMENTAL AND COMPREHENSIVE
IMPLEMENTATION

Most downtowns in need of revitalization did not reach their current condition overnight. Typically, the downward spiraling of an urban area was prompted not by a single cause but rather by a complex assortment of factors that, in concert, conspired to bring the area down. Similarly, no quick fixes are available for the long-term revitalization of downtowns. Sustainable improvements to a downtown's physical condition and economic health will not come about because of a new stadium, convention center, or aquarium. In fact, many large projects fail to spread positive economic impacts beyond the distance of a few blocks, as evidenced by Baltimore's Inner Harbor Aquarium and New Orleans's Super Dome. Instead, downtowns that have made dramatic comebacks have typically done so through a series of small but steady steps—"trickle up" rather than "trickle down." Those incremental steps have also been comprehensive in nature. Rather than focusing on one or two strategies for the downtown, such as design or marketing, or only one sector of the downtown, such as retail, a holistic approach has been employed by the most successful downtowns.

PLAN FLEXIBILITY AND CONTINUITY

Just as a downtown is an ever-evolving organism, the downtown plan should be as well. In order to take advantage of new opportunities and to address unforeseen setbacks, every downtown plan should be implemented with flexibility and a clear understanding of what can and cannot be compromised. A well-written plan will draw a distinct line between the two. By providing a set of principles to guide planning, later decisions can adhere to those principles that cannot be

Figure 6-1. It is easy to get caught up in the details of a downtown plan during the implementation stage, but it is critical that the plan's stewards, from time to time, step back and reconsider what really matters. Source: The Walker Collaborative / Ben Johnson

compromised and make the plan consistent. For example, it may be acceptable that the plan's recommended location for a future parking garage is replaced by another location, so long as the garage is equally strategically located where parking is most needed and the design principles for parking structures are followed. Such principles might include limiting garage access to a secondary street, the provision of ground-floor retail space on the street frontage, and an exterior design with a contextual architectural character. Likewise, because of changing circumstances, a low-priority plan recommendation may need to

---

Even Smooth-running Downtowns
Need an Occasional Tune-up

Anyone who has ever spent time in Virginia's Old Town Alexandria is keenly aware that it is a shining model for downtowns across the country. Although it is located within the dynamic metropolitan area of Washington, D.C., and enjoys a population base of approximately 7.5 million people—considerable advantages over the typical small to midsize American downtown—it still offers inspiration. Among its many advantages are its strong historic character, high level of design and physical maintenance, rich range of retail and dining offerings, waterfront, and Metro transit station, all of which translate into some of the highest real estate values and rental rates in the country. However, even a place such as Old Town Alexandria, which appears to have it all, cannot afford to be content and simply maintain the status quo.

Prompted by a variety of factors, including the usurping of ground-floor retail space by offices, flooding at the lower end of King Street, and the anticipated negative impacts of the September 11, 2001, terrorism attacks on future tourism, Alexandria's community leaders grew concerned about the future economy and tax base of Old Town. Consequently, they commissioned a study to examine a multitude of issues to ensure the long-term viability of the area, regardless of its current market strength. The study addressed the following objectives:

• Retention of ground-floor retail uses despite increasing rents and pressure from office space demand
• Retention of local independent retailers in the face of national and regional chains that can afford higher rents

- Provision of better public access and activation of the waterfront, which is currently underused and obstructed by private uses
- Redevelopment and improvements for several blocks near the Metro transit station, including enhancing unattractive building facades and providing an identity for the area
- Unification of Old Town's two primary business associations
- Addressing the potential negative economic impacts of the events of September 11, 2001, on the "lower end" of King Street, which is most heavily dependent on tourism

- Dealing with parking issues stemming from ineffective parking management

To the casual observer, Old Town Alexandria has very few problems. Moreover, to the seasoned downtown revitalization specialist, its various needs may seem somewhat trivial relative to those of the typically struggling downtown. Nevertheless, no downtown is so successful that it can afford not to conduct ongoing planning, and Old Town Alexandria is a shining example of a historic mixed use district not simply resting on its laurels.

be upgraded to a moderate- or high-priority recommendation at some point, even though its substance remains intact. In addition to keeping plans flexible without compromising their spirit and intent, continuity is another important consideration. Downtown plans should never be allowed to gather dust. Instead, they should be routinely revisited and adjusted to meet new conditions and to remain relevant.

FINAL THOUGHTS

Many downtowns have used a master plan as a vehicle for successful revitalization, management, and sustainability. Downtown plans should never be prepared simply for the sake of planning. Instead, they should be commissioned only with implementation in mind. The planning process should use experienced professionals and extensive public input, and it should energize the community with a renewed interest in the downtown. The plan itself should be based on solid research, comprehensive in its approach to revitalization, carefully thought out, and supplemented by graphics that paint an inspiring picture of the future. As important, the plan should include an implementation strategy that provides a clear road map to success, should be interpreted flexibly without compromising what is important, and should be routinely revisited and adjusted as needed.

A plan is not a panacea for every downtown, and the work required to produce it will represent only a small fraction of the work required to actually resuscitate the downtown. Regardless, the adage "To fail to plan is to plan to fail" unquestionably contains at least a thread of truth. Many downtowns are blessed with an assortment of factors allowing them to achieve every measure of success. For such downtowns, the creation of a plan may not be their top priority, although even they will need a strategy to stay the course and perpetuate their prosperity. For those downtowns not so blessed, a solid master plan and the process that accompanies it can be the difference between success and failure. Simply put, no matter what state of affairs a downtown might be in, good or bad, a master plan is one of the most effective ways to optimize its long-term performance.

References

Alexander, Christopher. 1977. *A Pattern Language: Towns, Buildings, Construction.* New York: Oxford University Press.

Ball, Jennifer. 2002. *Street Vending: A Survey of Ideas and Lessons for Planners.* Planning Advisory Service Report no. 509. Chicago: American Planning Association.

Beemer, C. Britt, and Robert L. Shook. 1998. *Predatory Marketing.* New York: Broadway Books.

Bloom, Joshua. 2005. "Surveys." *MainStreet News* 217 (April).

Broberg, Brad. 2005. "If You Rebuild, Will They Come?" *Common Ground* (summer).

Bunnell, Gene. 2002. *Making Places Special: Stories of Real Places Made Better by Planning.* Chicago: APA Planners Press.

Dittmar, Hank, and Gloria Ohland, eds. 2004. *The New Transit Town: Best Practices in Transit-oriented Development.* Washington, D.C.: Island Press.

Dono, Andrea. 2006. "Market Analysis: Going It Alone." *Main Street News* 225 (January/February).

_____. 1997. "1997 Great American Main Street Awards." *Main Street News* 132 (May).

_____. 2004. "Patience & Persistence Pay Off." *Main Street News* 209 (August).

Dunphy, Robert T. 2006. "Developing Around Transit: Challenges for Cities and Suburbs." Washington, D.C.: Urban Land Institute. Available at www.uli.org/AM/Template.cfm?Section=Home&CONTENTID=54587&TEMPLATE=/CM/ContentDisplay.cfm.

Edwards, John D. 1994. *The Parking Handbook for Small Communities.* Washington, D.C.: Institute of Transportation Engineers.

Erlewine, Meredith, and Ellen Gerl, eds. 2004. *A Comprehensive Guide to Business Incubation.* 2d ed. (rev.). Athens, Ohio: National Business Incubation Association.

Florida, Richard. 2002. *The Rise of the Creative Class: And How It's Transforming Work, Leisure, Community and Everyday Life.* New York: Basic Books.

Fregonese Calthorpe Associates. 2003. *City of Denton Downtown Master Plan.* Portland, Ore.: FCA.

Glisson, Linda S. 1997. *Main Street Success Stories: How Community Leaders Have Used the Main Street Approach to Turn Downtowns Around.* Washington, D.C.: National Trust for Historic Preservation.

Grava, Sigurd. 2003. *Urban Transportation Systems: Choices for Communities.* New York: McGraw-Hill.

215

Hayhow, Sally. 1995. *A Comprehensive Guide to Business Incubation*. Athens, Ohio: National Business Incubation Association.

Jacobs, Jane. 1961. *The Death and Life of Great American Cities*. New York: Random House.

Johnson, Jan Thomas, and William McLeod. "1997 Great American Main Street Awards." *Main Street News* 132 (May).

Katz, Peter. 2004. "Form First: The New Urbanist Alternative to Conventional Zoning." *Planning* (November).

Kostof, Spiro. 1992. *The City Assembled: The Elements of Urban Form Through History*. New York: Bulfinch Press.

Kuntsler, James Howard. 1994. *The Geography of Nowhere: The Rise and Decline of America's Man-made Landscape*. New York: Free Press.

Ledebur, Larry, and William Barnes. 1993. *All in It Together: Cities, Suburbs, and Local Economic Regions*. Washington, D.C.: National League of Cities.

_____. 1992. *Metropolitan Disparities and Economic Growth: City Distress and the Need for a Federal Local Growth Package. Research Report on America's Cities*. Washington, D.C.: National League of Cities.

Leinberger, Christopher. 2005. "Turning Around Downtown: Twelve Steps to Revitalization." Washington, D.C.: Brookings Institution Metropolitan Policy Program (March).

Lennertz, Bill, and Aarin Lutzenheiser. 2006. *The Charrette Handbook*. Chicago: APA Planners Press.

Lynch, Kevin, and Gary Hack. 1984. *Site Planning*. 3d ed. Cambridge, Mass.: MIT Press.

Moore, Terry, Stuart Meck, and James Ebenhoh. 2006. *An Economic Development Toolbox*. Planning Advisory Service Report no. 541. Chicago: American Planning Association.

National Association of Realtors. 2005. "Revitalization Meets Smart Growth." *Common Ground* (summer). Available at www.realtor.org/smart_growth. nsf/docfiles/summer05revit.pdf/$FILE/summer05revit.pdf.

National Business Incubation Association. 1992. *Bricks and Mortar: How to Find and Design the Best Business Incubator Facilities*. Athens, Ohio: NBIA.

Otto, Betsy, Kathleen McCormick, and Michael Luccese. 2004. *Ecological Riverfront Design*. Planning Advisory Service Report nos. 518/519. Chicago: American Planning Association.

Parking Consultants Council. 2000. *The Dimensions of Parking*. 4th ed. Washington, D.C.: Urban Land Institute.

Poger, Elliot. 2005. "Diagonal Parking on Castro Likely to Have a Trial Run." *The Noe Valley Voice* (March).

Poynter, Chris. 2005. "Downtown Arenas Beat Suburbs in Race for Cash." *The Tennessean*, May 1, E:1.

Rypkema, Donovan. 2005. "Keeping It Local." Speech at Tennessee Preservation Trust Annual Conference, Chattanooga, Tenn., April 8.

_____. 2004. "The Emergence of Neighborhood Business Districts." *Main Street News* 209 (August).

_____. 1994. *The Economics of Historic Preservation: A Community Leader's Guide.* Washington, D.C.: National Trust for Historic Preservation.

Schmidtz, Adrienne, and Deborah L. Brett. 2001. *Real Estate Market Analysis.* Washington, D.C.: Urban Land Institute.

Smith, Thomas. 1988. *The Aesthetics of Parking.* Planning Advisory Service Report no. 411. Chicago: American Planning Association.

VanBellingham, Luke. 2006. "Member Mania!" *Main Street News* 225 (January/February).

Veregge, Nina. 1993. "Transformations of Spanish Urban Landscapes in the American Southwest, 1821–1900." *Journal of the Southwest* (winter).

Walker, Chris, and Mark Weinheimer. 1998. *Community Development in the 1990s.* Urban Institute Publication no. 7552. Washington, D.C.: Urban Institute.

Walljasper, Jay. 2005. "Shopkeepers Are Antidote to Big Boxes." Available at www .mlui.org/growthmanagement/fullarticle.asp?fileid=16780.

Zelinka, Al, and Susan Jackson Harden. 2005. *Placemaking on a Budget: Improving Small Towns, Neighborhoods, and Downtowns Without Spending a Lot of Money.* Planning Advisory Service Report no. 536. Chicago: American Planning Association.

Index

219

Discussion Questions

1. What caused the physical and economic deterioration that many downtowns experienced over the past several decades?
2. What are the benefits of having a healthy downtown?
3. Why is it important to have a strong public input process when creating a downtown plan?
4. Downtown planning requires a multidisciplinary approach. What specific disciplines are involved, and how are various downtown planning issues intertwined?
5. What are the advantages of conducting a market analysis as part of a downtown planning process? How might the findings be used to benefit the downtown?
6. Why is it important to preserve and rehabilitate a downtown's historic buildings? What advantages do historic buildings lend to a downtown?
7. Urban public spaces include streetscapes, parks, and plazas. What are the ingredients of a good public space?
8. Parking is often cited as a challenge for downtowns. What are some effective strategies for creating and managing parking, both on-street and off-street?
9. Centralized retail management (CRM) is an approach originally used by suburban shopping malls to manage and market a mall and its individual tenants. How can CRM be applied to a downtown?
10. What are some of the "magic bullets" that struggling downtowns sometimes adopt, and why do they often fail to achieve the desired results?
11. What techniques are used to effectively market and promote downtowns?
12. How can a community's zoning and development standards either discourage or encourage revitalization? What types of code revisions are typically needed to implement a new downtown plan?
13. What are some of the funding mechanisms used to help finance downtown revitalization, both for individual properties and for a downtown as a whole?
14. Once a downtown plan has been prepared and adopted, what steps should be taken to implement it?

About the Author

Philip L. Walker, AICP, resides in Nashville, Tennessee, where he spends his working hours as the principal of The Walker Collaborative, LLC. With more than 20 years of professional experience in all areas of city planning, he specializes in downtown revitalization. His public-sector roles have included serving as the executive director of the Pensacola, Florida, Downtown Improvement Board and the city planning director for Natchez, Mississippi. Walker's earlier private-sector experience includes associate positions with consulting firms based in Princeton, New Jersey, and Cambridge, Massachusetts. He has been a consultant to the National Main Street Center, as well as numerous local Main Street programs and municipalities. He is a frequent speaker at national and regional conferences on the topic of downtown master planning.

Walker holds a bachelor's degree in historic preservation from Middle Tennessee State University, a master's degree in urban and regional planning from the University of Florida's College of Architecture, and a master's degree in real estate development from Harvard University's Graduate School of Design. He has been a member of the American Institute of Certified Planners since 1989. Walker lives with his wife, Kathryn, and daughter, Katie Rush, in a National Register Historic District near downtown Nashville.